HOCKEY HALL *of* FAME

MVP

TROPHIES & WINNERS

1963–64 Hart winner, Jean Beliveau, holds the Hart Memorial Trophy, while Gordie Howe, the 1962–63 Hart winner, looks on.

HOCKEY HALL *of* FAME

MVP

TROPHIES & WINNERS

Bob Duff & Kevin Shea

The 2011 Conn Smythe Trophy winner, Tim Thomas.

FIREFLY BOOKS

A FIREFLY BOOK

Published by Firefly Books Ltd. 2011

Copyright © 2011 Firefly Books Ltd.
Text copyright © Hockey Hall of Fame
Images copyright as listed on page 212
All rights reserved.

FIRST PRINTING

Publisher Cataloging-in-Publication Data
Duff, Bob.
    Hockey Hall of Fame MVP trophies and winners /
Bob Duff and Kevin Shea.
[216] p. : photos. ; cm.
Includes index.
Summary: The history and origin of the NHL's three MVP
trophies: the Hart Memorial Trophy, the Ted Lindsay
Award and the Conn Smythe Trophy, plus profiles of all
trophy winners and examinations of multiple winners,
controversies and surprises.
ISBN-13: 978-1-55407-886-8
1. Hockey – History. 2. Hockey players -- History. I. Shea,
Kevin. II. Title.
796.962/09 dc22   GV846.5D844   2011

Library and Archives Canada Cataloguing in Publication
Duff, Bob
    Hockey Hall of Fame MVP trophies
and winners / Bob Duff and Kevin Shea.
Includes index.
ISBN 978-1-55407-886-8
    1. Hockey—Awards. 2. Hockey—History. 3. Hockey
players—Biography. I. Shea, Kevin, 1956– II. Title.
GV846.5.D84 2011   796.962'64   C2011-904223-1

Published in the United States by
Firefly Books (U.S.) Inc.
P.O. Box 1338, Ellicott Station
Buffalo, New York 14205

Published in Canada by
Firefly Books Ltd.
66 Leek Crescent
Richmond Hill, Ontario L4B 1H1

Cover and interior design: Gareth Lind, LINDdesign

Printed in Canada

*The publisher gratefully acknowledges
the financial support for our publishing program
by the Government of Canada through
the Canada Book Fund as administered
by the Department of Canadian Heritage.*

PREVIOUS PAGE: Bobby Orr, the winner of the Lester B. Pearson Award as the NHLPA's Most Outstanding Player for the 1974–75 season, and a three-time winner of the Hart Trophy as the NHL's MVP as voted by the Professional Hockey Writers' Association, flies through the air after scoring the 1969–70 Stanley Cup-winning goal 40 seconds into overtime of Game 4. Orr received the first of his two Conn Smythe Trophies for his dominance in the 1970 playoffs. He won his second Conn Smythe for his performance in the 1972 playoffs.

PAGE 8: The base of the Hart Trophy, displaying the mid-1980s dominance of Wayne Gretzky.

A close up of the top of the Ted Lindsay Award, featuring a sculpture of Ted Lindsay in his Detroit uniform, which replaced the Lester B. Pearson Award as the NHLPA's top prize in 2010.

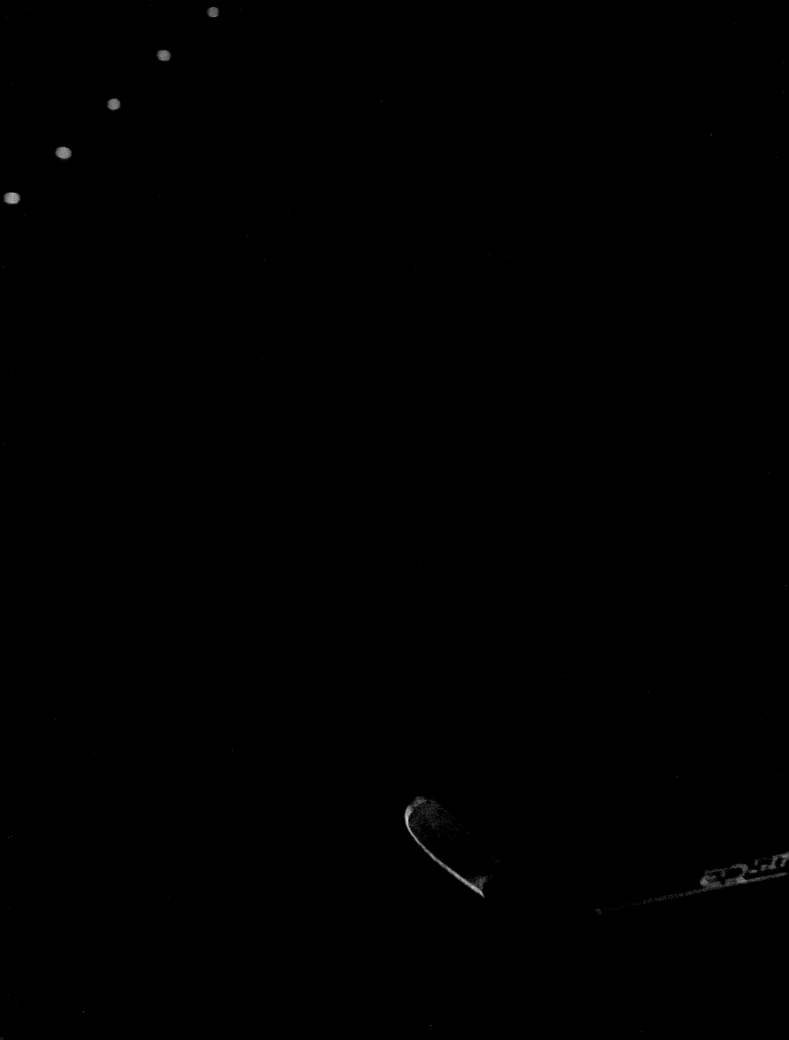

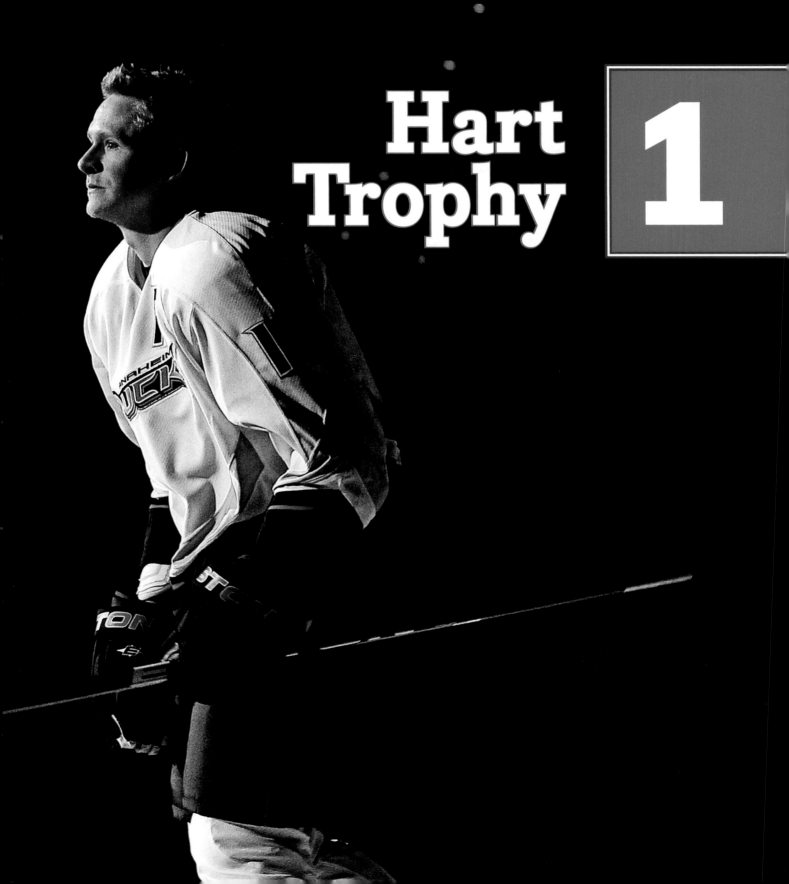

Hart Trophy

HART
MEMORIAL TROP
REPLACING THE
DR. DAVID A. HART TROP
Presented to the
NATIONAL HOCKEY LEAGUE
as its
MOST VALUABLE PLAYER
Award

The Hart Memorial Trophy, which replaced the original Dr. David A. Hart Trophy in 1963.

CHAPTER 1
Birth of the Hart Trophy

IT WAS A warm spring night, Ottawa Senators center Frank Nighbor recalled in 1925, when he received a message from Lady Byng, wife of Lord Byng, Governor General of Canada, asking Nighbor to drop by the Governor General's residence at Rideau Hall in Ottawa when he had a free moment.

Nighbor quickly made an appointment and upon arrival, was escorted by Lady Byng into a large drawing room, where a huge, shiny silver trophy was prominently displayed on a table. She held up the impressive cup for Nighbor to examine, and then she posed a question: Did he think the National Hockey League would accept it as a trophy to be awarded annually to the NHL's most sportsmanlike player?

Nighbor nodded and, in fact, suggested that no doubt the league would be delighted by the offer.

"Then," Lady Byng said, "I present this trophy to Frank Nighbor as the most sports-manlike player for 1925." (The impromptu ceremony made Nighbor the answer to a legendary hockey trivia question.)

A year earlier, Nighbor, a four-time Stanley Cup winner with the Senators during his NHL career, was also the recipient of the first-ever Hart Trophy as the player adjudged to have been the most valuable to his team during the regular season.

It would be wonderful to be able to offer a similar poetic and romantic tale about the birth of the Hart Trophy, the NHL's oldest individual award. Wonderful—but not factual.

"Ruth of Hockey to be Selected," announced the headline in the January 30, 1924, edition of *The Border Cities Star*, proclaiming hockey's newest trophy and its first award to be presented to an individual player. The reference referred to major-league baseball star George Herman "Babe" Ruth, the New York Yankees slugging outfielder who was named most valuable player of the American League in 1923.

"Dr. David A. Hart of Montreal has donated a trophy for the hockey player in the NHL, who, in the opinion of a board of judges to be appointed from Montreal, Toronto, Hamilton and Ottawa, is the most valuable player to his team," the story reported.

"Under the deed of gift, the trophy must be won three times, not necessarily in succession, before becoming the absolute property of any players," although there is no record of any player who accomplished this feat ever keeping, or seeking to keep, the Hart Trophy. Montreal Canadiens center Howie Morenz became the first three-time Hart Trophy recipient when he won the award in 1927–28, 1930–31 and 1931–32, but did not make a bid to maintain permanent possession of the award.

And the Winner Is...

NHL president Frank Calder announced the final voting on March 10, 1924, the first year of the Hart Trophy. The results produced one of the closest races in the history of the award with the winner, Frank Nighbor, finishing with 37 points, one better than Montreal Canadiens defenseman Sprague Cleghorn and two points more than was tabulated by Toronto St. Patricks netminder John Ross Roach. Also receiving votes were Ottawa defenseman Georges Boucher, Hamilton forward Billy Burch, Howie Morenz of Montreal, Hamilton goalie Vernor "Jake" Forbes, Hamilton defenseman Samuel "Goldie" Prodgers and Toronto forward Cecil "Babe" Dye. (Among that group, Burch would join Morenz among the Hart Trophy winners' fraternity the following year.)

Lord Byng presented the trophy to Nighbor on March 11, 1924, prior to the second game of the Canadiens–Senators NHL championship playoff.

"His Excellency, the Governor-General, presented the Hart Cup to Frank Nighbor as the teams lined up," the March 12, 1924, edition of the *Montreal Gazette* reported. "The Cup was awarded to the Ottawa center as being the most valuable player to his team in the NHL during the past season."

The Gazette made note of the apparent strong relationship between Nighbor and Lord Byng. "The presentation of the Hart Trophy to captain Frank Nighbor of the Senators by His Excellency, Lord Byng, and the latter's introduction to Sprague Cleghorn were also occasions for outbursts," the *Gazette* reported.

By modern standards, Nighbor would have proven an unlikely Hart recipient. Helping Ottawa to a first-place finish that season with a 16–8–0 record, Nighbor had been tied for eighth in league scoring with 11 goals and 6 assists in 20 games. Interestingly, Ottawa teammate Cy Denneny, who'd led the league with 22 goals, received paltry support from Hart voters. But, in following the original mandate set out to determine the winner, it was Nighbor's character, leadership and all-around ability that made him such a worthy candidate as the first Hart winner.

Though not a physical player, Nighbor was known as the master of the sweep check (not to be confused with the poke check): Nighbor would hold the length of his stick along the ice and sweep it across the path of attackers, claiming the puck with this move almost every time.

"Frank Nighbor is the greatest defensive player I've ever seen," former Ottawa manager Tommy Gorman proclaimed in a 1946 interview with the *Ottawa Citizen*. "He was by far the greatest defensive center in the game."

The Ottawa Auditorium was even constructed with Nighbor in mind, designed to play to his strength. The boards surrounding the ice surface were egg-shaped, forcing puck carriers to cut further inward the closer they got to the Senators' net, and right into the octopus-like reach of Nighbor's stick.

"There never was anyone to compare to Nighbor as an all-around hockey player," noted Dave Gill (who coached the Senators to the 1926–27 Stanley Cup) in a 1939 interview in the *Windsor Daily Star*. "In his prime, Nighbor could skate as fast as the best. He did everything so smoothly, so methodically, and with such precision that his effectiveness perhaps was not as apparent as in others. But the reverse was true. Nighbor, while not as flashy as some, certainly was more effective."

The top three vote getters for the first Hart Trophy (Nighbor, Cleghorn, Roach) offered distinctive personalities and not just because each played a different position on the ice. While Nighbor (nicknamed the "Pembroke Peach") was known as hockey's most gentlemanly player, Cleghorn took up permanent residence at the opposite end of the spectrum—and in the penalty box. During the 1921–22 season, Cleghorn had led the NHL with 80 penalty minutes in the 24-game campaign.

Once described as all three Hanson Brothers (those bespectacled hooligans from the hockey cult film *Slap Shot*) rolled into one, the *Ottawa Citizen* called Cleghorn "the present-day disgrace of the national winter game," after he injured three Senators players during a February 1, 1922, game at Ottawa. The following season, the Toronto St. Patricks sent a letter to NHL president Frank Calder, requesting that he advise Cleghorn to tone down his behavior.

Lady Byng was reported to have been in attendance at that infamous Ottawa game in which Cleghorn sent Nighbor, Denneny and Eddie Gerard to hospital with injuries. In fact, it was believed that the 1924 Hart Trophy voting

also played a role in Lady Byng's introduction of an award for gentlemanly play, so fearful was she that the Cleghorns of the hockey world would continue to garner too much of the attention.

Roach drew attention as well, but for reasons of size. At five-foot-five and 130 pounds, the diminutive dynamo was the first rookie to backstop an NHL team to the Stanley Cup when he guided the St. Patricks to the 1921–22 title. A feisty, acrobatic netminder, Roach was nicknamed "Little Napoleon" and was such a leader on a weak Toronto team (which finished 10–14 the following season), he was named captain, the first goaltender ever to receive such an honor in league history.

Ballot Boxing

While Lady Byng made her own choice of Nighbor as first recipient of her trophy, a panel of seven hockey writers from the four National Hockey League cities was charged with the task of determining the inaugural winner of the Hart Trophy. The jury of voters consisted of Baz O'Meara of the *Ottawa Journal*, Elmer Ferguson of the *Montreal Herald*, C.W. McQueen of the *Toronto Mail and Empire*, Bobby Hewitson of the *Toronto Telegram*, Albert Leberge of *La Presse*, Montreal, Paddy Jones of the *Hamilton Herald* and Walter MacMullen of the *Hamilton Spectator*.

Each writer was asked to provide a list of eight players to Calder. Those eight players were to be ranked in order of preference, as to who, in their judgment, were the most valuable players to their respective teams during the 1923–24 season. Eight points was allotted to the first-place finisher on each ballot, seven for second place, and so on down to one point for the eighth player on every list.

In 1942–43, the first season of the Original Six, two writers from each of the half-dozen NHL cities were charged with the task of determining the winner of the Hart. By now, 10 players were named on each ballot, with a 10-9-8-7-6-5-4-3-2-1 tally depending on where they were listed on the voting card.

During an October 30, 1946, dinner to honor General John Reed Kilpatrick, president of Madison Square Garden Corporation, NHL president Clarence Campbell discussed possible further changes to the process of determining the Hart victor. He suggested the possibility of the formation of a hockey writers' association with chapters in each NHL city and including all active writers covering the NHL. "I'm not sure at present just what we will do," Campbell said. "It probably won't take place this season anyway."

There was a subtle change to the Hart Trophy voting during the 1946–47 season, regardless. The voting list increased to three writers or radio broadcasters in each of the six cities. Then, in the 1950s, with the advent of televised games, TV broadcasters were also included in the voting mix.

A dramatic change to the voting for all NHL awards was introduced for the 1953–54 season: a mid-season vote was included in the process, and would count for 50 percent of the total vote for each trophy. The two votes would be tabulated at season's end, and the player with the most total votes would receive the award.

In 1966–67, the final season of the six-team league before the NHL added expansion franchises in St. Louis, Los Angeles, Pittsburgh, Philadelphia, Oakland and Minnesota in 1967, the league introduced a season-ending awards banquet to present its trophies to the winners.

Chicago center Stan Mikita made history that spring of 1967 when the Czech-born Mikita became the first European-born winner of the Hart Trophy, but he really ruffled feathers the

following season. Already booked for a family vacation in Fort Lauderdale, Florida, Mikita wouldn't change plans when he won the Hart again in 1967–68 and declined to attend the May 10, 1968, banquet in Montreal. "He's under no obligation," NHL director of publicity Ron Andrews told *The Canadian Press*. "There's nothing in his contract that obliges him to attend these functions."

Both Clarence Campbell and Chicago club owner William Wirtz unsuccessfully sought to sway Mikita, but his no-show meant there was no one to accept the Hart, as well as the Art Ross and Lady Byng Trophies, all of which Mikita had captured for the second straight season.

Campbell took Mikita's no-show in stride. "I talked with him earlier and he indicated then that he wouldn't be available, so it's not too surprising," the NHL president said.

"He wanted to spend his time with his family in Florida, which comes first with him. I wanted him to fly up for the day, but he declined."

As for Mikita, he blamed the NHL for poor planning. "It seems to me that every time something comes up, they let you know at the last minute," he said. "[Campbell] called me on Wednesday [May 8]. We had made plans right away after the playoff [loss] against Montreal. I'm sure they knew about a week after the season ended who the trophy winners were.

"If they had let me know then, I wouldn't have told anybody and it would have been a surprise, as I guess it was. They just didn't give me enough time on it."

For the 1968–69 season, the Hart Trophy voting was handed to the NHL Writers' Association, with three writers in each of the 12 NHL cities casting ballots, a pattern that remained in place into 1980, when by that time there were 21 teams in the league, but still

Stan Mikita accepts the Hart Trophy from NHL president Clarence Campbell in 1967 at the NHL's annual award ceremony. The Hart win made Mikita the first European-born winner of the award.

three voters in every NHL city, for a total of 63 ballots cast.

As the NHL grew to 30 teams, the ballots per city were reduced to two, along with two at-large bids for national writers, a number that remained in place as the new century dawned. However, when veteran *USA Today* hockey writer Kevin Allen was named president of the PHWA (Professional Hockey Writers Association) in 2003, he set out to entirely revamp the voting procedures.

"Basically, we used to be just two votes per team," Allen said. "We only had 62 people voting when I took over and my feeling was that we had a few years when there were some odd votes. Every once in a while, we'd have some sort of goofiness. One year, [Boston Bruins defenseman] Ray Bourque didn't appear on somebody's ballot, and if he'd even have gotten a fifth-place vote, he would have won the Norris Trophy. We had some instances when there were some odd votes, and

my feeling was that, No. 1, even one or two odd votes, when you're only casting 62, really makes a difference. And No. 2, for our membership to be meaningful, we needed to have more people involved in the process."

Allen wanted to make the voting process of the NHL awards a more inclusive process. "The league mandated that we still needed some sort of geographic balance," Allen said. "Rather than do it by team, what I decided to do was do it by conference. I broke it down so that we'd have an even amount of voters from each conference, regardless of what team they covered.

"Last year, we had 63 [voters] from the Western Conference and 63 from the Eastern Conference. And then we add in what I call the at-large voters, people with a national perspective who cover the entire league. You start adding in three guys from *The Hockey News,* and people like myself and Pierre LeBrun and Scott Burnside from ESPN, and suddenly, you've got another 30 people. So we've gone to over 150 voters each season."

The larger mandate has also meant that those who are tardy with their ballots are no longer essential to the outcome. "If you're late, your vote isn't counted anymore," Allen explained. "We used to have to chase people down. Now, we always end up with a voting count between 130 and 135. This seems to have worked out really well. We haven't had any of what I would consider oddities in the voting."

Each voter lists five Hart finalists on their ballot, ranking them 1 to 5, with a 10-7-5-3-1 points system employed to determine a winner. Three finalists are announced by the NHL, and the winner is revealed during the annual NHL awards show.

While this new system may be delivering a wider mandate, knowledge of the subject matter is still a requirement for a writer to receive a Hart ballot. "There's a misnomer where people believe that everyone in the association gets a vote," Allen said. "That's not true. I still pay attention to how many years you've been a member. You've got to be at it awhile before you start to get a vote, or you have to have some credentials that make you, in my mind, more qualified. For example, if there's a new beat writer for the New York Islanders, and they're traveling home and away, they would probably get a vote immediately, because they're spending so much time in the hockey environment. But somebody just coming in as a back-up writer would have to wait a few years before they'd get a vote."

Babe Pratt, the 1943–44 recipient of the Hart Trophy is pictured with the original trophy, donated to the NHL by Dr. David A. Hart in 1924.

Pay the Man

Big news was made at the NHL meetings in Montreal on September 4, 1946. While the headlines announced that Clarence Campbell had succeeded Mervyn "Red" Dutton to serve as the third president in NHL history, also revealed at the meeting was that starting with the 1946–47 season, all winners of the NHL's major trophies—the Hart, Vezina, Lady Byng and Calder Memorial Trophies—would be the recipients of $1,000 bonus checks provided by the league.

Amazingly, that solitary $1,000 prize remained the sole monetary amount awarded the Hart winner up until 1965, when the prize awarded was bumped to $1,250, though most teams would match any prize monies earned by their players. For the 1968–69 season, the Hart winner's bonus money was increased to $1,500, and a runner-up prize of $750 was introduced.

It stayed that way until the 1987–88 season, when the Hart winner's share was upped to $3,000, with $1,500 presented to the runner-up. In 1992, the Hart prize money took a quantum leap forward, and the winner now receives $10,000. Second place is good for $6,000 and the third-place finisher garners $4,000. Most NHL players today have significant bonus clauses written into their contracts, which pay them handsomely should they win one of the NHL's awards.

Changing Hardware

During the NHL governors meeting of February 9, 1960, in Montreal, the decision was made to retire the original Hart Trophy, which was beginning to show signs of wear and tear, to permanent residence within the Hockey Hall of Fame. A second trophy was commissioned and was dubbed the David A. Hart Memorial Trophy.

Detroit Red Wings right-winger Gordie Howe was the first to receive the new version of the Hart Trophy. He previously had won the award in 1951–52, 1952–53, 1956–57 and 1957–58 and would win it again in 1962–63, making Howe one of just two players to earn both versions of the Hart Trophy. Montreal Canadiens center Jean Beliveau won the original Hart Trophy in 1955–56 and won the Hart Memorial Trophy in 1963–64.

Who's Got Hart?

A daring robbery the night of April 9, 1969, at the site of the Hockey Hall of Fame and Canadian Sports Hall of Fame on the Canadian National Exhibition grounds in Toronto saw thieves get away with some of the NHL's most coveted prizes, including the original Hart Trophy. Also stolen were the Calder Memorial and Conn Smythe Trophies.

Stunned by the development, Hockey Hall of Fame curator Lefty Reid struggled to place an estimate on the value of the missing silver trophies. "Unofficially, I'd have to say they were worth about $10,000," Reid told *The Canadian Press*. "But how can you put a value on trophies like that?

"Whoever it is [that the stole the trophies] has to be a kook. None of these trophies is market-able. It's like stealing a Rembrandt. What would they ever do with them?"

The thieves gained entrance to the Hall by removing a cylinder lock from one of the doors at the main entrance to the building, then smashed open the glass cases holding the trophies with a shovel. As well as the NHL prizes, the brazen robbers got away with about 100 medals won by turn-of-the-century speedskater Fred J. Robson of Toronto and approximately 40 medals that had been presented to hockey legend and Hall of Fame member Dan Bain, who captained the Winnipeg Victorias to a pair of Stanley Cups. The thieves were thwarted in their attempts to make off with the Lou Marsh Trophy, awarded annu-ally to Canada's athlete of the year. Apparently, the trophy's heavy marble base proved to be a deterrent.

"If anybody really wanted them that badly, we would gladly supply them with miniatures of each of them," Clarence Campbell told reporters. If kidnapping was their goal, Campbell was quick to point out that the thieves would be sadly disap-pointed. "There is no way in which we would consider cooperating if asked to pay ransom for the return of the trophies," the NHL president told reporters. "We could be prepared to pay a reasonable reward, but only through the police."

As it turned out, no reward was necessary. Shortly after *Hockey Night in Canada* broadcaster Brian McFarlane appealed over the airwaves for the return of the legendary awards during the telecast of a Boston Bruins–Montreal Canadiens Stanley Cup semifinal game on April 10, 1969, Toronto police received an anonymous telephone call informing them of the approximate location of the missing trophies.

The trophies were found housed in green plastic garbage bags in a shed behind a vacant home in surburban Etobicoke, just west of Toronto. All three trophies were intact. "It's a great thrill to recover something like these," Metro police holdup squad Detective Harold Lambert told *The Canadian Press*. "When my boy found out I had the trophies, he wanted to bring all his school chums around to see them."

Toronto police chief James Mackey was of the opinion that the blanket media coverage of the robbery made it impossible for the thieves to sell the trophies.

Campbell, while relieved by the safe return of the hockey awards, remained stunned by the actions that were taken by the thieves, who were never caught. "I don't know how anyone could perpetrate such an act," he said. "As far as I know, the Hall of Fame has no enemies, and while the NHL might have, it's a strange way to react, as the trophies are not much use to anyone."

What's in a Name?

The NHL's divisions were recast in 1993–94. That season, the historical handles on the four divisions (Smythe, Norris, Patrick and Adams) were dropped and replaced with the geographic names Northeast, Atlantic, Central and Pacific.

Then, late in 2009, the NHL pondered the thought of modernizing its hardware and renaming its trophies, again opting to overlook its own

history. The thinking among NHL executives in regards to the awards was that they were mostly named after owners of teams and people who never played in the league. Instead, the league wanted to rename certain trophies after famous players.

Originally, the Hart was named in 1924 after Dr. David A. Hart, father of Cecil Hart, who was manager-coach of the Montreal Canadiens from 1926 to 1932 and again from 1936 to 1939. (It was the elder Hart who had donated the award.) Art Ross, the former manager-coach of the Boston Bruins, had presented the scoring trophy to the league in 1947. Frank Calder was NHL president from 1917 until his death in 1947 and was honored with the rookie award being named for him. The Norris family donated that trophy in 1953 to honor the memory of the patriarch of the family, James Norris, the former owner of the Detroit Red Wings.

The new suggestions were that the Hart Memorial Trophy, for the most valuable player, would be named instead after Gordie Howe; the Art Ross, for scoring, would be changed to the Wayne Gretzky Trophy, named for the most prolific scorer in league history; the Norris Trophy, given to the NHL's top defenseman, would be named after Bobby Orr, who revolutionized the position, and who had won the award more than any other defender; and the Calder Trophy, for rookie of the year, would instead be named after Pittsburgh great Mario Lemieux, who won the award in 1984–85.

"It's nothing more than an idea being kicked around at this point in time," said NHL deputy commissioner Bill Daly, and the idea went no further.

CHAPTER 2
The Harts of Hockey

THE NATIONAL HOCKEY League was still in its childhood, all of four years of age in 1921, when Canadiens owner George Kendall died, and his widow announced that the team would be sold at auction.

A trio of prominent Montreal businessmen banded together in pursuit of the team. They were led by the flamboyant Leo Dandurand, who carried a French-Canadian handle, but also a birth certificate listing his place of birth as Bourbonnais, Illinois. Well-known in Montreal sports circles, Dandurand was a former National Hockey Association referee and was as shrewd a promoter as he was an investor.

Joe Cattarinich was a former Canadiens netminder with an eye for talent. In fact, after an exhibition game with Chicoutimi in 1910, Cattarinich recommended to his bosses that they drop him and sign the Chicoutimi netminder, a fellow by the name of Georges Vezina. A quiet, efficient sort who preferred to operate in the background, after hockey, he'd succeeded in the tobacco industry.

The third member of this triumvirate, a collective which became known in Montreal as the Three Musketeers, was Louis Letourneau. He was a carefree sort, someone who'd made his fortune in the operation of thoroughbred horse-racing tracks, and therein lay the problem.

When the Canadiens went on the auction block in the fall of 1921, the three were in Cleveland, where the summer meet of racing was winding down. Thinking fast, Dandurand contacted a Montreal acquaintance, Cecil Hart, whom he knew to be reliable and trustworthy. Hart, at the time, was a prominent figure in the Montreal amateur sports scene.

Hart was deployed to act as agent for the three at the auction, and to go to whatever means necessary to acquire the Canadiens.

Also in the bidding were two other groups—Tom Duggan of the Mount Royal Arena Company, which was home rink to the Habs, and NHL president Frank Calder, who was representing unnamed Ottawa interests.

According to authors Chrys Goyens and Allan Turowetz in their book *Lions in Winter*, the bidding opened at $8,000 and Hart quickly upped the ante to $8,500. Calder requested time to consult with his backers and the auction was put on hold for a week.

When they resumed, Duggan quieted the room by laying ten crisp $1,000 bills on the table. Undaunted, Hart phoned Dandurand and relayed the status of the auction. Once more, he was told to use whatever means necessary to purchase the team. Hart returned, immediately offering $11,000. That ended the battle. The Canadiens belonged to Dandurand, Letourneau and Cattarinich.

"I was acquainted with Cecil Hart for some 35 years," Calder once explained in an interview with the *Montreal Gazette*. "He was a fine person, instrumental in fostering many branches of sport [in Montreal]. He gained a circle of friends wherever he went."

Hart continued to work for the team, and though he was never listed as having an official capacity, his value and loyalty to the Canadiens was unquestioned. "Cecil Hart was a sportsman, a hail-fellow-well-met, a kindly man, an earnest man, a humorous man, a man of unshakable convictions—and genuine to the core," Marc T. McNeil wrote in the *Montreal Gazette*.

One of the first moves Hart made after the Three Musketeers acquired the Canadiens was to recommend to them a speedster from Stratford, Ontario, that he'd seen in action on Montreal ice playing for the Canadian National Railway team from that city against the Montreal CNR squad.

Cecil Hart seen here in 1938–39, his last year of coaching in the NHL.

Ernie Sauve, a member of the Montreal club, had advised Hart that he ought to get to Mount Royal Arena to check out this Stratford Streak in action, and Hart obliged. The youngster, who was all of 18 at the time, darted to and fro and left the opposition grasping at air in their bids to halt his many dangerous rushes, most of which resulted in scoring plays that provided the Stratford club with a hearty, one-sided victory.

That player's name was Howie Morenz.

Hart only watched Morenz play for a few minutes, but it was more than enough to make up his mind. The Canadiens offered Morenz a contract, and when the shy center hedged on turning pro and asked out of the deal he'd signed, Hart traveled to Stratford, peeled off $850 and laid it on the kitchen table in the Morenz home as a signing bonus. The deal was done.

After signing with the Canadiens on September 30, 1923, Morenz would win the Hart Trophy three times during his NHL career, more than any other player in franchise history.

Deft Organizer

Although Cecil Hart was born in Bedford, Quebec (in 1883), the family moved to the Montreal suburb of St. Lambert when he was a child. Hart became a prominent figure in the Montreal amateur sports scene, and his first love in sports was baseball. He pitched and played shortstop, but it quickly became apparent that his true genius lay in organization and leadership. At the age of 14 in 1897, he organized the Montreal Stars team to compete in the Montreal City Senior League, winning six championships (1906, 1907, 1910, 1911, 1916, 1917), covering all bases as the team's manager, promoter, publicist and statistician. "Cecil thought more of his Stars than of his right hand," Calder recalled in a 1940 interview with the *Montreal Gazette*.

Among his ballplayers were future hockey stars such as Art Ross and Odie and Sprague Cleghorn. "Cecil was a great friend of mine for many years, dating back to [our] early baseball days with the Stars," Odie Cleghorn told the *Gazette*.

Hart expanded the Stars into senior hockey, winning city league titles in 1916 and 1917. In 1916, Hart gathered his Montreal Stars squad and traveled to Pittsburgh for a challenge match against the senior amateur team in that city run by Roy Schooley. "The Montreal Stars are managed by one of the shrewdest hockey experts in Canada, Cecil M. Hart," reported the *Pittsburgh Press*.

Hart also operated the famed and unbeaten Dimanche Matin hockey team, a sort of Harlem Globetrotters on ice consisting of many ex-pros, including Hart and former Canadiens player Dave Campbell, whose team name was derived from the weekly Sunday morning games they'd host against all comers at Montreal's Mount Royal Arena. A favorite trick, devised by Hart, was to play the national anthem prior to each game. As the unsuspecting and patriotic opponents lined up to pay their respects to the flag, one of the Dimanche Matin players would scoop up the puck, race in on the vacant goal and give his squad a 1–0 lead. "Cecil was probably one of the most beloved of figures in the sports world," Clarence Campbell told the *Montreal Gazette* in a 1940 interview.

A Big Year

The year of 1924 proved to be a dramatic one in the annals of the Hart family, and it was Cecil's father, Dr. David A. Hart, who got the ball rolling. On January 29, 1924, he donated a trophy to the NHL to be awarded annually to the player adjudged most valuable to his team, the first award to recognize individual achievement in NHL history. In his honor, it was dubbed the Hart Trophy.

Nine months after Dr. Hart donated his trophy, his son also finally officially made it to the NHL. On October 11, 1924, Montreal was awarded a second NHL franchise—the Maroons—and Cecil Hart was named manager of the club. Hart's decision to accept the position was not reached easily. He first consulted with Dandurand, not wanting to cross his lifelong friend. Dandurand enthusiastically endorsed the idea and Hart accepted the position with the Maroons.

He set out quickly to build one of the NHL's first expansion teams from the ground up, grabbing two Stanley Cup veterans and future Hall of Famers from the Ottawa Senators: goaltender Clint Benedict and right-winger Harry "Punch" Broadbent. Hart signed defenseman Dunc Munro, captain of Canada's 1924 Olympic gold-medal-winning squad, to a pro contract, and paid the Toronto St. Patricks $8,000 for another Stanley Cup veteran, Reg Noble.

It was the latter deal that proved to be Hart's undoing. Even though Noble's moves kept the

Maroons in playoff contention for much of the 1924–25 NHL season, team executives questioned Cecil's wisdom when it came to spending so much on a player who was closer to the end than the beginning of his playing days.

The two sides waged an ongoing battle of wits, with Hart seeking to maintain complete control of the players on and off the ice, and of all hockey operations, including trades and other methods of acquiring talent. With the two sides at an impasse, team officials demanded Hart's resignation. When he refused, he was fired by the Maroons on February 8, 1925, and replaced by former NHL defenseman Eddie Gerard.

There was also family bereavement for the Harts to deal with that year. Dr. David Hart, Cecil's father and the man who presented the NHL with the Hart Trophy, died June 30, 1925, in Montreal. He was 81.

Marooned in Montreal

Hart's decisions while with the Maroons proved to be genius a year later. With Benedict, Munro, Broadbent and Noble all playing significant roles, the Maroons, a second-year NHL team, won the Stanley Cup in the spring of 1926.

Although within days of his dismissal from the Maroons, Cecil Hart was hired by the Canadiens to fill the position of assistant manager, the Maroons experience left a bitter taste in his mouth. Afterward, the almost-always affable Hart never tired of beating them or chiding the organization during his tenure with the Canadiens.

"It will be sickening to see what you fellows will write about your big red team," he complained to reporters whenever the Maroons got the better of the Canadiens. "They were lucky, that's all. See what we do to them next time."

When the Canadiens lived up to that billing and handed the Maroons a shellacking, Hart's tone changed. "Now let's see what you can write about your big red team," he'd tell the assembled media after a Canadiens triumph over their crosstown rivals. "It ought to be good after what we did to them tonight."

Hart never missed a chance to needle the Maroons. When the injury-plagued Canadiens battled deep into the 1938 playoffs, a post-season that the Maroons had missed out on, Hart was appalled that the media wasn't more complimentary to his team's pluck. "Now, if it had been the Big Red Machine," he roared, "adjectives would have been piled sky-high to herald their gallantry."

While the Maroons that Hart built won the 1925–26 Stanley Cup, his new employers, the Canadiens, floundered through a last-place finish that season and dealt with the tragic death of longtime netminder Georges Vezina, who was ravaged by the effects of tuberculosis and ultimately succumbed late in the NHL season.

Dandurand, who'd been running the team and was finding it draining on his health and well being, determined a change was in order and on September 25, 1926, named Hart to be his successor as manager.

That was the season in which the NHL usurped its big-league rival, the Western Hockey League, and acquired the rights to all of that league's players. Assets were quickly snapped up. Boston grabbed Eddie Shore, the New York Rangers snared the Cook brothers, Bill and Bun, and Frank Boucher, while Detroit added Frank Fredrickson.

Hart wasn't asleep at the switch, though. Among his first moves was to sign Saskatoon goaltender George Hainsworth to fill Vezina's skates. Next, he added a solid, two-way defenseman—Calgary's Herb Gardiner.

They proved to be shrewd moves. At the end of the season, Hainsworth earned the first-ever

The 1929–30 Stanley Cup champion Montreal Canadiens, managed by Cecil Hart.

Vezina Trophy as the NHL's top goaler, while Gardiner, who wore sweater No. 1, normally reserved for netminders, even though he patrolled the blue line, captured the nod from the voters for the Hart Trophy.

"Cecil Hart has bolstered his club fully 50 percent over 1925–26," reported the *Montreal Gazette.*

Taking Charge

The Canadiens were revitalized under Hart's leadership, winning 28 of 44 games in 1926–27 to finish second in the Canadian division behind eventual Stanley Cup champion Ottawa. Best of all for Hart, they shut out the Maroons in four successive meetings that season.

Hart assembled an all-star lineup. He put Morenz on a line between Aurel Joliat and first Billy Boucher, then later Johnny "Black Cat" Gagnon, and they were among the

most dangerous units in the league for years. Hainsworth proved to be the NHL's most reliable goalie, and Gardiner was a rock along the blue line.

The following season, they moved to top spot as Morenz netted 33 goals, won the scoring title and his first Hart Trophy. Another first-place finish followed in 1928–29, but the best was yet to come. Even though they fell to second spot behind the hated Maroons in 1929–30, Hart's Canadiens found their gear in post-season play. They handled Chicago and the New York Rangers in the first two playoff rounds without tasting defeat, setting up a final showdown with the powerhouse Boston Bruins.

The Bruins steamrolled the NHL that season, posting a 38–5–1 mark for an astonishing .875 winning percentage that remains the league record today. Boston forward Ralph "Cooney" Weiland set an NHL single-season scoring mark with 73 points.

Boston had gone through the entire season without losing successive games when they lined up to face the Canadiens in the best-of-three Cup final series, but proved no match for the Habs. Hainsworth blanked Boston 3–0 in the opener and the Canadiens were 4–3 winners in Game 2, capturing their first title since 1923–24, and Hart's leadership was being credited for their success.

"Cecil Hart has undoubtedly the most glittering record of any manager in the National Hockey League," the *Montreal Gazette* reported. "Greatly respected as a hockey tactician, Hart is even more noted for the spirit of fight he injects into his charges. He has a knack for maintaining complete harmony in a team and the loyalty and respect of every member of it."

The following season, Montreal was back on top of the standings in the regular season, and bested Chicago in a thrilling five-game final series to defend their Cup title, joining the Ottawa Senators (1919–20, 1920–21) as the only NHL teams to have worn successive crowns. Once again, Hart was the talk of the NHL.

"I know of no individual who could better inspire a hockey team to victory than Cecil Hart, the man who brought two successive Stanley Cups to Canadiens," Bruins owner Charles Adams said.

However, Hart also ran his own insurance business, so, as much as he loved the game, he found that hockey was placing too much demand on his time. He therefore decided, following the 1931–32 season, to step back from the sport to focus on his business. He was replaced as manager of the Canadiens by former Montreal star Edouard (Newsy) Lalonde.

Hart Transplant

During his time away from the Canadiens, Hart wasn't exactly gone from hockey completely. He still found time to run the Verdun Maple Leafs of the Quebec Senior Hockey League.

In 1933, the Sportsman's Association of Montreal initiated a new fundraising event, a golf tournament that was combined with a dinner to recognize someone who'd given of his time to further the cause of sports in the city. The first winner of the award was Cecil Hart. Eventually, as the event became an annual affair, the award was named the Cecil Hart Trophy.

There's another Hart Trophy in existence as well. The bauble that goes annually to the champions of the Montreal High School Hockey League has been known since 1940 as the Cecil Hart Memorial Trophy.

Meanwhile, the Canadiens floundered in the years that Hart was away and in 1936, there were rumblings that he might return to the job. Those rumors became fact on July 30, 1936, when Canadiens player-coach Sylvio Mantha relinquished the latter position, and Hart was rehired to take over the team. As in 1926, he immediately set out to reshape the squad, and he did so by going back to the future.

One of Hart's first moves was to reacquire Morenz, who had floundered since a 1934 trade sent him to Chicago and a further deal moved him on to the Rangers. Hart immediately reunited Morenz with Joliat and Gagnon and the line reignited its old fire.

"I couldn't help giving everything for a coach like Cecil Hart." Aurel Joliat told Jack Calder in the *Regina Leader-Post*. Joliat won the Hart Trophy in 1933–34, and three Stanley Cups, but didn't rate any of them No. 1 on his highlight reel.

"I'll tell you the biggest thrill I ever got out of hockey," Joliat explained. "It was when

Canadiens brought Cec Hart back as coach and brought Howie Morenz back from New York. That put us right back in the league and I felt like a kid again."

To strengthen the defense, Hart acquired Babe Siebert from Boston. "I never had a player who gave me more on or off the ice," Hart said of Siebert, who won the Hart Trophy that season.

Last-place finishers in 1935–36, the Canadiens now raced to the top of the standings, and even old rivals were complimenting Hart's work. "Cecil, old boy…you've got a great team and you took them from the bottom right to the top," Toronto Maple Leafs owner Conn Smythe said.

Then tragedy struck. Taken hard into the boards by Chicago defenseman Earl Seibert during a January 28, 1937, game at the Montreal Forum, Morenz badly fractured his left leg. His condition worsened in hospital and shockingly on March 8, 1937, Morenz died, the victim of a pulmonary embolism.

Hart had lost not only his best player, but his best friend. Death came on so suddenly, that Hart, racing to be at Morenz's bedside, couldn't make it in time. "I can't talk about it," a devastated Hart told the *Ottawa Citizen*. "It is terrible—a thunderbolt."

Howie Morenz Jr., only 10 when his father died, remembers the compassion that Hart showed their family. "I remember Cecil Hart coming to our house in the middle of night to offer condolences to my mother," Morenz Jr. recalled.

"At first, everyone came around to see us. But after everyone else stopped showing up, Cecil Hart was always there. He would check in on us regularly, almost every week, to see if there was anything we needed, or anything he could do for us."

Minus Morenz, the Canadiens fell in a tight best-of-five-game playoff series to the eventual Cup champion Detroit Red Wings, losing the deciding game in overtime. "I still feel a little upset, for I can't believe yet that [the Red Wings] beat us," Hart told the *Montreal Gazette*. "Well, I guess all I can do now is get busy on next year."

"If Howie hadn't died, we'd have won the Stanley Cup [that] year," Joliat added. "He was a great Howie."

Despite the loss of the Cup, Montreal fans were so delighted by the turnaround in the team's performance that supporters raised enough cash to present Hart with a new automobile in the summer of 1937.

The Canadiens slumped to third in 1937–38, and were sixth in the seven-team league the following campaign when word started to leak that Hart might be fired. "This business of making the manager the goat does not always work out," Canadiens president Ernest Savard explained to the *Montreal Gazette*, seeking to stem the tide of the scuttlebutt. "Cecil is going to stay. He can't go out on the ice and skate and score for them, and he can't give them brains when they are standing face-to-face with a goalkeeper. It is not his fault. It is the fault of the players. We need players who can score, but try and get them."

Soon, though, even Savard turned against his coach and in January 1939, Hart tendered his resignation. "I am amazed that before giving me the slightest intimation of this possibility, President Savard should discuss it with the newspapers and let the public know first," Hart told *Montreal Herald* sports editor Elmer Ferguson. "I've done my part. If some of the others on the club had done their parts as faithfully as I did, we wouldn't be in the last place today."

Trend Setter

Hart was unique among his peers in his era, for he was an NHL coach who'd never played the game at an elite level. Rangers manager Lester Patrick, who'd known Hart since they were kids growing up in Montreal, felt this issue to be immaterial.

"Hart is one of the best managers who ever sat on a hockey bench," Lester Patrick said at the 1938 New York Hockey Writers' dinner. "We played together as kids on [the] flooded lots of Montreal and I count Cecil as one of my best friends. I went on as a player, but Cecil never made the big-time. That doesn't mean, though, that he has no knowledge of hockey. After all, you can be a dramatic critic without even making an attempt to write a play.

"Cecil's very lack of big-time experience is one of the things that makes him a great leader. He still has the attitude of the fan. I wish I had his fresh viewpoint. Every night behind the dasher, he's still the kid watching his first hockey game. [Canadiens players] Aurel Joliat, Pit Lepine, Marty Burke and Georges Mantha are all heroes to him."

In 1938, Hart and Detroit manager Jack Adams combined to make a little history when they took their respective teams on a tour of Britain and France. "We've had a successful trip," Hart told *The Canadian Press* after 8,500 people watched the final game of the tour in Southampton. "The boys played wonderful hockey and I'm sure they've sold the professional game in a big way to British and French fans.

"We turned thousands away. I never saw anything like it. If they ever get any big rinks over there, the game is a cinch to go."

Hart did find the English customs to be somewhat confusing. "Afternoon tea. Good heavens, when they're at afternoon tea, the King himself couldn't talk to them," he said. "We were idle from Tuesday of one week until Saturday. I wanted to play Thursday night. 'We'll pack 'em in,' I said. But no, they were afraid of hurting the Saturday gate. So when we turned 4,000 away Saturday night, the promoter came to me and said, 'Hart, I wish I'd taken your advice.' I said, 'With your money and my brains, you'd be a success.'"

As much as he was known for his hockey mind, Hart's wit was equally charming and often biting.

Prior to the 1937 Stanley Cup final between Detroit and the New York Rangers, Hart declined to offer a prediction. "I've already picked Canadiens to beat Detroit," Hart said. "Toronto to trim Rangers. Boston to take Maroons and finally Maroons to beat Rangers. You can't expect me to try again."

When NHL referee Bill Stewart was named manager of the Chicago Black Hawks in 1937, Hart cabled him a congratulatory message. "Bill, I want to congratulate you most warmly on your appointment as manager of the Black Hawks," it read. "I'm glad you got the job, because it will take you off the ice as a referee. And I hope you keep it permanently, so you'll stay off the ice. You were no good out there, anyway."

When the Canadiens embarked via steamship for their trip to Europe in the spring of 1938, Hart allowed that he had a plan in place if he got into any trouble while across the pond. "I won't give my right name," he explained. "I will use the name [of Maroons manager] Tommy Gorman."

Hart was also capable of great diplomacy. Asked at a dinner in New York which team would meet the Canadiens in the Stanley Cup final, Hart quipped, "Either Rangers or Americans—but I must confess that when they asked the same question in Boston, I said, 'the Bruins.'"

Hart Stopped

Becoming a fan of the sporting world after he was relieved of his duties by the Canadiens, besides hockey games, Hart was a regular at baseball and boxing matches, and his passion for professional wrestling was well known in Montreal circles. He'd often bemoan the fact that he'd be forced to miss a bout at the Forum when the Canadiens were embarking on a road trip.

In April of 1940, Hart fell seriously ill, and was hospitalized in May. Bed-ridden for a three-week sojourn, he was sent home, with little hope being held for his recovery.

He made his farewell public appearance in June, attending the same Montreal Sportsmen's Association dinner that first honored him in 1933. Letourneau was to be the 1940 honoree and Hart didn't want to miss his friend's day.

Once the life of the party, the Hart that showed up to the country club that afternoon was frail and drawn, able to move slowly and only with the aid of the cane. He left early, and Letourneau when speaking of Hart during his acceptance speech, was forced to pause, remove his glasses, and pat away tears with his handkerchief.

Hart died July 16, 1940. He was 56 years old. "Associated with Les Canadiens during the years when the team was the toast of professional hockey, Cecil Hart's name was known wherever the sport was played. He developed some of the game's greatest stars and it was while he was at the helm that Canadiens became known to hockey followers everywhere as the Flying Frenchmen," wrote Jack Coffman in the *Ottawa Citizen*.

Quickly, tributes poured in regarding Hart's legacy. "Cecil Hart was one of the finest men ever to be connected with the National Hockey League," Gorman told the *Montreal Gazette*. Added Jules Dugal, who replaced Hart as Canadiens coach: "I always found Cecil to be one of the finest of sportsmen when we worked together with the Canadien hockey club."

Even the men in the middle offered praise. "Knowing Cecil for many years, having played with him and against him in hockey, and also officiating in games when he handled the Canadiens, he was to me a great sportsman," NHL referee-in-chief Cooper Smeaton said.

In 1986, Cecil Hart received further recognition from his home city when he was inducted into the Jewish Sports Hall of Fame. "Run, don't walk, to get tickets for [the] ceremony at the [Montreal] YM–YWHA, where the late Cecil Hart will be among those inducted into the Jewish Hall of Fame," wrote Red Fisher in the *Montreal Gazette*. "I don't have to remind you that Hart won back-to-back Stanley Cups with the Canadiens in the 1930s, or that the Hart Trophy is named after his family. Three former winners of the Hart—Elmer Lach, Jean Beliveau and Guy Lafleur—will be there, and so will [then Canadiens president] Ronald Corey, the honorary chair of the event. And oh, yes: hockey's greatest individual award has been loaned to the 'Y' for the occasion. Sounds like an affair no hockey fan would want to miss."

Had he been alive, you can be sure of one thing: Cecil Hart wouldn't have missed it for the world.

Ted Kennedy is awarded the Hart Trophy for the 1954–55 season, as well as a commemorative platter by Clarence Campbell on Ted Kennedy Retirement Night at Maple Leaf Gardens in 1955.

CHAPTER 3
Controversies and Surprises

IT ISN'T OFTEN that a player is tabbed as the most valuable in his chosen sport and feels the need to apologize. As he accepted the Hart Trophy as the National Hockey League's MVP following the 1953–54 season, Chicago Black Hawks goaltender Al Rollins was in no mood to celebrate.

Considering Rollins' numbers for the season—a 3.46 goals-against average, 12 wins in 70 games and 242 goals against (60 more than any other team had allowed)—his restrained approach appeared appropriate. When taking into account the beating he took from the press after his Hart win was announced, people were left to wonder who it was that actually voted for Rollins.

"We can't recall when the experts made a more idiotic selection," wrote Elmer Ferguson in the *Montreal Herald*. "If this sort of mawkish, sentimental voting is to become a permanency, it's better we should scrap all the awards and turn over their allocation to the league or the governors or the coaches."

Writing in the *Montreal Star*, Baz O'Meara

was another who felt that it might be time for the voting procedures to be altered. "Our own preference was for [Montreal right-winger] Maurice Richard, and this was not dictated by devotion to Canadiens or Richard friendship or sentiment," O'Meara opined. "Nearly everybody thought [Detroit defenseman Red] Kelly would win the award, but he has had plenty of honors and awards this year. Our own idea is that there should be some other method of selection, some method by which referees and linesmen should be allowed into the panel."

Not everyone with a pen and a column was down on Rollins, though. "It's just possible that Detroit's Red Kelly, Canadiens' Maurice Richard, and Leafs' Harry Lumley were more valuable to their teams in the strict sense of the word," noted Red Burnett of the *Toronto Star*. "However, from our point of view, the hungry-looking, six-foot-two native of Vanguard, Saskachewan, rates the coveted Hart Trophy—maybe they should spell it 'heart' in this case—for courage, if nothing else."

Over the years, the netminder grew even more puzzled by the development of his Hart worthiness that season. Offering an assessment during a 1968 interview with the *Spokane Spokesman-Review*, Rollins was of the opinion that his Hart was a year late, feeling that his work in leading the Black Hawks to the playoffs during the 1952–53 season, Chicago's first post-season action since the 1945–46 campaign, was an MVP-worthy performance.

"I thought I played well for Chicago in 1952–53," Rollins said. "It was a pretty good club. We went seven games, losing to [eventual Stanley Cup champion] Montreal in the semifinals. That year, I finished second in the Hart voting to a guy named Gordie Howe.

"The next year, we didn't make the playoffs, and I didn't feel I had much chance to win anything, but that's when I got the Hart. Maybe they felt sorry for me."

Certainly, his peers at the time agreed with such sentiment regarding Rollins and the 1952–53 season. "If we make the playoffs, I think some consideration should be given to Al Rollins for the Hart Trophy," Black Hawks general manager Bill Tobin opined to Dink Carroll of the *Montreal Gazette*.

* * *

If Rollins's win was the most controversial in Hart history, then the following season produced the most shocking winner of the trophy. That season, the voters opted to give the Hart to long-time Toronto Maple Leafs captain Ted "Teeder"

Kennedy, a great player, but one who was clearly past his best-before date by that point of his career.

In fact, Kennedy had already indicated he would give up the game at season's end, and many viewed his Hart win as a sentimental sendoff from writers who'd always admired his work with the Leafs and felt he probably should have won at least one Hart during his stellar career.

"I don't know if I deserved the Hart or not in the past," a seemingly embarrassed Kennedy told *The Canadian Press*. "But the way I saw it, I was of less value to my club last season than I was in some of the other years."

Kennedy finished eleventh in NHL scoring during the 1954–55 season with 10–42–52 numbers from 70 games. His 10 goals were the fewest ever recorded by a forward who won the Hart Trophy. His 42 assists were third in the league, however, it should be noted. Kennedy and Rollins remain the only Hart winners who failed to earn a spot on either of the NHL's season-ending First or Second All-Star Teams since selection of the teams was inaugurated following the 1930–31 season.

Maple Leaf Gardens' president Conn Smythe, while admittedly biased, would tolerate none of the anti-Kennedy talk, and hoped to convince his captain that the Hart win indicated he should stick around for another season. "It justifies Kennedy's decision to play an extra year and also mine," said Smythe, noting that Kennedy had pondered retirement following the 1953–54 campaign.

"Kennedy's record for our club last season was as fine as it ever was. The club was poorer, but Kennedy's goals-for and goals-against average was about the same as in other years."

Perhaps working on Kennedy's side was the reality that there was no clear-cut favorite for

1954–55 Vezina Trophy winner Terry Sawchuk, seen here stopping a Leaf attack, may have been the most worthy candidate for the 1954–55 Hart nomination, but it was Ted Kennedy, in his final NHL year, who won the award.

the Hart that season. Perennial contender Howe of Detroit slumped to 62 points, not even good enough to lead his own team. Montreal's Maurice Richard looked to be on his way to his first NHL scoring title and likely his second Hart when his on-ice antics induced a brawl in a game at Boston, during which he attacked an on-ice official, and he was suspended for the rest of the regular season and playoffs by NHL president Clarence Campbell. Teammate Bernie "Boom Boom" Geoffrion nipped the Rocket by a point for the title, but perhaps suffered backlash from those who felt he benefited from Richard's suspension.

Even the management of the Canadiens seemed to understand and accept their fate in this ordeal. "I want to regain for Maurice Richard what he had before that night, and I hope he will be the leading scorer next season and win the Hart Trophy," Canadiens managing director Frank Selke told the *Ottawa Citizen* after the 1954–55 campaign.

Looking at that season, the best Hart candidate was probably a goalie. Detroit's Terry Sawchuk won the Vezina and topped the NHL in wins (40) and shutouts (12), but the aloof Sawchuk was far from popular with the writers, and never even factored into the voting. Those writers instead voted Toronto netminder Harry Lumley, who won just 23 games for a third-place team that played .500 hockey (24–24–22) as runner-up to Kennedy, another puzzler from what was without a doubt the strangest Hart ballot of them all.

* * *

Not that affairs of the Hart haven't resulted in strange, surprising outcomes in other seasons.

The Boston Bruins rewrote the NHL record book during the 1929–30 season. Taking advantage of new rules which allowed forward passing in all zones, the Boston juggernaut produced an NHL-best 38–5–1 record for an .875 winning percentage that still reigns as the league record.

Leading the assault was Bruins center Ralph "Cooney" Weiland, who shattered the NHL single-season points mark of 51 established by Howie Morenz of the Montreal Canadiens in 1927–28, garnering 73 points, including a league-leading 43 goals, to win the scoring title by 11 points over New York Rangers center Frank Boucher.

By modern Hart Trophy standards, this would have been no contest. Weiland would have proven the runaway winner when the votes were tabulated. But that wasn't the case in the spring of 1930. When the Hart winner was announced, it was Montreal Maroons center Nels Stewart, author of 39 goals for the Canadian Division-leading Maroons, who won the award with 101 voted points, 7 better than a Boston player who wasn't Weiland, but rather defensive defenseman Lionel Hitchman. Weiland finished well up the track in third with 79 voted points.

Another benchmark for scoring was established in the NHL during the 1944–45 season, when Canadiens right-winger Richard proved to be the league's first 50-goal scorer. But it wasn't the trigger-man who was recognized, but the man who fueled the Rocket, Canadiens center Elmer Lach. He finished as NHL scoring leader with 80 points, including a league-record 54 assists, and his helping hand earned Lach a near-landslide victory in the Hart voting, garnering 116 of a possible 120 points. Richard was a distant second at 79 points, and even though he'd established an NHL record for goal scoring, no one questioned the outcome of the voting. "As Lach goes, so go Canadiens," noted the *Ottawa Citizen*.

* * *

From the mid-1950s through the late 1960s, the Hart was decided in a two-tiered voting system. A mid-season ballot in January counted for 50 percent of the ballot, with the other half cast at the end of the regular season. This format led to an unusual situation during the 1955–56 season, when Montreal Canadiens center Jean Beliveau won the Hart, despite finishing second in both halves of the balloting.

When the January vote totals were made public, New York Rangers goaltender Lorne "Gump" Worsley led Beliveau by a 55–53 margin. Worsley faded in the second half, but when Toronto center Tod Sloan exploded and finished with 37 goals, he garnered 72 second-half votes, compared to 43 for Beliveau, who won the NHL scoring title for the first-place Canadiens with 47 goals and 88 points. Overall, though, when both halves were tabulated, the totals were thus: Beliveau 94, Sloan 86 and Worsley 72.

"No one will hold a tag day for Beliveau," suggested Frank Selke, who was reportedly paying his star player $25,000 per season.

Detroit GM Jack Adams spoke out in favor of Sloan. "If it hadn't been for Sloan, the Leafs wouldn't have made the playoffs," Adams told the *Montreal Gazette*, before lamenting, "Beliveau is the best player to come into the game since Gordie Howe. He carried the Canadiens all season."

* * *

Even those who have won the Hart can find shock and awe when the results are tabulated. Pittsburgh Penguins center Mario Lemieux was certain he'd walk off with the trophy following the 1988–89 season, and not without cause. Lemieux ran away with the scoring title, registering 199 points, 31 points better than runner-up Wayne Gretzky of the Los Angeles Kings. On top of that, he'd led the Penguins to their first playoff appearance in six seasons.

Yet, when the Hart was presented at the NHL Awards banquet, Gretzky was the one who heard his named called for the ninth time, much to the chagrin of the Pittsburgh captain. "In the past, they gave the Hart to the best player or top scorer," Lemieux groused to *The Associated Press*, noting that 11 of the previous 12 Hart winners also captured the Art Ross Trophy. "I don't know why it changed. Nothing in this league makes sense. The facts are there."

On the eve of his 2005–06 Hart Trophy win, San Jose Sharks center Joe Thornton was busy lobbying—for one of the other finalists, right-winger Jaromir Jagr of the New York Rangers. "Definitely Jagr," Thornton suggested to Jason Diamos of *The New York Times* when asked who he thought would walk away with the Hart. "New York hasn't made the playoffs in eight years. That's his team. He's carried them all year. I think he's the best player in the world."

Sometimes, the surprise comes when no one wins. That was the case in the spring of 1968, when Canadiens coach Hector "Toe" Blake, himself a former Hart winner with the Habs, lamented that his team was shut out of the award, even though Montreal topped the standings during the regular season and swept to the Stanley Cup.

"Who finished first this season?" Blake asked in *The Vancouver Sun* as he watched Chicago's Stan Mikita pick up the Hart ahead of Canadiens captain and two-time Hart winner Beliveau. "We did. We're in the finals and we've done everything we're supposed to do, but still not one of our players gets an award. What do we have to do to get one?"

The No-Playoff Payoff

Over the years, the debate about the language of the Hart Trophy, which is supposed to go to the player adjudged to be the most valuable to his team, has led to an obvious debate: should the Hart go to a player from a non-playoff team? The naysayers insist that their argument is based on purely simple logic. How valuable can a player be to a team that fails to qualify for post-season play? Could they not have missed the playoffs just as easily without him?

This debate was part and parcel of the argument against Chicago's Al Rollins in 1953–54, who was the second such player to be recognized with a Hart. The first was Brooklyn Americans defenseman Tommy Anderson during the 1941–42 season, but that selection was based around a number of factors.

The Amazin' Amerks, as they were jokingly known within NHL circles, were placed on life support that season, taken over by the league, forced to sell off the majority of their top players just to pay their bills and survive to play another day.

Amidst this sea of chaos, Anderson, an eight-season NHL veteran, dropped back from his usual left-wing position to fill in along the blue line and was nothing short of sensational, producing career highs in assists (29) and points (41). "Anderson gained, rather than lost, effectiveness as a scorer as a result of his switch to a post behind the blue line," noted the *Calgary Herald*.

"The naming of Anderson as holder of the coveted individual award came as little surprise, since the stocky veteran's play with a last-place club had made it evident he would be one of the top contenders," declared the *Ottawa Citizen*.

The 1958–59 season was a true anomaly. The third player to win the Hart and miss the playoffs was Rangers right-winger Andy Bathgate.

Playing on two wonky knees—a left one with a metal plate and a right one in need of surgical repair—Bathgate finished third in the scoring race with 40 goals and 88 points, but the Rangers won just 3 of their last 20 games and were nipped for the fourth and final playoff spot by Toronto by the scant margin of a single point.

"It's not Bathgate's fault," Rangers' publicity director Herb Goren proclaimed in the *Montreal Gazette*. "The man scored 40 goals. The defense sprung a few holes." Gordie Howe of the Red Wings, who finished last in the standings, was the runner-up in Hart balloting. At mid-season, Howe and Wings goaltender Terry Sawchuk stood 2–3 in Hart voting, even thought the Wings were stumbling along at a middling 16–16–3 mid-season mark.

The post-season debate was put on hold until the 1987–88 season, when Mario Lemieux was awarded the Hart even though his Pittsburgh Penguins finished last in the Patrick Division standings. Lemieux ended Wayne Gretzky's eight-year reign as Hart Trophy winner and seven years as the NHL's leading scorer. Lemieux chalked his win up to anti-Gretzky sentiment among the voters. "A lot of people are tired of him, but I can't see why," Lemieux, who received 54 of 63 first-place votes, told Dave Molinari of the *Pittsburgh Press*.

Oilers coach and general manager Glen Sather, while admitting bias, felt the award should have gone to Gretzky or Edmonton goaltender Grant Fuhr. "I wouldn't have voted that way, but of course, the other two guys play on my hockey team," Sather said. "I think when it comes to the world's best hockey player, and you're going to pick the most valuable player in the league, the man who gets you into the playoffs and wins the playoffs for you is the most valuable hockey player."

A similar debate preceded the announcement of the 2001–02 Hart winner. Calgary Flames right-winger Jarome Iginla, one of the three finalists, led the NHL in goals (52) and points (96), but Calgary was second-last in the Northwest Division, failing to qualify for post-season play. This led some in the media to question whether he deserved to be a Hart contender, but a past Hart winner under similar circumstances rose to Iginla's defense.

"Iginla should be judged on how he performed and what he did for the team," Bathgate stated to Mike Russo of the *Beaver County Times*. As it turned out, Iginla and Montreal Canadiens netminder Jose Theodore tied in points in the Hart balloting, but Iginla lost out in the tie-breaker because Theodore garnered more first-place votes.

Six years later (2008), Washington Capitals left-winger Alexander Ovechkin faced an almost identical scrutiny. He'd led the Caps on a memorable charge from last overall in the 30-team NHL early in the season to a chance to make the playoffs, topping the NHL in goals (65)—an NHL record for left-wingers—and points (112) in the process; but as Washington entered the last game of the season needing a win to qualify for the Stanley Cup tournament, questions were posed as to the validity of Ovechkin's Hart candidacy.

"Even if the Capitals fail to land a playoff berth, don't even think of delivering the Hart Trophy to anyone other than Ovechkin," penned *Montreal Gazette* writer Red Fisher on the eve of that game.

The point proved to be moot. The Capitals won their last game of the season by a 3–1 count over the Florida Panthers, earning the Southeast Division title and a playoff spot. A few months later, Ovechkin was presented with the Hart Trophy at the NHL Awards.

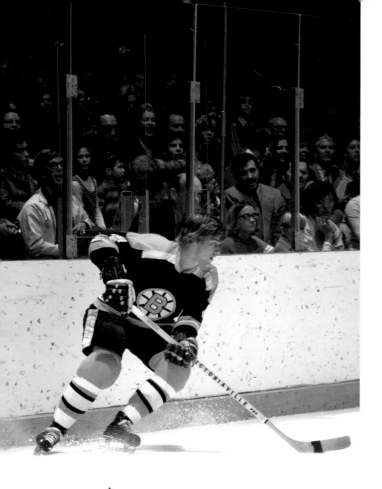

Eight-time Norris Trophy winner Bobby Orr is one of only two defensemen to win the Hart more than twice. Orr won the award three times in succession (1969–70 to 1971–72) while Eddie Shore won the trophy a total of four times over his 14-year career.

The Defense Rests

When Eddie Shore of the Boston Bruins was awarded the Hart Trophy as MVP of the league in 1938, it marked the fifteenth occasion in NHL history that the trophy had been meted out. Six of those trophies went to defensemen. Shore's triumph was the fourth season in succession that voters had deemed a member of the league's blue-line corps as the NHL's most valuable player.

During the first 31 years of Hart Trophy balloting, defensemen won the award nine times, with five different blue-liners being recognized. Boston's Shore won it four times, a record for overall Hart wins he held until Gordie Howe bettered him in 1960. Fellow Bruin Babe Siebert, Tommy Anderson of the Brooklyn Americans, Ebbie Goodfellow of the Detroit Red

Wings, Babe Pratt of the Toronto Maple Leafs and Herb Gardiner of the Montreal Canadiens were the other rearguards who were voted as the NHL's most valuable player during this time frame. Curiously, though, three of the winners (Anderson, Goodfellow and Siebert) were converted forwards.

Since 1955, Hart presentations have proven thin for the blue line. *Edmonton Journal* writer Jim Matheson described it as an "either-Orr" proposition for defensemen. "Either your name is Bobby Orr," Matheson wrote, "or you don't win it." In point of fact, Hart victories by defensemen in the aforementioned time frame account for four in total: three in a row to Boston wunderkind Orr (1969–70, 1970–71, 1971–72) and just one since then, to Chris Pronger of the St. Louis Blues in 1999–2000. And that win came by a scant point over Pittsburgh Penguins right-winger Jaromir Jagr, even though Pronger had a year that was difficult to overlook. He also won the Norris Trophy as top defenseman, registering career highs of 14 goals and 48 assists for 62 points and finished with a league-high plus-52.

Pronger also led all skaters in ice time per game, averaging 30:14, but seemed to understand the reasoning as to why so many defensemen are blown past by Hart voters. "We have our own award and some people think the Hart is more forward driven," Pronger said of the defensive blight when it comes to Hart ceremonies. "Maybe we need to change the mindset. Defensemen are just as important to a hockey club as a star forward."

Pronger's reasoning for the gap is sound, at least up to a point. "From the time Orr left the league, Wayne [Gretzky] and Mario [Lemieux] were there," he said. "They deserved everything they got."

New York Islanders Hall of Fame blue-liner

Denis Potvin, the Hart runner-up in 1975–76, thinks voters aren't paying enough attention to the sport when they overlook the value of a solid defenseman. "Most hockey people will tell you that defense is the hardest position to master," Potvin, a three-time Norris Trophy winner, told Michael Buteau of *Bloomberg News*. "You need the person who creates the offense by negating the other team's offense."

Even those who earn their paychecks for scoring goals seem to understand why it's so easy to overlook the overall contribution of a top defender to the success of an NHL team. "As a defenseman, you don't get the same publicity as a forward," Detroit Red Wings center Henrik Zetterberg said. "If you score goals and are doing the stuff that ends up in highlights, you get noticed. If you're doing good things in your own end, if you're not a real hockey fan, you don't see that. That's part of the reason why a defenseman doesn't get recognition."

The Wings need look no further than their own dressing room to see a Hart-worthy candidate who's been passed over countless times. Detroit captain Nicklas Lidstrom has won the Norris Trophy as the NHL's most valuable defenseman seven times, but has never finished in the top two places in Hart balloting.

"We talk about this every single year," Wings coach Mike Babcock said of Lidstrom's lack of Hart love. "I don't know. I have no idea. A few years back, I thought Nick was in the running and he never was. We think he's the best defenseman in the game. He's an elite person and a great leader and he's so important to this hockey club."

No less a source than Hall of Famer Steve Yzerman, Lidstrom's long-time Detroit teammate and currently general manager of the Tampa Bay Lightning, insists Lidstrom was the best player he ever played with in the NHL. "He's the best player

every night," added Wings rearguard Niklas Kronwall. But apparently not when the Hart votes are tabulated.

"He was voted player of the decade," Babcock said of Lidstrom. "He's one of the best of all-time. That's all I can tell you."

Wings GM Ken Holland, who was assistant GM of the team when they drafted Lidstrom in 1989, is baffled by his captain's Hart-less career. "I can't tell you he should have won the Hart Trophy, but there's no doubt in my mind he should have been a finalist for the Hart Trophy a number of times," Holland said.

Lidstrom himself, the only player to win an NHL individual award at least six times and never even finish as a Hart runner-up, is at a loss to explain why defensemen get the shaft when it comes to selecting an MVP. "That's a good question," Lidstrom said. "I'm not sure. I think especially during the regular season, people are focused on the points that the players are getting. Usually, a lot of points will get you close to the Hart. That could be one reason."

Perhaps another is Pronger's theory that both defensemen (Norris) and goaltenders (Vezina) have their own MVP trophy, sort of like the Cy Young for pitchers in baseball, which has made it rare for a hurler to garner an MVP award in that sport. "That could be true," Lidstrom admitted. "I never thought about it that way, but they do have trophies for the top D and the top goalie."

Apparently, it is a consideration of those holding Hart ballots. In the history of the award, which dates back to 1924, there have only been five occasions when no forward finished either first or second in the voting. The last time was in 1972, when Orr won the Hart and Montreal Canadiens goaltender Ken Dryden finished as runner-up. The other years included 1970 (Boston's Bobby Orr, Chicago Black Hawks goalie Tony Esposito), 1962 (Canadiens goalie Jacques Plante, New York Rangers defenseman Doug Harvey), 1954 (Chicago goalie Al Rollins, Detroit Red Wings defenseman Red Kelly) and 1937 (Boston defenseman Babe Siebert, Chicago defenseman Lionel Conacher).

In fact, 1937 marked the only occasion in Hart Trophy history when the top two vote-getters were both rearguards.

No Goal

No one questions that it takes a lot of heart to play goal in the National Hockey League. Still, when it comes time to select the NHL's most valuable player, for the most part, goaltenders have been left a Hart-less bunch.

Since 1962–63, goaltenders have been awarded the Hart Trophy (which, according to the NHL Guide and Record Book, is presented annually "to the player adjudged to be the most valuable to his team") three times. In that same time frame, a goalie has been honored with the Conn Smythe Trophy as MVP of the Stanley Cup playoffs on 15 occasions.

While goaltending is considered the most important aspect of playoff success, the significance of the position is often taken for granted during the regular season. "Playoffs are shorter, not as long as an 82-game season," reasons Vancouver Canucks goalie Roberto Luongo, runner-up in the 2006–07 Hart Trophy balloting. "You need to have a hot goalie to make it all the way and when you do have that, most of the time you do stand out."

The only goaltender to win back-to-back Hart Trophies puts forth an interesting theory as to why his brethren are so often shut out when it comes to consideration for the NHL's most valuable player award. "Why have goalies had so much trouble winning this?" Dominik

Hasek asked rhetorically. "I think it was because of [Wayne] Gretzky and Mario Lemieux in the 1980s, for sure. They made it tough on goalies."

On and off the ice, apparently. But that only covers one decade of NHL play, and the Hart has been up for grabs since 1924. You can't blame all of this lack of goalie love on The Great One and Super Mario. Prior to Hasek's successive wins with the Buffalo Sabres in 1996–97 and 1997–98, it had been a long dry spell for netminders. They'd gone Hart-less since Plante won the award in 1961–62.

The three winningest goaltenders in NHL history, Martin Brodeur, Patrick Roy and Terry Sawchuk, as well as the top three on the all-time NHL shutout list, Brodeur, Sawchuk and George Hainsworth, own zero Hart Trophies.

Johnny Bower, who won four Stanley Cups and two Vezina Trophies with the Toronto Maple Leafs, was named MVP of the American Hockey League in three straight seasons, a league record. But he only came close to winning the Hart once during a Hall of Fame NHL career.

The Hart derby was a three-man race during the 1960–61 season. Toronto left-winger Frank Mahovlich raced to an early lead, but was stalked by Montreal right-winger Bernie "Boom Boom" Geoffrion in the second half. Beyond them, an old war horse was keeping pace, turning aside shots and turning heads. It was Bower. Rangers netminder Gump Worsley, Bower's old pal, was lobbying hard for some love to be thrown the way of the goaltenders' union.

"They say he's 47 or 48 or something like that," Worsley told Dink Carroll of the *Montreal Gazette*. "But he's been playing great hockey for Toronto. I'd say he's the fellow who's been keeping the Leafs up there. I think he's saved more games for them than Mahovlich has won. If I had a vote for the Hart Trophy, I'd give it to him."

Ultimately, Geoffrion, who scored 50 goals that season and won the NHL scoring title, got the nod over Bower in the voting.

* * *

While Boston's Bobby Orr was rewriting the scoring record book for NHL defensemen during the 1969–70 season, collecting 33–87–120 totals to become the first rearguard to win the NHL scoring title, Chicago's rookie netminder Tony Esposito was doing his best to put a stop to all that offensive nonsense. Esposito posted 15 shutouts, the most in the league since George Hainsworth of the Montreal Canadiens posted 22 zeroes in 1928–29, and that led his coach Billy Reay to stump for Tony O as the man with the most Hart.

"Certainly I think he should win it," Reay told Jim McKay of the *Windsor Star* during the 1970 Stanley Cup playoffs. "Why? Because he was instrumental in us finishing first. What does a guy have to do? He lifted the team all season. He had 15 shutouts. He also had 15 one-goal games. There's altogether too much emphasis placed on scoring statistics by some of the people who pick these things."

Again, like Bower, Esposito was left to take the runner-up position behind Orr, even though so few goals got behind him.

Canadiens Jose Theodore, the 2001–02 Hart winner, is the most recent netminder to receive the award, joining Hasek, Plante, Roy Worters of the New York Americans (1928–29), Charlie Rayner of the New York Rangers (1949–50) and Al Rollins of the Chicago Black Hawks (1953–54). Theodore still finds it stunning that he won the award.

"I was pretty much a new guy; I just wanted to make a name for myself, and things just started picking up the year before," Theodore said. "And then when the season started, I was ready for a big season, and things just worked out. You've got be lucky in a way, you have to, and we had a team that worked really hard, and it was a great season."

Looking at the rarity of goalie wins, Theodore treasures his Hart. "That's why it's so special," he said. "It's a hard award to get, for a player or for a goalie. Looking back now, I realize that it's something that I'm proud of, something in my career that I achieved. It's something I'm proud of achieving, but you know, when you play in this league, you want to win the Stanley Cup. But obviously for a goalie, you need it to fall at the right timing, and you need to have a good team in front of you. But I think goalies are a big part of today's game."

Someday, perhaps, even Hart voters will get a better handle on recognizing that reality of the game.

The Hart Offensive

To some, the honor was long overdue. "It was a long time coming, but the National Hockey League's highest individual honor finally caught up with 33-year-old Milt Schmidt," *The Associated Press* reported May 8, 1951, as the veteran captain of the Boston Bruins was announced as winner of the Hart Trophy for the 1950–51 season.

A long-time all-star who'd led the NHL in scoring during the 1939–40 season and runner-up in the Hart balloting in 1946–47, the Bruins center finished up the track in fifth spot in the scoring race during the 1950–51 campaign. Schmidt's 61 points in 62 games were 25 in arrears of Art Ross Trophy winner Gordie Howe of Detroit, and he scored 20 goals fewer than Hart runner-up Maurice Richard of the Montreal Canadiens.

Regardless, Schmidt led Boston in scoring and carried the Bruins back into the playoffs after a one-season absence, and was the unanimous choice in voting for the center position on

Johnny Bower dives to stop the Montreal attack. In 1960–61, Bower posted a league-high 33 wins, was named to the NHL's First All-Star Team and was awarded the Vezina Trophy, but was edged out by Montreal's Bernie Geoffrion for the Hart.

the NHL's First All-Star Team, polling 40 of a possible 54 points in Hart balloting.

"Schmidt has been the main cog in the Bruins' offense this season, despite playing the last few weeks with his left knee heavily bandaged because of a torn ligament," noted the *Calgary Herald* early in Boston's Stanley Cup semifinal series with the Toronto Maple Leafs.

Schmidt was typical of the Hart Trophy winners of the award's first three decades. A true leader in every sense of the word, he could beat you with his skill, but also earned a reputation as a fierce competitor, playmaker, and someone who was handy to have around when trouble started on the ice. He was equally adept on the power play or the penalty kill.

In short, Schmidt could do it all. "He never plays a bad game and he never has a bad practice," Bruins coach Lynn Patrick told the *Montreal Gazette*. "Even in the workouts, he hates to lose." Patrick labeled Schmidt the greatest two-way

player who ever lived, putting him ahead of the likes of past Hart winners Frank Nighbor and Nels Stewart as the craftiest player in NHL history.

In terms of the Hart Trophy, Schmidt could also be affixed with the title as the last of his kind to win the award. Certainly, the season after his victory marked a turning point in the way the Hart was awarded.

Howe won it the following season, launching a tradition in which the league scoring champion would come to be considered the favorite to walk off with the Hart.

The Hart had been in existence for more than 30 years by the mid-1950s, but it was clear to those who followed the NHL that the landscape for choosing the winner was changing. Early Hart winners were certainly true to what the award was intended to represent: "the player adjudged to be most valuable to his team."

The first winner (for the 1923–24 season), Ottawa Senators center Nighbor, didn't rank anywhere near the NHL scoring leaders, but was recognized for the role he filled as the glue that kept the defense-first Senators in lock-step to their system for success.

Many of the early winners followed a similar protocol in terms of their selection. In 1924–25, voters opted for Billy Burch, the crafty, play-making center of the first-place Hamilton Tigers, over more flashy scorers such as Toronto's Babe Dye, Ottawa's Cy Denneny, and the Montreal Canadiens duo of Howie Morenz and Aurel Joliat.

Multiple NHL scoring champions of the 1920s and 1930s, the likes of New York Rangers right-winger Bill Cook, Toronto Maple Leafs right-winger Charlie Conacher and New York Americans left-winger Dave "Sweeney" Schriner never were awarded the Hart. Since 1950, every player who has won at least two NHL scoring titles has won a Hart Trophy with the exception of Canadiens center Dickie Moore, the NHL scoring leader in 1957–58 and 1958–59.

It's not that the early voters never went for the big-time scorers when choosing a Hart winner. It's more that they did it on occasions when it was warranted. Consider the case of Montreal Maroons center Nels Stewart.

Breaking into the NHL during the 1925–26 season, Stewart put together the most impressive rookie performance in league history. He led the NHL in goals (34) and points (42) and carried the second-season Maroons to second overall in the NHL. They became the first expansion franchise to win the Stanley Cup that spring.

Two seasons later, center Howie Morenz of the crosstown Canadiens topped the NHL in goals (33), assists (18) and points (51), the latter a new league standard, and became just the second player to lead the NHL in all three major offensive categories. His performance also allowed the Canadiens to run away with the NHL's regular-season title. Montreal's 26–11–7 slate put them eight points clear of any other team. So powerful was Morenz's performance that after the season, the New York Rangers were reported to have offered $50,000 for his services. "As far as the Rangers and Morenz are concerned, there has been no such deal," Habs manager Leo Dandurand told the *Ottawa Citizen*. "Canadiens will not sell any of their players. Money cannot buy them."

Morenz won a scoring title and the Hart again in 1930–31, leading Montreal to top spot in the Canadian Division of the NHL, and he was recognized as the most complete offensive package in the game. "Although Morenz won his greatest renown for his spectacular lone rushes, circling his own goal and darting and swerving through the entire opposing team to score, he is also a great playmaker and passes unselfishly," reported the *Edmonton Journal*. "His record of assists resulting in goals is almost as high as his total for goals scored."

Canadiens left-winger Hector "Toe" Blake was another scoring champ who proved a worthy Hart recipient. In 1938–39, his 47 points not only topped the league, but it also helped lift a woeful Habs squad into the final playoff spot. Two years later, Boston center Bill Cowley ran away and hid with the scoring title, winning by 18 points, including an NHL-record 45 assists. Cowley became the first player in NHL history to win the scoring title, Hart Trophy, lead his team to first overall in the regular season and to a Stanley Cup in the playoffs.

As exceptional as those performances were, it's important to remember that they were the exceptions and not the rule. The player who won the most Hart Trophies between 1924 and 1951 was a defenseman, Boston's Eddie Shore, who was voted the award four times. Shore's final win came in 1937–38, and NHL scoring leader Leafs Gordie Drillon (the most recent Maple Leafs player to lead the league in scoring) didn't even factor in the voting for the Hart. Chicago left-winger Paul Thompson, a distant third in scoring, was runner-up and Babe Siebert of the Bruins, Shore's defense partner, finished third in the voting.

Flashy scoring alone did not warrant Hart consideration, a fact of life that began to change shortly after Schmidt's 1950–51 win.

Not long afterward, people in the game began to question exactly what the Hart stood for, and whether those assessing the MVP had lost their way. "Wouldn't it be simpler to award the trophy to the best player in the league?" *Montreal Gazette* writer Dink Carroll asked readers in 1956. "Or shouldn't that be the index? If he's the best player in the league, the chances are he's the most valuable to his team."

More and more, as time passed, voters seemed to agree with this assessment. The numbers are there to be tabulated and these numbers don't lie. From 1924 to 1951, 8 of 28 Hart winners were also NHL scoring champions, an average of 28 percent. From 1952 to 2011, 34 of 59 winners have also been league scoring champion, a 58 percent average. Since 1966, the percentage jumps to 61 percent (28 of 46 winners). Factor into the equation the player who finished second in scoring or the skater who was the NHL leader in goals and that number jumps to a colossal 52 of the last 60 Hart winners, an astonishing 86 percent.

"I think if you win the Art Ross, I think it gives you a better chance," said San Jose Sharks center Joe Thornton, who won both the Art Ross and Hart Trophies during the 2005–06 season. "I

think that's why I thought [2009–10 Hart winner Vancouver's Henrik] Sedin had a real good shot. If you win the Art Ross, I think you have a better shot at winning the Hart, especially as a Western player."

The last time an Art Ross Trophy winner wasn't a Hart finalist was in 1993–94, when Wayne Gretzky—coincidentally the man with more Harts (nine) than any other player—didn't get the nod. But Detroit center Sergei Fedorov, runner-up to The Great One in the scoring chase, was awarded the Hart.

So why this long love affair with those who light the red lamp behind the net the most? Certainly, expansion has played a role. In the days of the six-team NHL, writers saw each player frequently with 14 games against each opponent. Today, with 30 teams, it's possible that a voter might not see a Hart candidate play at all in person over the course of a season, making statistics much more of a factor when determining a winner.

Since 1967, the Hart has gone to a forward on 35 occasions. Only three of those players didn't finish among the top two in the NHL scoring race—center Bobby Clarke of the Philadelphia Flyers in 1974–75, who ended up sixth overall in scoring, center Mark Messier of the New York Rangers, who was also sixth in the scoring charts during his Hart-winning campaign of 1991–92, and 2011 winner Corey Perry, who finished third in league scoring, one point out of second place.

"The guys who score the most get voted on for the Hart," succinctly observed Detroit Red Wings coach Mike Babcock, a fact of life all players have come to recognize.

How the West Was Shunned

Marcel Dionne remembers what it felt like to be a big fish in the biggest sea, and yet, still feel like a man alone on an island. "You got to play, but there were no highlights," said Dionne, a Hockey Hall of Famer who is fourth on the NHL all-time goals list after scoring 731 times during an 18-season career, the majority of which were spent in relative obscurity skating on the west coast for the Los Angeles Kings.

Four times, Dionne was picked to the season-ending NHL All-Star Team. He won the Art Ross Trophy in 1979–80, and finished second in scoring on three other occasions, but never won the Hart Trophy, finishing once as runner-up in the voting to Edmonton's Wayne Gretzky in 1980.

"It was difficult to get noticed," Dionne recalled. "I remember in 1975–76, I scored 50 goals in Los Angeles and coming into towns, people didn't even know I played the whole year at right wing. They thought I was playing at center. When the all-star selection came, they voted me at center. It just shows you the lack of knowledge that some of these guys had at the time. Sometimes, there's writers who don't like you, or they don't get to see you as much."

Long before TSN and ESPN initiated 24-hour coast-to-coast sports coverage and nightly highlight packages, before NHL Center Ice beamed every game played each night into the living rooms of all hockey fans, games played on the west coast tended to fall into a hockey black hole of sorts.

Though there have been NHL teams situated in the Pacific Time Zone since 1967, it wasn't until Gretzky of the Kings in 1988–89 that a player from a west coast club was voted the Hart Trophy as most valuable player in the league.

"That was a different era, admits longtime *USA Today* hockey writer Kevin Allen, current president of the Professional Hockey Writers' Association (PHWA). "I think information on hockey was harder to get then. I wouldn't

probably argue with those who say that in the 1970s, it was difficult for a guy on the west coast to get attention. We couldn't get any information about them. It was very, very difficult."

Things have changed of late. Three times since 2006, west coast players—center Joe Thornton of the San Jose Sharks (2006), center Henrik Sedin of the Vancouver Canucks (2010), and right winger Corey Perry of the Anaheim Ducks (2011)—were awarded the Hart. Three other Canucks—forward Markus Naslund (2003), goaltender Roberto Luongo (2007), and forward Daniel Sedin (2011)—finished as runners-up in Hart balloting over the past decade.

"Now there's a little bit more coverage," Dionne said. "TSN and *Hockey Night in Canada*, now they carry some games. Now, you can watch highlights. You see the top 10 goals every week, and scoring all those goals, I think I would have made top 10 goals of the week once in a while."

Still, even those who've lifted the Hart Trophy insist there's a geographic bias against players from west coast teams. "I just think, I know personally, from watching games as a young kid, or even with Boston, you really never watched the west coast because the games started so late," Thornton said. "I kind of think there still might be a bias there."

Henrik Sedin shared Thornton's view of the situation. "There's still the time difference there," Sedin said. "Watching games back home, there's still a lot of Toronto media that don't know what's going on out in our place. I think it's [bias] still there."

While both admit there's more opportunity than ever to view action on the Pacific Time Zone, neither buys that the majority of people are making the effort to become informed. "It's true, but I just don't think people know too much about the west still," Thornton said. "It's just the time difference. I don't think too many people are going to go on the Internet and check out stats and scores the next day."

Dionne, who operates a sports memorabilia company based out of Niagara Falls, Ontario, witnesses from his sales how the east dominates the marketplace. "That's in all sports, not just hockey," Dionne said. "I have a sports marketing company and I sell licensed products. It's the Yankees and Red Sox in baseball. San Francisco wins [the World Series in 2010], and nobody cares.

"It's the same thing with football. The Steelers versus Green Bay in the Super Bowl was great. The Patriots are big. The Giants. In the NBA, the Lakers control things, but when the Celtics came back big, it meant a lot to the business."

Kevin Allen, who oversees the voting on all NHL awards handled by the PHWA, doesn't entertain the notion that any of these anti-west arguments hold water for even a moment. "It's interesting," Allen said. "A few years ago, there was a issue when somebody from the San Jose Sharks was up for the award. [Mark] Purdy [of the *Orange County Register*] wrote a column in which he suggested it was impossible for a west coast guy to win the Hart.

"That's all nonsense. Historically, that wasn't the case. *The Hockey News* put together a study over the last 25 years and found out that was not even close to being accurate. We've tended to be more generous to Western Conference people than Eastern Conference people. In fact, if there

was a bias at all, it was probably in the voting [conducted by NHL general managers] for the Vezina. It was mostly Eastern Conference guys who won that award forever and a day.

"I don't personally believe there is ever an issue today, where most of us own the NHL Center Ice package and we can watch games from everywhere any night. The information superhighway allows us to know everything about what's going on with the league.

"We have so much information now, it's almost information overload. I don't think it matters where you play. I think the fact that we've had two west coast guys [win since 2006] is merely a coincidence. I think people want to look at that as not just the Western Conference, but as a particular Pacific Time Zone bias against Vancouver and L.A., San Jose and Anaheim, but the truth is, over the years, there haven't been a lot of great [Hart] candidates from out there."

Allen maintains a 50-50 balance between media covering both Eastern and Western Conference teams when assigning voters, but doesn't think that it matters as much as say, 25 or 30 years ago.

"It's completely different now," Allen said. "I don't think that there's any kind of bias. I don't particularly think it's imperative to have the East-West balance in the voting that I do have. If you're a qualified voter, you're a qualified voter. The league is interested in maintaining that geographic balance, so I try to accommodate them."

Wayne Gretzky holds the record for the most Hart Trophy victories, with nine.

CHAPTER 4
Seminal Seasons and Multiple Winners

The Great One's Goblet

You try to compare, and you quickly realize how incomparable the achievement truly rates in the history of professional sports: nine MVP awards, eight of them in succession.

When you get right down to the heart of the matter, the Hart Trophy truly belonged to Wayne Gretzky.

In 1935, when Frank Boucher won the Lady Byng Trophy for the seventh time in eight seasons, the NHL presented the original trophy to the New York Rangers center for good. It was his to keep. Boucher announced at the time that he no longer wanted to be considered for the award, so that someone else might have a chance to win it.

For most of the 1980s, it looked like that was the only way someone other than Gretzky was going to win the Hart. During his eight-season reign as MVP of the NHL, the eight runners-up in the Hart balloting were eight different players, exhibiting how Gretzky was the one

who delivered the goods season after season.

Just when you thought he couldn't get better, Gretzky would take out his eraser and do another number on the NHL record book. In 1980–81, Gretzky shattered the league mark for assists, garnering 109 to better Bobby Orr's previous NHL standard by seven. That same season, his 164 points won Gretzky his first Art Ross Trophy, and toppled Phil Esposito's single-season points standard of 152.

A great beginning, but The Great One only became even greater. The next season, Gretzky achieved an NHL scoring trifecta, wiping out his own barriers for assists (120) and points (212), and obliterating Esposito's 76-goal mark set in 1970–71 by lighting no less than 92 red lamps, and set an NHL standard for goals that remains on the books to this day. He collected his 100th point in his 38th game of the season, another NHL record.

"His vision and thought process were always unmatched by any athlete in any sport," former

Wayne Gretzky poses with the Hart and the Art Ross Trophies. Gretzky also holds the record for the most Art Ross wins, with ten.

New York Islanders general manager and fellow Hall of Famer Bill Torrey said. "That extra-special bit of insight. He always had it."

Gretzky's dominance was unheard of and has been unseen since he left the game. During the 1983–84 season, Gretzky collected a point in a league-record 51 consecutive games, scoring 61 goals and 92 assists over that span. Had he opted to take the rest of the season off, those point totals alone would have been enough to garner him the scoring title by 27 points over his nearest rival, Edmonton teammate Paul Coffey.

It was more than mere numbers that added up to Gretzky's total greatness. That same season, he led the Oilers to their first of four Stanley Cups over his next five seasons with the team. "The greatest leader, both on and off the ice, that I've ever played with is Wayne Gretzky," Coffey said.

Gretzky followed up the next year by leading the Oilers to another Cup and breaking his own assists record, dishing out 135 helpers. He also recorded his league-record thirty-fifth hat trick. "He's a fabulous player," said former NHL player and coach Tom Webster, who coached Gretzky in Los Angeles. "When you have a Wayne Gretzky in your lineup, it just elevates everyone. He's such a natural. Some of those plays he made are ones I still only dream about making."

There seemed to be no height he couldn't reach. The 1985–86 campaign was Gretzky's most productive as an NHLer. He rewrote the assists record even further, dishing out 163 of them, enough to win the Art Ross Trophy by 22 points if he hadn't scored a goal all season long. But Gretzky netted 52 of them, and his total of 215 points was also a new NHL standard.

Gretzky's eight straight Harts put him into an exclusive category. No other player has ever been voted the award more than three seasons in succession. After Gretzky's nine wins, Gordie Howe ranks second with six career Harts.

Gretzky's last Hart triumph was the result of a transcending moment in the game's lore. After leading Edmonton to the 1987–88 Stanley Cup, Gretzky was traded by the Oilers to Los Angeles. It was the biggest trade in NHL history and involved five players, three draft picks and a reported $15 million in cash.

He was the show in L.A., and he didn't disappoint, leading the Kings from eighteenth overall to fourth in the league during his first campaign in California.

Even though Pittsburgh's Mario Lemieux, the reigning Hart winner, won the Art Ross Trophy as NHL scoring champion, the Hart balloting wasn't even close, with Gretzky tabulating 267 of a possible 315 votes, including 40 of the 63 first-place nods. It was the first time since Gretzky's inaugural Hart victory in 1979–80 that the Hart Trophy winner wasn't also the NHL scoring champ.

"It means more to me this time than ever before," Gretzky said as he accepted the ninth Hart of his NHL career. "I think the very first one I won was something I would never forget … but [this] is real special."

On the big stage in Los Angeles, Gretzky led the game to previously unthinkable possibilities. He did for hockey what the Beatles did for rock and roll. Their music gained them fame, but it was their engaging personalities which turned the Fab Four into living legends.

Gretzky transcended the game like Michael Jordan on the hardwood, Babe Ruth at the plate, Muhammad Ali in the ring, or Pele on the pitch. Ask anyone from Timmins to Timbuktu. Even if they don't know hockey, they know of Gretzky. "No player has done as much for their game as you've done for ours," NHL commissioner Gary Bettman told Gretzky.

Gretzky's MVP accomplishments put him atop the heap in all the major North American sports. San Francisco Giants slugger Barry Bonds was a seven-time National League MVP and won the award a record four successive seasons from 2001 to 2004. Kareem Abdul-Jabbar won a record six MVP awards in the National Basketball Association, but never more than two in a row. Indianapolis Colts quarterback Peyton Manning holds the National Football League record with four MVP awards, but no NFL player has ever been named MVP more than two years in succession.

Perhaps the most amazing aspect of Gretzky's dominance of his game like no other athlete is that his motivation to be the best was driven by a devout concern that he wouldn't be good enough to measure up. "My whole sports life, from the time I was six years old, I've always played with this fear of failure," Gretzky said. "I remember the first time I tried out for a minor hockey team, I was scared to death that I wouldn't make the team.

"That same fear of failure motivated me to do my schoolwork as soon as I got home from school. The effects of that fear carried over and created the respect I have for other players and other teams and the preparation I put in before every game."

Amazingly, as a youngster, Gretzky dreamed of a career as a professional athlete, but it had nothing to do with rinks. "When I was growing up, I used to tell everyone that I was going to be a baseball player," Gretzky said. "I had harbored thoughts of playing in the NHL, but I never told anyone, because I always figured I wouldn't have the size and strength to make it. A serious notion of playing pro hockey never crossed my mind until I played in the world junior tournament [in 1978]."

Gretzky, 16 at the time, led all scorers with 17 points in six games and was named the top forward in the tourney, as Canada won the bronze medal. "I was going up against guys who were 19 and 20 years old and I did well," Gretzky said. "When I left that tournament, for the first time I said, 'I'm going to be a pro hockey player.'"

When Gretzky retired following the 1998–99 season, the Hockey Hall of Fame waived the usual three-year waiting period and inducted him immediately. There was a grassroots movement suggesting the NHL should rename the Hart the Wayne Gretzky Trophy, but The Great One, ever respectful to the history of the game, would hear none of it. Other legends have passed from the ice, he pointed out. The NHL existed for 62 years without Gretzky.

"No player is bigger than the game," Gretzky noted.

And no player made the game bigger than he did.

Mr. Hockey's Hardware

One fall, when Gordie Howe ("Mr. Hockey") was a youngster growing up in Saskatoon, Saskatchewan, the Detroit Red Wings held their training camp in that city. Howe knew Detroit was housed at the Bessborough Hotel, and like a lot of kids, angled for a way to get to his favorite player—Red Wings forward Sid Abel.

"A friend of mine was a bellhop at the hotel," Howe recalled. "And when Abel wanted anything, he'd let me take it up to Sid." It may have been the first time that Mr. Hockey elbowed his way to where he wanted to go. It certainly wasn't the last.

Howe convinced Abel to let him carry his skates to the arena, one future Hart Trophy winner helping another, just as they would on the ice a few years later.

Legendary players in their own right, superstars Bobby Hull and Wayne Gretzky, both of them also multiple Hart Trophy winners, can regale listeners with stories of how, as youngsters, they approached Howe with trepidation, seeking his autograph.

"My parents took me to Detroit," recalled Hull, who was 10 at the time. "I was bashful and kind of held back while the other kids crowded toward [Howe]. But after I saw the other kids got Howe's autograph, I got braver and asked him for it."

Gretzky's tale of his first encounter with Howe follows a similar path. "The first memory I have of Gordie is meeting him as a 10-year-old," Gretzky said. "A lot of times, when you meet your idol, you come away disappointed.

"That wasn't the case with Gordie. He's such a kind, wonderful person to everyone he meets. My father and Gordie Howe are probably the two men who have had the most profound effect on my life. Any recognition he gets is totally deserved."

These anecdotes, while appreciated by Howe, leave him speechless, simply because he can't remember a specific signature from the midst of millions he's scrawled across countless pieces of paper and items of memorabilia over his lengthy time as hockey's No. 1 ambassador.

"I can't remember," Howe admitted of such stories. "People are always pulling that stuff with me."

Until the arrival of Gretzky, no other player captured the collective conscience of the hockey world the way Howe did. No wonder they gave him the handle "Mr. Hockey."

He was referred to as a superstar and a geriatric legend. And at a time in life when some are under doctors orders taking heart medication, Howe was still slugging it out with the best hockey players in the world at the age of 52. In fact, Howe scored more goals in his 50s (fifteen) than he did at 18 in his rookie NHL season of 1946–47 (seven).

He was 24 when he won his first Hart Trophy, at the time the youngest player to win the award since 23-year-old Nels Stewart of the Montreal Maroons back in 1925–26. By the time he was collecting his then-record sixth Hart, Howe had celebrated his 35th birthday, making him the oldest forward ever to be voted the award. And he wasn't done yet with being the best of his league. At age 46, after ending a two-year retirement to join the Houston Aeros and make sporting history skating with his sons Mark and Marty as teammates, Howe was named MVP of the World Hockey Association.

"I recall the time I saw Gordie shoot a goal," remarked veteran Detroit Lions defensive lineman Alex Karras at a 1970 testimonial dinner in Howe's honor held in Windsor, Ontario, prior to the start of Howe's 25th NHL season in 1970. "I was so excited, I took the pacifier out of my mouth."

Howe won the Hart Trophy and Art Ross Trophies six times each, and both stood as NHL records when he finally gave up the game for good in the spring of 1980. He was chosen to the NHL All-Star Team in all but 5 of his 26 seasons, and rated among the league's top five scorers each season for 20 consecutive seasons between 1949–50 and 1968–69.

"Gordie also holds the record for the most practices," Doug Barkley, his old Detroit team-mate and coach, joked with the *Montreal Gazette* in 1971. "He's unbelievable."

When he retired from the NHL the first time following the 1970–71 season, Howe held 22 indi-vidual NHL records. His best offensive season as an NHLer was assembled during the 1968–69 season, when he finished third in NHL scoring with 44–59–103 totals. He was 41 at the time.

"It's the greatest sports story ever written," assessed Don Blackburn, Howe's last NHL coach with the Hartford Whalers.

Clarence Campbell, NHL president for all but one of Howe's 26 seasons, credited him with converting hockey from a Canadian to a North American sport. "Howe is a perfect example to two countries of what a perfect athlete should be," Campbell told *The Canadian Press* in 1971.

Apparently, there was merit in Campbell's words, for upon Howe's retirement in September 1971 (his first retirement) Howe received a congratulatory telegram from United States President Richard Nixon. "As a friend and fan, I wholeheartedly applaud the tremendous contri-butions you have made to the game of hockey and to the lives of its many enthusiasts by your splendid sports career," Nixon wrote.

Howe made the NHL record book his personal plaything. He shattered the NHL single-season scoring record in 1950–51 with 86 points, then tied it the following season, as he won his first Hart Trophy. As far as Detroit GM Jack Adams was concerned, there was nothing on the ice that Howe couldn't accomplish.

"He's great because he's big," Adams told the *Windsor Star*. "Because he's the cleverest stick-handler in the game, because he shoots with either hand, because he's aggressive, so nobody rides him off on a play, because he's one of the surest skaters on the ice."

The next season (1952–53) was the first Howe played without Abel as his center on Detroit's Production Line, and pundits wondered how good he'd be without his set-up man. How about better than anyone in the history of the game? Howe pushed the single-season standard to 95 points as he repeated as Hart Trophy winner.

Detroit returned to the top of the NHL standings in 1956–57, led by Howe, who topped the league in goals (44) and points (89). Howe finished first in the NHL in goals five times and in assists on three occasions. In 1950–51 and 1952–53, he led the NHL in goals, assists and points in the same season. In 1957–58, Howe won his fourth Hart Trophy, tying Eddie Shore for the all-time record. "Howe is the best player in hockey, great on defense and scores goals when we need them the most," Abel, now Detroit's coach, told *The Associated Press*. "Howe makes everything look easy. But he knows instinctively what to do and does it without too much effort. We'd be in a heck of a fix without him."

Howe snapped the tie with Shore in 1959–60, winning his fifth Hart as he lifted a Detroit team from last place to a playoff spot, matching his career points-per-game ratio of 1.07. "You've got to say he's likely the greatest player that ever played, or likely ever will play," offered Hull, runner-up to Howe in the 1960 Hart balloting. "He does everything well."

Howe won Hart and Art Ross Trophies, No. 6 each, following the 1962–63 season, when he led the NHL with 38 goals and 86 points. All in his seventeenth season in the league, at the age of 35.

"Gordie is the undisputed leader of the team," Abel told the *Windsor Star*. "They look to him to start things and get us going. When Gordie starts barreling in, he seems to get us moving."

Following his 1962–63 Hart triumph, Howe was named *The Canadian Press* Athlete of the Year. "Everyone who ever played with or against Gordie Howe knows he is the greatest," former New York Rangers coach Murray "Muzz" Patrick said.

That sentiment followed Howe wherever he went, even to the WHA when it seemed illogical that a man closer in age to 50 than 40 could still dominate games. In 1973–74, when Howe won his seventh major-league MVP award after he was named top player in the WHA, he joined Hull (1972–73, 1974–75) as the only players to be recognized as MVP of both the NHL and WHA. Eventually, the WHA honored Howe by renaming its MVP award the Gordie Howe Trophy. "It's hard to say how much Gordie means to hockey,"

offered two-time WHA scoring champ Andre Lacroix to *The Associated Press*. "He's the star of every game, just because he's still in it at 46 and because he's the greatest that ever lived."

When the WHA's New England Whalers held a celebration to honor Howe's 50th birthday in 1978, the guest list read like a who's who of Hart Trophy recipients. Among those on hand to fete Mr. Hockey were four-time Hart winner Eddie Shore, three-time Hart winner Bobby Orr, two-time Hart winner Bobby Hull, and Sid Abel, the 1948–49 recipient of the Hart Trophy.

"There have been so many years and so many exciting moments that they all blend into one," Howe said after scoring his 800th NHL goal with the Hartford Whalers on February 29, 1980. He left the NHL for good at the end of that season, at the age of 52. "I probably have another half year in me," Howe told *The Associated Press* upon announcing his second retirement from the NHL on June 5, 1980. "But I'd hate to go out after 32 years and find out in the middle of winter I've run short."

Howe's own recollection of the game he dominated through nearly five decades displays the heart this six-time Hart winner gave to hockey. "There could be no better way to make a living than in hockey," Howe told Hal Bock of *The Associated Press*. "It's been great to me and I only hope that in my own way, I've helped it along."

Fear not, Gordie. You helped plenty.

And how.

An Old-Time Hart Hero

He is worshiped as the patriarch of old-time hockey by Reggie Dunlop and the Hanson brothers in the 1977 hockey cult film *Slap Shot*, and in reality, in old-time hockey circles, Eddie Shore was the first player to take a dominant role in terms of the Hart Trophy selection.

During the first 15 years of the trophy's history, Shore was voted the Hart Trophy as the MVP of the NHL four times, a total that stood as the record for Hart victories by one player until Detroit Red Wings right-winger Gordie Howe won his fifth career Hart in 1959–60. Shore remains the only defenseman to win four Harts, one of the few marks that Bobby Orr, a legendary Boston blue-liner of a later era, can't lay claim to as his property. "He is one of the finest sportsmen I ever met," Toronto manager Conn Smythe told the *Calgary Herald* of Shore in 1933.

Shore was a player for all seasons, a man whom all fans could discover a reason to love or despise. His rink-length rushes with the puck were the stuff of legend. His bodychecks had no equal in the punishment they dealt out. His eccentricities off the ice and his rugged, often

disdainful persona made Shore Public Enemy No. 1 in all opposing arenas. He was often referred to as the most applauded and most booed player in NHL history.

It could be argued that no player shaped a permanent destiny for a franchise in the way Shore molded the Bruins in his image. Throughout Bruins history, they've remained true to Shore's base characteristics—explosive, entertaining, and tough to play against.

Throughout his hockey days, right up until the time in the mid-1960s when he was forced to abdicate as owner of the Springfield franchise of the American Hockey League following a player revolt, Shore was a polarizing figure in the game. He purchased the Springfield club for $40,000 while still a Bruins player in 1939, proposing he'd play for both teams. Bruins owner Charles Adams wouldn't stand for it and traded Shore to the lowly New York Americans.

No matter what he got himself into, though, Shore's status as hockey legend was never in doubt. "You didn't have to be a baseball fan to know who Babe Ruth was, and you didn't have to follow racing to recognize the name of Man O' War," wrote John Lardner in the *Milwaukee Journal* in 1940. "They were a front-page man and a front-page horse. The same thing applies to Eddie Shore. Eddie is the only player in hockey known generally to the people who ignore hockey."

Perhaps because Shore made it so hard to ignore him. "Shore is Mr. Hockey, just as Ruth was Mr. Baseball," Lardner continued. "Shore has the same quality of excitement that Ruth had. A simple gesture from Eddie will make them rise in their seats. And he shares Ruth's talent for getting into trouble and making stories."

Lardner marveled at the way Shore could both dominate games and antagonize opponents.

"A dozen of the toughest men in hockey have sworn to get him. He can protect his goaltender with the strength of three men and he skates forward big, tough and elusive, to shovel passes up to the wings and threaten the enemy goal."

Not bad for a guy who looked nothing the part when he first arrived in the big show. "He was the worst looking hockey player I ever saw when he broke in," said New York Rangers manager Lester Patrick, who first saw Shore in action with the Regina Capitals of the old Western Canada Hockey League.

"That's right," said Shore, refusing to dispute Patrick's scouting report. "At least it's not exaggerating much. I couldn't get out of my own way on the ice. You know, I never played hockey—legitimate hockey—till I reached college. Most of these fellows were at it as soon as they could walk. But I thought I knew it all, and that probably helped me as much as it hurt me. I even convinced the coaches that I knew it all. That's why they let me keep playing."

Coming to Boston after the Western League went under in 1926, Shore learned the fine art of defense from veteran practitioners Sprague Cleghorn and Lionel Hitchman, both Hart Trophy runners-up during their careers with the Bruins. By the late 1920s, he was already establishing a reputation as the league's best all-around defender.

Shore was someone who could beat you with his skill, or his fists. "I never went looking for fights, but if somebody else started one, I gave it all I had," Shore explained. "After all, hockey fans come to see individual players as well as teams. If a player doesn't let 'em know he's there, why should they come see him?"

Of all the legendary Hart winners, none savored the spotlight to soak in its gleam with the fervor that Shore opted for. The Bruins played up Shore's flamboyance to the hilt. Shore would make solo pre-game entrances to Boston Garden, accompanied by blaring music, covered in a scarlet-lined cloak like a Spanish matador entering the ring to fight a bull.

Shore was able to walk this walk because between the boards, he always delivered the goods. A Hart runner-up to Montreal Canadiens center Howie Morenz in 1930–31, Shore was voted the award in 1932–33, collecting 27 assists, an NHL record for defenseman, for the first-place Bruins that season.

Shore wasn't afraid to utilize his Hart Trophy success in contract battles with the Bruins. Following his first MVP award, Shore held out in the fall of 1933, seeking better contract terms from the Bruins, for whom he often played 50 minutes of ice time per game. "I figure if I am to play 60 minutes a game, and I can save the Boston club some money, due to the fact that they do not have to employ another defenseman, then, at least, I should receive something extra for my time," Shore told the *Regina Leader-Post*.

Shore's most infamous incident came during a December 12, 1933, game at Boston against the hated Leafs. Dumped by a bodycheck from Toronto defenseman King Clancy, Shore mistakenly thought Leafs winger Irvine "Ace" Bailey was the culprit, and cut the legs out from under him. Bailey's head hit the ice with a sickening thud. He underwent emergency brain surgery to save his life and never played in the NHL again. Toronto tough guy Red Horner then decked Shore, cutting open the Boston defenseman for stitches. "Eddie did a bad thing and got what he deserved," Horner said.

Afterward, Shore was distraught, and claimed no memory of the incident. He came to the area in the arena where Bailey was being tended to by physicians to offer an apology, which Bailey accepted. Twice Shore sought to visit Bailey in his Boston hospital and was refused permission. "I never held any animosity toward Bailey and there was no malice on my part for him," Shore said in a sworn statement given to NHL managing director Frank Patrick. "I was partially dazed by a fall immediately previous to my collision with Bailey. I have no recollection of seeing Horner or being hit by him. I first woke up in the Bruins' dressing room. I have never intentionally injured anyone in my entire hockey career." Shore was suspended for 16 games by NHL president Frank Calder and took a Bermuda vacation during that time to try and come to terms with his actions.

He rebounded from the near-tragic circumstances with Bailey to capture his second Hart in 1934–35, leading all NHL rearguards with 26 assists and 33 points. The following season, he was again recognized by Hart voters as his veteran influence kept a Boston team so riddled by injury it suited up 29 players in contention for the Stanley Cup. Playing against arch-rival Montreal with three broken ribs, Shore scored twice and set up another goal in a Boston victory. "He'd be a star in any era," former New York Rangers forward Muzz Patrick told *The Canadian Press*.

The next season (1936–37), Shore was limited to 18 games due to a cracked vertebra, and even Shore wondered if hockey was all over for him. "I don't know how this will affect me," he told *The Canadian Press*. "I want to know what I can do and what I can't do. If I can't get in there as I used to, I won't play, but if I can recover completely, I'll play again."

That fall, Shore came to training camp a driven and determined man. "Eddie Shore is in the best physical condition I have ever seen him,"

Bruins president Weston Adams exclaimed in the *Windsor Star*.

Shore's final Hart triumph came following that 1937–38 campaign, his third-last NHL season. Voters saw a different Shore that season, one who limited his offensive forays, but played defense with much attention to detail. "Hockey is not only a game of the swift, but of the intelligent," Shore explained to the *Edmonton Journal*.

After his fourth Hart Trophy victory, Shore, then 36, was determined to show he was worthy of his elite status: he reported to training camp in the fall of 1938 for his twelfth NHL season below his playing weight of 185 pounds. "Maybe it will help me to show some of these kids a burst of the old-time speed," Shore remarked to *The Associated Press*. "I have never felt better. Every day for the past two months I have been working from dawn to dusk harvesting my wheat [on his farm in Duagh, Alberta], and then, to prove to myself I was in shape, I drove the family over the road from Edmonton to Boston, making the trip in a bit more than five days, and that's no rest cure."

In his final full season as a Bruin, Shore helped Boston to an NHL-best 36–10–2 regular-season mark and a Stanley Cup title. When Shore retired in 1940, his 284 points stood as the NHL career mark for defensemen. He was elected to the Hockey Hall of Fame in 1947 and never lost his spirit for the game.

"Ah, we had some fun," Shore said of his times in the NHL in a 1967 interview with *The Canadian Press*. "Remember, though, half those yarns you hear about me aren't true at all."

The other half?

"Well, let's just say we had some fun," Shore said with a chuckle.

1996–97 · 1997–98
DOMINIK HASEK

CHAPTER 5
Hart Trophy Winners

1923–24
Frank Nighbor
OTTAWA SENATORS

By modern Hart Trophy standards, the veteran Ottawa center would have proven to be a surprise winner. Nighbor finished ninth in NHL scoring with 11–6–17 totals in 20 games, but was recognized for his defensive play and leadership role as much as for his offensive output. "To me, he certainly was tops," Ottawa defenseman King Clancy said. Nighbor was known for his calm, cool demeanor on the ice and his unyielding dedication to Ottawa's defense-first system. "Frank was a sensational star for the Senators," Ottawa general manager Tommy Gorman told the *Ottawa Citizen*. Nighbor was inducted into the Hockey Hall of Fame in 1947.

1924–25
Billy Burch
HAMILTON TIGERS

Doormats of the NHL, last-place finishers in each season from 1920–21 through 1923–24, the Hamilton Tigers jumped to first overall in 1924–25 and center Burch was honored for his role in the turnaround. He led the Tigers with 20 goals and was eighth in NHL scoring with 27 points. A crafty playmaker, Burch was the first American-born Hart Trophy holder, but although he entered the world in Yonkers, New York, Burch's family relocated to Toronto when he was a youngster, and he learned all his hockey in Canada. He was inducted into the Hockey Hall of Fame in 1974.

1923–24 FRANK NIGHBOR

1924–25 BILLY BURCH

1925–26
Nels Stewart
MONTREAL MAROONS

Few players broke into the NHL with the fanfare of "Old Poison." Signed in June from an amateur club in Cleveland, left-winger Stewart became the first and only rookie to win the Hart Trophy, leading the NHL in both goals (34) and points (42), while displaying that he wasn't to be messed with, collecting 119 penalty minutes in 36 games. His goal total stood as the NHL record for rookies until Gilbert Perreault bettered it in 1970–71.

1926–27
Herb Gardiner
MONTREAL CANADIENS

Acquired from the Calgary Tigers following the 1926 demise of the Western Hockey League, Gardiner was a stalwart leader for the Canadiens. A first-year NHLer at age 35, he became the first defenseman to win the Hart, playing every minute of all 44 regular-season games, as the Canadiens posted the lowest goals-against average. Gardiner's 6–6–12 totals are the smallest offensive output from a non-goaltender Hart winner. Another curious note: he's also the first player to wear sweater No. 1 to win the Hart. Canadiens netminder George Hainsworth wore No. 12 during the 1926–27 season. He was inducted into the Hockey Hall of Fame in 1958.

1927–28
Howie Morenz
MONTREAL CANADIENS

A surprising eighth in the Hart voting the previous season despite finishing third in NHL scoring, Montreal's speedball center left no doubt as to who would win the Hart that season. Morenz led the NHL in goals (33), assists (18) and points (51), as the Canadiens topped the regular-season standings by eight points over Boston. A stellar gate attraction throughout the league, Morenz

1925–26 · 1929–30 NELS STEWART

was often referred to as the Babe Ruth of hockey. His dominance showed in the voting. Out of a possible 140 votes, Morenz received 123. Morenz's win marked the first time that teammates had won the Hart in successive seasons. He was inducted into the Hockey Hall of Fame in 1945.

1928–29
Roy Worters
NEW YORK AMERICANS

The diminutive puckstopper nicknamed "Shrimp" loomed large between the pipes for his club and even larger in Hart Trophy lore. Worters became the first netminder to be judged MVP, as the Amerks finished second in the Canadian Division with a 19–13–12 record. Only two goalies posted a better GAA than Worters (1.15) and his 13 shutouts tied for second in the NHL. Regardless, his selection was open to controversy. "There is to be no question about Worters' class as a net guardian," opined the *Ottawa Citizen*, "…but

Pre-Hart Winners

The National Hockey League first presented the Hart Trophy to its most valuable player following the 1923–24 season. Prior to that, had there been an MVP selected in the league, who would have won? Allow us to speculate.

1917–18
Joe Malone
MONTREAL CANADIENS

The *Regina Leader* offered a word of warning to the rest of the NHL on the eve of the 1917–18 season that proved to be an accurate prediction of things to come. "It is a safe bet that [Canadiens manager] George Kennedy did not consult [opposing NHL goalies] Clint Benedict, Bert Lindsay and Sammy Hebert before putting Newsy Lalonde, Didier Pitre and Joe Malone on the same line," the paper reported. "Goal getting averages should be sky high this winter." Malone produced 44 goals in 20 games, an NHL single-season mark that stood until 1945 and a goals-per-game ratio of 2.2 that remains the league standard. He collected three or more goals in seven games, including a trio of five-goal outbursts. Malone was enshrined in the Hockey Hall of Fame in 1950.

1918–19
Edouard "Newsy" Lalonde
MONTREAL CANADIENS

The first player in league history to top the NHL in goals (22), assists (10) and points (32) in the same season, Lalonde carried the Habs to top spot in the first half of the season and a place in the NHL playoffs against Ottawa. The *Calgary Herald* lauded the Canadiens center for his "bursts of speed, his superb stickhandling and his cool, calculated attacks, frequently fatal in respect to bulging the nets." Lalonde was a 1950 inductee into the Hockey Hall of Fame.

1919–20
Clint Benedict
OTTAWA SENATORS

During an era when scoring ruled the game, Benedict shut the door, posting five shutouts and a 2.40 goals-against average (GAA), both NHL records. No other netminder posted a GAA below four. He set the tone early, opening the season with back-to-back shutouts, and led the

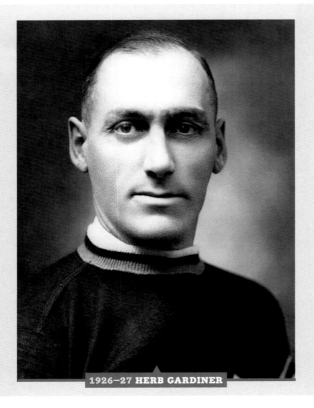

1926–27 **HERB GARDINER**

1927–28 · 1930–31 · 1931–32
HOWIE MORENZ

in this writer's opinion, Billy Burch was just as useful to the Americans as their great little goalie, and Frank [King] Clancy was more useful to the [Ottawa] Senators than Burch was to his team." Worters became a Hall of Famer in 1969.

1929–30
Nels Stewart
MONTREAL MAROONS

Becoming the first two-time Hart winner, Stewart's victory was among the surprises of Hart Trophy history. He'd finished fourth in goal-scoring with 39, behind Ralph "Cooney" Weiland (43), Aubrey "Dit" Clapper (41), and Howie Morenz (40), but had helped lead the Maroons to first in the Canadian Division, leading the division scoring race for much of the season. The NHL's first 300-goal scorer, Stewart was inducted into the Hockey Hall of Fame in 1962.

1930–31
Howie Morenz
MONTREAL CANADIENS

Winning his second NHL scoring title and equaling a career high with 51 points, the superstar Canadiens center joined Nels Stewart as a two-time Hart winner and continued to turn heads. "I would suggest that Morenz was the fastest and greatest two-way center in the game," New York Americans general manager Tommy Gorman said. In a five-year stretch from 1926–31, during which Morenz won two Hart Trophies, the meteoric superstar led all NHL snipers with 143–65–208 totals. He was a unanimous selection to the NHL's first-ever All-Star Team in 1930–31.

1931–32
Howie Morenz
MONTREAL CANADIENS

Setting two standards, Morenz won the Hart for a record third time and became the first player to

1928–29 **ROY WORTERS**

win the award in successive seasons, establishing his dominance as the top player of his era. He finished third in NHL scoring as the Habs wound up first overall in the NHL. "There was only one Canadiens player who won three MVPs," points out Howie Morenz Jr. His father also may have been the only Hart winner to combine crime fighting with hockey excellence. Finding an armed intruder inside his mother-in-law's home, Morenz disarmed the gunman with an old hockey trick, pulling the burglar's topcoat up over his head.

1932–33
Eddie Shore
BOSTON BRUINS

After knocking on the door for years, a Boston defender finally copped the Hart. The Bruins finished atop the NHL standings and Shore, their powerful and colorful defenseman, led all NHL blue-liners and was third on the team in scoring

PRE-HART WINNERS

NHL with 19 wins in 24 games. "Benedict did the best work of his career," offered *The Vancouver Sun* in assessment of the lanky netminder's 1919–20 campaign. "His work bordered on the marvelous." "Benedict's performance reached the high-water mark in goalkeeping exhibitions," Lester Patrick said. He was inducted into the Hockey Hall of Fame in 1965.

1920–21
Eddie Gerard
OTTAWA SENATORS

The captain and the conscience of the Senators, Gerard was a clean player in a time when pro hockey was rife with hooligans and stick swingers. Not that he didn't play a hard game, known for delivering stiff bodychecks, but never used his stick as a weapon. His work on the blue line enabled Ottawa to allow an NHL-low 75 goals. "[Gerard] is one of the most valuable all-around players in the National Hockey League," reported the *Quebec Telegraph*. He was inducted into the Hockey Hall of Fame in 1945.

1921–22
Harry Cameron
TORONTO ST. PATRICKS

The first NHL defenseman ever to record a four-goal game and the first NHLer to ever collect a Gordie

Howe hat trick (goal, assist, fight in same game), Cameron established single-season NHL records for defensemen with 18 goals and a league-leading 17 assists, finishing fourth in the league scoring race. His goals total stood fourth until 1941–42, while his assists mark was the standard until 1929–30. Cameron was inducted into the Hockey Hall of Fame in 1962.

1922–23
Georges Vezina
MONTREAL CANADIENS

A team in the midst of a roster transition, the Canadiens scored a league-low 73 goals, but became a playoff club thanks to the sensational work of their veteran netminder, Georges Vezina, who allowed three goals or fewer in 18 of 24 games, including a pair of shutouts. Vezina had started every game in Montreal's goal since the birth of the NHL in 1917. "He was a standup goaler and he made a lot of saves with his stick," Canadiens defenseman Sprague Cleghorn told the *Montreal Gazette*. Vezina was voted into the Hall of Fame in 1945.

1932–33 · 1934–35 · 1935–36 · 1937–38
EDDIE SHORE

1933–34 **AUREL JOLIAT**

with a career-best 27 assists and 35 points. Shore's 27 helpers were an NHL record for a defenseman and one shy of the 28 posted by league-leader Frank Boucher of the New York Rangers. Shore was a unanimous choice on defense for the NHL's First All-Star Team.

1933–34
Aurel Joliat
MONTREAL CANADIENS

With linemate Howie Morenz slumping to eight goals and reigning Hart winner Eddie Shore of Boston suspended for a hit that nearly killed Toronto's Ace Bailey, Montreal's mighty atom rose to the fore. Known for his distinctive black ball cap and at 33, the oldest player on the Canadiens roster, Joliat tied for third in the NHL with 22 goals and was considered the best stickhandler in hockey. Relegated to Second Team status on the NHL All-Star squad behind Toronto's Harvey "Busher" Jackson, Joliat was the first Hart winner

not named a First All-Star since team selection was introduced in 1930–31. He was enshrined in the Hockey Hall of Fame in 1947.

1934–35
Eddie Shore
BOSTON BRUINS

Rebounding from a 1933–34 campaign which began with a contract holdout and included a lengthy NHL suspension for a cheap hit on Toronto's Ace Bailey, Boston's belligerent blue-liner was back to his old self. Shore's 26 assists and 33 points led all NHL defenders for the first-place Bruins, and he became the first defenseman with two Harts on his résumé. His close call with Bailey didn't deter Shore. A Shore bodycheck left Montreal Maroons forward Jimmy Ward hospitalized in January with a concussion, and he traded blows with Georges Boucher in a February game against St. Louis, leading Eagles manager Clare Brunton to call for disciplinary action.

1936–37 **BABE SIEBERT**

1938–39 **TOE BLAKE**

1935–36
Eddie Shore
BOSTON BRUINS

Joining Howie Morenz as a three-time Hart winner, even though his point totals dropped from 33 to 19, Shore was credited for his leadership role in keeping a Boston team that was in transition among the contenders, despite utilizing 29 players during the campaign. Shore and Boston partner Babe Siebert were named the defense pair on the NHL's First All-Star Team, the sixth of eight times Shore would receive such recognition during his career. Shore was inducted into the Hockey Hall of Fame in 1947.

1936–37
Babe Siebert
MONTREAL CANADIENS

A sensational scorer who helped the Maroons win the 1925–26 Stanley Cup, Siebert transitioned to defense late in his career and was

a First All-Star at the position with Boston in 1935–36. Moving back to Montreal to play for the first-place Canadiens in 1936–37, Siebert joined former teammate Eddie Shore and ex-Hab Herb Gardiner as the only defensemen to win the Hart. Siebert, who led all NHL defenders in 1936–37 with 28 points, proved adept at using his size, strength and balance on his blades for moving players off the puck.

1937–38
Eddie Shore
BOSTON BRUINS

Rebounding from a serious back injury that scuttled his 1936–37 season, Boston's Shore won the Hart for a record fourth time, and it was the fifth time in eight seasons that he'd finished first or second in the voting. More of a defensive presence than an offensive threat at this point in his career, Shore, 35, and a 12-year veteran, was stalwart at the back end as Boston rolled to an

1939–40 **EBBIE GOODFELLOW**

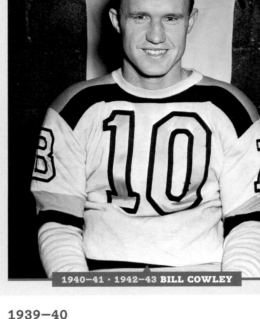

1940–41 · 1942–43 **BILL COWLEY**

NHL-best 30–11–7 slate, once more earning First All-Star Team status. Described as older, balder, and slower, Shore was said to have replaced the rage of his youth with the cunning of experience.

1938–39
Toe Blake
MONTREAL CANADIENS

Originally passed over in 1934 by the Canadiens and left to sign with the crosstown rival Maroons, Blake was acquired by the Habs the following season. He blossomed on a weak Montreal squad, winning the NHL scoring title with 24–23–47 numbers, and earned First All-Star Team status at left wing. His work ethic and performance at both ends of the ice helped the Habs garner the sixth and final playoff spot in the now seven-team, one-division NHL. Blake was inducted into the Hockey Hall of Fame in 1966.

1939–40
Ebbie Goodfellow
DETROIT RED WINGS

Another high-scoring forward who made the switch to the blue line, Goodfellow helped Detroit to back-to-back Stanley Cups in 1935–36 and 1936–37, but in the 1939–40 season, he was recognized for his work in holding a young Red Wings team together enough to earn fifth place and a playoff spot. Described by Wings coach Jack Adams as the rallying force of the hockey club, Goodfellow finished second in team scoring with 11–17–28 totals. Goodfellow was inducted into the Hockey Hall of Fame in 1963.

1940–41
Bill Cowley
BOSTON BRUINS

Collecting 45 assists, the Boston center, skating on a line between Roy Conacher and Eddie Wiseman, shattered the previous NHL single-

1941–42 **TOMMY ANDERSON**

1943–44 **BABE PRATT**

season mark for helpers of 37, set by Toronto's Joe Primeau in 1931–32. "Bill sets up the smoothest plays you could hope to see," Bruins coach Ralph "Cooney" Weiland told the *Regina Leader-Post*. Cowley finished as NHL scoring champion with 62 points, 18 better than any other player.

1941–42
Tommy Anderson
BROOKLYN AMERICANS

Never before had a player from a non-playoff team been awarded the Hart Trophy, but that changed in 1941–42. Anderson switched from left wing to defense, anchoring the back end for a cash-strapped team taken over by the league and forced to sell most of its top players in order to survive. He collected 41 points, a new NHL record for blue-liners, and earned First All-Star Team status (his first as an NHLer) with the last-place Amerks. He was the first Hart winner who would not earn enshrinement in the Hockey Hall

of Fame and the first player to win the award in his farewell NHL season.

1942–43
Bill Cowley
BOSTON BRUINS

Finishing second in NHL scoring with 72, and equaling his own NHL mark with 45 assists, the Bruins center won his second Hart in three years, joining Eddie Shore, Howie Morenz and Nels Stewart in the multiple-Hart-winners fraternity. It is interesting to note that Cowley and Montreal Canadiens forward Toe Blake were the only winners of the Hart still active in the NHL. Cowley was inducted into the Hockey Hall of Fame in 1968.

1943—44
Babe Pratt
TORONTO MAPLE LEAFS

Some hockey purists frowned on the performance of the Leafs defenseman, who established a single-season scoring record for NHL rearguards with 57 points, including 17 goals. They felt Pratt spent too much time up ice, and did not pay enough attention to his work at the other end of the rink. But the First All-Star Team selection was recognized for his ability to keep a Toronto club, decimated by personnel losses due to the war effort, in contention. At the conclusion of the regular season, Leafs fans presented Pratt with a $100 Victory Bond, which he immediately donated to the Red Cross. Pratt was inducted into the Hockey Hall of Fame in 1966.

1944—45
Elmer Lach
MONTREAL CANADIENS

Faced with a choice between the passer and the shooter, the Hart Trophy panel opted for the former. Looking past the NHL record 50 goals scored by his right-winger Rocket Richard, the MVP trophy went to Lach, Richard's center, who led the NHL in scoring with 80 points, including a league-record 54 assists. In fact, it was one of the almost unanimous choices in Hart history, Lach garnering 116 of a possible 120 points. Just three years earlier, Lach had broken his left arm when crashing into the boards at the Montreal Forum and was told by doctors that he'd never play again. NHL president Red Dutton officially awarded Lach the trophy April 6, 1945, during a Canadiens–Maroons oldtimers' game at the Forum, the first public presentation in the award's history. Lach was enshrined in the Hockey Hall of Fame in 1946.

1945–46 **MAX BENTLEY**

1945—46
Max Bentley
CHICAGO BLACK HAWKS

"Stop Max Bentley and you will stop the Hawks." That was the rallying cry of NHL opponents, but it was a strategy easier spoken than implemented. Returning to the NHL after serving two years in the Canadian army, Chicago's dipsy doodle dandy led the league in scoring with 31–30–61 totals, skating on a line with his brother Doug and Bill Mosienko. Bentley was the first Black Hawk to win the Hart, and NHL president Clarence Campbell made a special trip to Chicago to present him with the trophy prior to a November 21, 1946, game with Detroit. Bentley was inducted into the Hockey Hall of Fame in 1966.

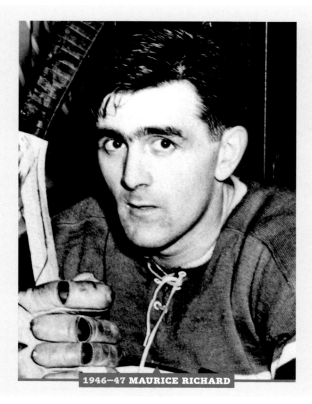

1946–47 MAURICE RICHARD

1947–48 BUDDY O'CONNOR

1946–47
Maurice Richard
MONTREAL CANADIENS

Potting 45 goals, 15 more than any other player, Montreal's fiery right-winger with a nose for the net showed his doubters he was the real deal, putting up those numbers despite the loss of his center Elmer Lach for 29 games due to a fractured skull. Richard collected 48 of a possible 54 points from Hart voters. Twelve of 18 voters put the Rocket first on their ballot, and the other six had him in second spot. His win meant all three members of Montreal's Punch Line—Richard, Lach and Toe Blake—were Hart winners, an NHL first. Richard was inducted into the Hockey Hall of Fame in 1961.

1947–48
Buddy O'Connor
NEW YORK RANGERS

Becoming the first Ranger to win the Hart, O'Connor also made history as the first player to win both the Hart and Lady Byng Trophies in the same season. Traded to the Rangers by the Montreal Canadiens at the start of the season, O'Connor collected 24–36–60 totals, finishing second in the scoring race, a point behind Montreal's Elmer Lach, and was second in assists, one behind Chicago's Doug Bentley. But despite all his hardware, O'Connor was only named to the Second All-Star Team, Lach taking the First Team nod at center. O'Connor was inducted into the Hockey Hall of Fame in 1988.

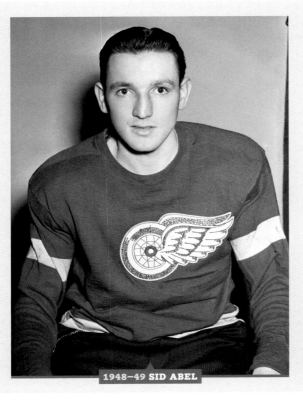

1948–49 SID ABEL

1949–50 CHUCK RAYNER

1948–49
Sid Abel
DETROIT RED WINGS

The Detroit captain and center of the Production Line led the NHL with 28 goals and was third in scoring with 54 points as the Wings finished first for the first season since 1942–43 with a 34–19–7 slate. "Sid had a soft heart, but when he hit the ice, he was very much a machine," linemate Gordie Howe said. Abel was selected center on the First All-Star Team for the first time in his career. He'd been tabbed the Second Team left-winger back in 1941–42. Abel was inducted into the Hockey Hall of Fame in 1969.

1949–50
Chuck Rayner
NEW YORK RANGERS

The second goaltender to win the Hart, Rayner almost singlehandedly carried the Rangers to the fourth and final playoff spot, winning 28 games

and posting six shutouts. The hardest part for the NHL was locating Rayner to inform him of his win. He'd embarked on a trip to a fishing camp in Kenora, Ontario, in which he shared ownership with fellow netminder "Sugar" Jim Henry, and couldn't be located. Rayner didn't warrant First All-Star Team status in 1949–50. That went to Montreal's Bill Durnan, the Vezina Trophy winner, while Rayner was the Second Team netminder. He was inducted into the Hockey Hall of Fame in 1973.

1950–51
Milt Schmidt
BOSTON BRUINS

Most hockey people felt that the Boston captain was long overdue for recognition. Finally, in his twelfth NHL season, Milt Schmidt, age 33, finally received his first individual honor. He helped the Bruins battle their way into the final playoff spot, finishing in a tie for fourth in NHL scoring with

1950–51 **MILT SCHMIDT**

1953–54 **AL ROLLINS**

61 points. Schmidt was a unanimous choice at center on the NHL's First All-Star Team and was known equally for his work as a checker as he was for his offensive production. He was inducted into the Hockey Hall of Fame in 1961.

1951–52
Gordie Howe
DETROIT RED WINGS

The man who became known world wide as Mr. Hockey finally ascended to his place atop the hockey world in the 1951–52 season. Howe netted a career-high 47 goals, and equaled his own NHL single-season record of 86 points, winning the Art Ross Trophy for the first-place Red Wings. Wings GM Jack Adams even suggested Howe could replace Sid Abel at center on Detroit's top line. "He's got everything it takes to make a great center," Adams told Dink Carroll. "But [then] we'd have to replace Howe at right wing." Howe was inducted into the Hall of Fame in 1972.

1952–53
Gordie Howe
DETROIT RED WINGS

In 1953, the Detroit right-winger joined Howie Morenz and Eddie Shore as the only players to win back-to-back Harts up to that time. The first player in history to lead the NHL in scoring three times, Howe won his third straight Art Ross Trophy with an NHL-record 95 points and a career-best 49 goals, but had a naysayer to his win in his own camp. "I think [Detroit defenseman Red] Kelly should get the Hart," Wings coach Tommy Ivan opined late in the regular season. Howe was among four Wings voted to the NHL's First All-Star Team in 1952–53.

1951–52 · 1952–53
1956–57 · 1957–58
1959–60 · 1962–63
GORDIE HOWE

1953–54
Al Rollins
CHICAGO BLACK HAWKS

Few Hart winners were a more surprising choice. Rollins backstopped a Chicago team that finished last overall at 12–51–7 and allowed 244 goals for a dismal 3.46 goals-against average. But the year before, Rollins had posted five shutouts, two of them coming in scoreless ties, and had come second in the Hart voting. "That Rollins is sensational," Boston coach Lynn Patrick declared to the *Christian Science Monitor*. Added defenseman Gus Mortson, a teammate of Rollins in Toronto and Chicago: "He was always a good goalkeeper, but he just didn't get the recognition that should have come his way in Toronto." Rollins joined Tommy Anderson (1941–42) of the Brooklyn Americans as the only Hart winners from last-place clubs.

1954–55
Ted Kennedy
TORONTO MAPLE LEAFS

Some viewed Kennedy's triumph as a sort of lifetime achievement award for the personable Toronto captain who was expected to retire at season's end. Hockey people disagreed. "Absolutely not," remarked Boston Bruins coach Lynn Patrick. "Kennedy is the man." Kennedy scored just 10 goals, the fewest ever by a Hart-winning forward. "He certainly is a fine player," Montreal GM Frank Selke remarked, "but he isn't the type to be selected on all-star teams." Kennedy was inducted into the Hockey Hall of Fame in 1966.

1955–56
Jean Beliveau
MONTREAL CANADIENS

Montreal, led by Beliveau, ended Detroit's seven-season reign as regular-season champions.

1954–55 TED KENNEDY

Beliveau topped NHL scoring that season with a league-high 47 goals and 88 points, both records for a center. He also set an NHL mark by registering a hat trick during one power play, leading the NHL to change the existing rule that a team must remain shorthanded for the entire two-minute duration of a minor penalty. "He's still developing," New York Rangers GM Frank Boucher told the *Montreal Gazette* of Beliveau. "He has a chance to become the greatest player in the history of hockey."

1956–57
Gordie Howe
DETROIT RED WINGS

Finishing with 89 points, Howe won his fifth Art Ross Trophy as NHL scoring leader by four points over linemate Ted Lindsay, as Detroit returned to the top of the NHL standings for the eighth time in nine seasons. December was an especially productive month for Howe. On

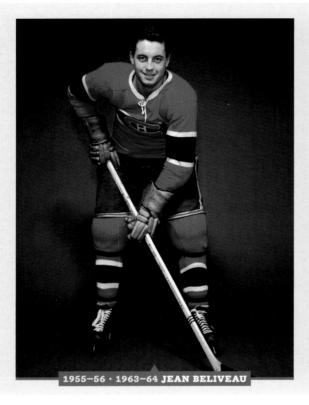

1955–56 · 1963–64 **JEAN BELIVEAU**

1958–59 **ANDY BATHGATE**

December 15, he surpassed the career goals total of Nels Stewart (325) to become the NHL's second all-time leader in goals, and recorded a career-high six-point game Christmas Day against the New York Rangers. "Guys like Howe and Lindsay don't come along in hockey very often," expressed Wings coach Jimmy Skinner to *The Associated Press*. Howe joined Howie Morenz and Eddie Shore as the only players to win at least three Hart Trophies.

1957–58
Gordie Howe
DETROIT RED WINGS

Becoming the first player ever to twice win back-to-back Harts, Mr. Hockey joined Eddie Shore (known himself as Mr. Hockey during his playing days) as the only four-time winners of the award. "You never know how he's going to come at you," Chicago goalie Harry Lumley said of Howe. Howe had moved past Elmer Lach's total of 408

to become the NHL's career-assists leader and finished second in the NHL with 33 goals, despite missing six games due to a rib injury.

1958–59
Andy Bathgate
NEW YORK RANGERS

Performing gamely on a pair of damaged knees, the Rangers right-winger not only captured his first Hart, he also ended the Gordie Howe–Maurice Richard stranglehold on the right-wing berth of the NHL's First All-Star Team for the first time since Toronto's Lorne Carr earned the honor in 1943–44. Bathgate won both halves of the balloting, even though his Rangers faded badly down the stretch and missed the final playoff spot by a point behind the surging Maple Leafs. Bathgate was inducted into the Hockey Hall of Fame in 1978.

1960–61 **BERNIE GEOFFRION**

1961–62 **JACQUES PLANTE**

1959–60
Gordie Howe
DETROIT RED WINGS

And then there was one. Winning the Hart for a record fifth time, Howe stood alone as the MVP of the NHL's MVPs. Leading the Wings in scoring with 73 points, while leading them back into the playoffs after a last-place finish the previous season, Howe surpassed Maurice Richard's 946 as the NHL's career scoring leader. He garnered 118 points in the voting, more than double the points of any other player.

1960–61
Bernie Geoffrion
MONTREAL CANADIENS

Geoffrion, son-in-law of three-time Hart winner Howie Morenz, missed six games in January due to an injured knee, and then went on a tear; he scored 23 times in the next 20 games, and joined Rocket Richard as the only NHLers to register

a 50-goal season. "The players kept telling me I could do it," Geoffrion told *The Canadian Press*. He also won his second NHL scoring title with 95 points. The left-winger was inducted into the Hockey Hall of Fame in 1972.

1961–62
Jacques Plante
MONTREAL CANADIENS

There were whispers that Plante's best days were behind him when the Canadiens five-year reign as Stanley Cup champions ended in the spring of 1961, and he gave way to Charlie Hodge between the Montreal posts for much of that season. But Plante silenced the skeptics in 1961–62, playing all 70 games, posting a league-leading 42 wins and capturing his sixth Vezina Trophy for the first-place Habs. He was inducted into the Hockey Hall of Fame in 1978.

1964–65 · 1965–66 **BOBBY HULL**

1962–63
Gordie Howe
DETROIT RED WINGS

Showing no signs of slowing down at age 35, Howe raced to his sixth scoring title with 86 points, his best season since 1956–57, and in the process, won the Hart for a record sixth time as well. Third after mid-season voting, Howe garnered 81 of a possible 90 points in the second half to run away with the award. "We've been talking for five years about him playing defense when he doesn't score goals anymore, but that day doesn't look any closer than it did five years ago," Detroit coach Sid Abel told the *Windsor Star*.

1963–64
Jean Beliveau
MONTREAL CANADIENS

"Le Gros Bill," as he was known in Quebec, set a record for the longest time passage between Hart triumphs, winning his second Hart eight seasons after his first. The Canadiens center posted a team-leading 78 points, including 50 assists, for first-place Montreal. "I was very pleased when I won it the first time, but this one gives me even more satisfaction," Beliveau, 32, told the *Montreal Gazette*. "When you reach a certain stage of your career, you begin to wonder how much longer you can play, so it's gratifying to win it at my age." Beliveau was inducted into the Hockey Hall of Fame in 1972.

1964–65
Bobby Hull
CHICAGO BLACK HAWKS

Thirty-two of the Chicago left-winger's 39 goals came in the first 32 games, so it was no surprise when Hull led the Hart voting by a country mile at mid-season—66 points over Detroit's Norm Ullman. But when the speedy skater with the heavy shot scored just seven goals the rest of the way, he barely hung on to win, garnering only

1966–67 · 1967–68 **STAN MIKITA**

15 second-half votes. Hull, who joined Buddy O'Connor as the only players to win the Hart and Lady Byng Trophies in the same season, was inducted into the Hockey Hall of Fame in 1983.

1965–66
Bobby Hull
CHICAGO BLACK HAWKS

Rewriting the NHL single-season scoring record book, Chicago's Golden Jet became the fourth player to win consecutive Hart Trophies. Finishing with 54 goals, Hull became the first player in NHL history to score more than 50 times in a season, and with an assist in his final game of the season, Hull won the Art Ross Trophy with a record 97 points. Toronto goalie Johnny Bower marveled at Hull's wicked shot. "The puck comes at you with such terrific speed, it's all over in a split second," he told Hal Bock of *The Associated Press.*

1966–67
Stan Mikita
CHICAGO BLACK HAWKS

Born in Sokolce, Czechoslovakia, Mikita immigrated to Canada as a youth, making him the first European-born Hart winner. Leading the Black Hawks to their first-ever first-place finish, Mikita tied teammate Bobby Hull's record of a year earlier, winning the Art Ross Trophy with 97 points. He also earned the Lady Byng Trophy, becoming the first player ever to turn this triple in the same season. In victory, Mikita praised linemates Ken Wharram and Doug Mohns. "I let them share in the trophies, but they're not going to share in the [prize] money," Mikita told *The Associated Press.*

1967—68
Stan Mikita
CHICAGO BLACK HAWKS

The fifth back-to-back Hart winner, Mikita won the Art Ross Trophy with 87 points and a career-high 40 goals, repeating his Hart–Art Ross–Lady Byng Trophy treble of the season before. "It's quite an honor, but I think right now, I'd trade all three for the Stanley Cup," Mikita told the *Montreal Gazette*. Black Hawks coach Billy Reay had nothing but praise for Mikita. "Mikita is all guts, 160 pounds of guts," Reay told the *Windsor Star*. Mikita became a Hockey Hall of Fame enshrinee in 1983.

1968—69
Phil Esposito
BOSTON BRUINS

The burly Boston center obliterated the previous NHL scoring mark of 97 points, becoming the league's first century man, winning the Art Ross Trophy with 126 points, including an NHL-record 77 assists. "One of his best virtues as a player is his patience with the puck," Boston coach Harry Sinden told the *Montreal Gazette*. "Esposito will always wait for the opposition defenseman or goaltender, or his own winger to make the first move. He will never give the puck away under any circumstances." Esposito entered the Hockey Hall of Fame in 1984.

1969—70
Bobby Orr
BOSTON BRUINS

In what was billed as the first annual Bobby Orr awards luncheon, the wunderkind Bruins defenseman walked off with three awards—the Hart, Art Ross and Norris Trophies. With 33–87–120 numbers, Orr became the first defenseman to ever lead the NHL in scoring, potting

1968-69 · 1973-74 **PHIL ESPOSITO**

30 goals and collecting 100 points in the season. He later added the Conn Smythe Trophy as Stanley Cup MVP, becoming the first player to sweep the Hart and Smythe in the same season. "[Orr's] the greatest thing I've seen in the past, the greatest thing in the present and if anything comes along in the future, I hope the Good Lord will let me stay around to see it," Boston GM Milt Schmidt told *The Associated Press*.

1970—71
Bobby Orr
BOSTON BRUINS

Shattering his own offensive records for blue-liners with 37–102–139 totals, the Boston defenseman repeated as Hart Trophy winner, becoming the sixth player to win consecutive Harts and the third to do it in the past seven seasons. Orr joined former Bruins rearguard Eddie Shore as the only defensemen to win the Hart at least twice. Orr's only concern was for the Stanley

1969–70 · 1970–71 · 1971–72 **BOBBY ORR**

Cup chance lost when the Bruins were upset by Montreal. "Any member of the Canadiens or Black Hawks like to trade two-for-one right now?" Orr asked of the two teams in the Cup final series.

1971–72
Bobby Orr
BOSTON BRUINS

Only 24, Orr continued making history, topping 100 points for the third straight season and becoming the first player to win the Hart three times in a row. Signed to a record five-year, $1 million contract prior to the season, Orr, playing much of the season in need of knee surgery, persevered to win his second Conn Smythe Trophy as playoff MVP as the Bruins added the Stanley Cup to their first overall regular-season finish. "Even on one leg, Bobby Orr is still the best thing out there," St. Louis Blues defenseman Bob Plager told *The New York Times*. Orr was inducted into the Hockey Hall of Fame in 1979.

1972–73
Bobby Clarke
PHILADELPHIA FLYERS

The first player from one of the 1967 expansion franchises to win the Hart. Clarke was also the first player from an expansion team to post a 100-point season but shrugged when someone suggested the Hart win indicated he was the world's best player. "Are you kidding?" Clarke remarked. "If it went to the best, Bobby Orr would win every year, hands down."

1973–74
Phil Esposito
BOSTON BRUINS

Named Canada's Athlete of the Year for 1973 after helping Canada beat Russia in the 1972 Summit Series, Esposito rebounded from off-season knee surgery to lead the NHL in scoring for the fifth time in six seasons with 68–77–145 totals. He became the first player to register four successive 50-goal campaigns. "Phil Esposito does what he wants to do with the puck," explained Bruins coach Bep Guidolin to Bruce Lowitt of *The Associated Press*. "That's why he's Phil Esposito."

1974–75
Bobby Clarke
PHILADELPHIA FLYERS

Rolling to an NHL-leading 113 points, the defending Stanley Cup champion Flyers followed the leadership of their captain. Clarke set a single-season NHL record for centers with 89 assists, but described the Hart win as being about effort more than talent. "Hard work is the equalizer," Clarke explained to *The Associated Press*. "If everyone worked as hard as he could, then naturally the best players would rise to the top. But not everyone is willing to work that hard."

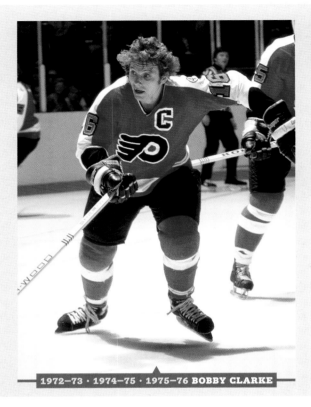

1972–73 · 1974–75 · 1975–76 **BOBBY CLARKE**

1976–77 · 1977–78 **GUY LAFLEUR**

1975–76
Bobby Clarke
PHILADELPHIA FLYERS

Earning First All-Star Team status, Clarke equaled his NHL mark for centers with 89 assists; finished second in NHL scoring; and led the Flyers to top spot in the Campbell Conference. "Clarke is the most valuable man I've ever seen in sports," Flyers coach Fred Shero told *Canadian Magazine*. Diagnosed as a diabetic at age 15, Clarke's work ethic and tireless commitment to excellence were an inspiration to everyone. Clarke was inducted into the Hockey Hall of Fame in 1987.

1976–77
Guy Lafleur
MONTREAL CANADIENS

Following in the long line of great Habs scorers, The Flower bloomed into a superstar. He won his second straight NHL scoring title with 56–80–136 numbers as Montreal set an NHL record by winning 60 games. Lafleur also set an NHL mark with a 28-game point streak. "If you really like what you're doing and concentrate on what you're doing, you can do a lot of things other guys can't do," was how Lafleur explained his on-ice dominance to *The New York Times*. Lafleur was enshrined in the Hockey Hall of Fame in 1988.

1977–78
Guy Lafleur
MONTREAL CANADIENS

Joining Howie Morenz as the only Canadiens player to win back-to-back Harts, Lafleur won his third successive scoring crown with 132 points and put his name alongside such other Habs greats as Jean Beliveau and Rocket Richard. "It's always nice to be compared with guys like Beliveau and Maurice Richard," Lafleur told *The Associated Press*. "I just go out there and if the team does well, maybe you win something."

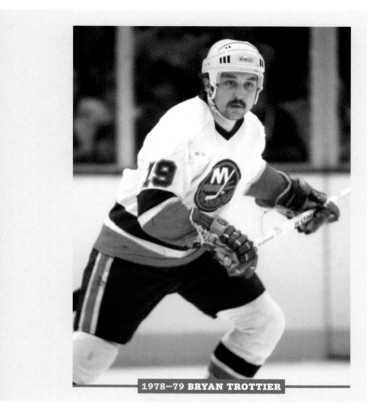

1978–79 **BRYAN TROTTIER**

1978–79
Bryan Trottier
NEW YORK ISLANDERS

His steady ascension to the top of the NHL was achieved in the 1978–79 season. Trottier, a fiery two-way competitor, led the NHL in scoring with 134 points, including a league-leading 87 assists, and the Isles supplanted Montreal as the NHL's No. 1 team, collecting a league-best 116 points. At 23, Trottier was the second-youngest Hart winner, bettered only by Bobby Orr, who was 22 when he first won the award in 1969–70. Trottier was inducted into the Hockey Hall of Fame in 1997.

1979–80
Wayne Gretzky
EDMONTON OILERS

Only 19, The Great One took the NHL by storm when he and the Oilers joined the league in the 1979 NHL–WHA merger. Collecting 137 points,

Gretzky helped Edmonton rally to capture the sixteenth and final Stanley Cup playoff position. "This makes me pinch myself a little bit," Gretzky told *The Canadian Press*. "Sometimes, I don't believe all this has happened to me."

1980–81
Wayne Gretzky
EDMONTON OILERS

Establishing new NHL standards for assists (109) and points (164), Gretzky won his first Art Ross Trophy as league scoring champion. "It's a tremendous feeling," Gretzky told *The Associated Press*. "It's great anytime you break a record." Word of Gretzky's second Hart triumph leaked out a day early when Edmonton television station CFRN got hold of confidential NHL documents listing the 1980–81 award winners. "I'm very excited, pleased and happy," Gretzky, the first player ever to win the Hart in each of his first two NHL seasons, told CFRN. "Anytime you win a trophy in the National Hockey League, it's exciting."

1981–82
Wayne Gretzky
EDMONTON OILERS

The Great One kept breaking records, turning the annual Hart Trophy announcement into a broken record itself. He won for the third straight season, joining Bobby Orr as the only players to do so. Gretzky achieved his Hart hat trick in spectacular fashion, rewriting the NHL scoring marks with 92 goals, 120 assists and 212 points. "My dad told me, when Gretzky was 14, 'Mark my words, there's one guy who can break your record,'" said Phil Esposito, previous holder of the goal-scoring mark at 76.

Hart Trophy

1982–83
Wayne Gretzky
EDMONTON OILERS

Joining Gordie Howe (six) and Eddie Shore (four) as a four-time Hart winner and becoming the first player to win the award four years in succession, Gretzky shattered a league mark for the third straight season, garnering 125 assists for the Edmonton club, which led the Campbell Conference with 106 points. "It's just as exciting as the first time," Gretzky said. "He turns defensive chances into offensive chances," Washington defenseman Rod Langway explained to *UPI*. When the puck is going one way, if somebody makes a bad play and he's there, he's gone. It's anticipation. It's acceleration. It's Gretzky."

1983–84
Wayne Gretzky
EDMONTON OILERS

Gretzky led the NHL in scoring for the fourth straight season with 87–118–205 totals for the first-overall Oilers. He also led the NHL with a plus-76 rating. And as he accepted his unprecedented fifth successive Hart Trophy, Gretzky no longer needed to lament, because for the first time, the Oilers were also Stanley Cup champions. Gretzky talked about what drove him to such heights. "You have to have a lot of personal pride," he explained to *The Canadian Press*. "And I respect every player I go on the ice against, so I know before every game that I have to give 100 percent."

1984–85
Wayne Gretzky
EDMONTON OILERS

Topping 200 points for the third time in four seasons, so dominant was Gretzky that his NHL-record 135 assists would have been enough alone to tie him for the scoring title with teammate Jari Kurri. Winning the Hart for the sixth time in a row, Gretzky tied his childhood idol Gordie Howe for the record number of Hart victories. "I'm overjoyed to get the sixth and tie Gordie," Gretzky told *The Canadian Press*. "He's one of the greatest who ever played. They can never take these six away from me, no matter what happens in the future."

1985–86
Wayne Gretzky
EDMONTON OILERS

Even The Great One seemed surprised when his name was called as the winner of his NHL-record seventh Hart Trophy. "I thought this was the year it was going to end for me," Gretzky admitted to *The Canadian Press*. Gretzky collected 52–163–215 numbers to lead the NHL in scoring, setting new NHL standards for assists and points, running away with the honor, polling 281 of a possible 300 points in the voting. He was inducted into the Hockey Hall of Fame in 1999.

1986–87
Wayne Gretzky
EDMONTON OILERS

The Art Ross Trophy came Gretzky's way for the eighth time, thanks to a 62–121–183 output for the first-overall Oilers, and what followed was his eighth straight selection as winner of the Hart Trophy. It caused The Great One to become reflective about his hockey career. "I don't know what the future holds for me," Gretzky told *The Associated Press*. "I was probably more drained at the end of this season than I have ever been. I love the game and everything about it, but … I want to be able to walk away from the game also."

1979–80 · 1980–81
1981–82 · 1982–83
1983–84 · 1984–85
1985–86 · 1986–87
WAYNE GRETZKY

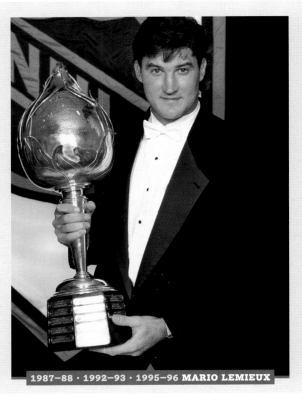

1987–88 · 1992–93 · 1995–96 **MARIO LEMIEUX**

1988–89 **WAYNE GRETZKY**

1987–88
Mario Lemieux
PITTSBURGH PENGUINS

Some saw it as a passing of the torch. After eight years as Hart Trophy winner and seven years as the Art Ross Trophy holder, Wayne Gretzky finally gave way on both counts to the new phenom on the block, Lemieux, who ran away with the scoring title, posting 70–98–168 numbers. Super Mario garnered 54 of 63 first-place votes, even though the Penguins were a last-place club, making him just the fourth player from a non-playoff team to be awarded the Hart. In victory, Lemieux seemed sheepish about unseating The Great One from his pedestal. "I was a little bit surprised to see the big spread," Lemieux told Dave Molinari of the *Pittsburgh Press*. "Wayne won this trophy the last eight years and from my point of view, he's still the best player in the world."

1988–89
Wayne Gretzky
LOS ANGELES KINGS

A shocking off-season trade from Edmonton to L.A. put Gretzky in Hollywood and into a different stratosphere of stars. Gretzky led the Kings to a 91-point season, their best record since 1981, and though he was vastly outdistanced in the scoring race by Mario Lemieux (199 to 168), he captured his ninth Hart Trophy, the first player to win the award with two different teams. "The first Hart Trophy I won was great; the eighth I won was great also," Gretzky told Damien Cox of the *Toronto Star*. "But [this] is really special for me because I enjoyed the year so much. It meant more this time than ever before." He was inducted into the Hockey Hall of Fame in 1999.

1989–90 **MARK MESSIER**

1990–91 **BRETT HULL**

1989–90
Mark Messier
EDMONTON OILERS

Ascending to the captaincy of the Oilers after the departure of Wayne Gretzky, Messier finished second in NHL scoring behind his old teammate with career-high 45–84–129 numbers and was recognized for his leadership abilities. In accepting the Hart, Messier shared the honor with his teammates. "This is a great reflection of the type of year we had as a team," Messier told *The Associated Press*. "It's a great way to end the season."

1990–91
Brett Hull
ST. LOUIS BLUES

Setting a record for right-wingers with 86 goals and helping the Blues to the second-best record in the NHL, "The Golden Brett" joined his dad Bobby Hull as the only father-son tandem to win the Hart Trophy. Bobby was a two-time winner in 1964–65 and 1965–66. "This brings me a little closer to what [Bobby] has done," Brett told Lance Hornby of the *Toronto Sun*. "It's a real feather in my cap." Hull appeared on all but one of 66 ballots cast by the Professional Hockey Writers' Association. He was enshrined in the Hockey Hall of Fame in 2009.

1991–92 **MARK MESSIER**

1993–94 **SERGEI FEDOROV**

1991–92
Mark Messier
NEW YORK RANGERS

Leading the Rangers to top spot in the NHL for the first time in 50 years, Messier joined former Edmonton teammate Wayne Gretzky as the only players to win the Hart with two different teams. "Somebody was asking me earlier how I felt about winning a second time when Wayne had won it nine times," Messier explained to Scott Morrison of the *Toronto Sun*. "I was surprised to win it once." Messier collected 107 points and was named center on the First All-Star Team that season, and was inducted into the Hockey Hall of Fame in 2007.

1992–93
Mario Lemieux
PITTSBURGH PENGUINS

In one of the most stirring performances in hockey history, Lemieux, diagnosed with

Hodgkin's disease on January 5, 1993, returned after an absence of 24 games, rallied to win the Art Ross Trophy by 12 points over Buffalo's Pat LaFontaine, and captained Pittsburgh to a club-record 17-game winning streak. "It's special because it recognized me for coming back from cancer and my [chronic] back, too," Lemieux (also awarded the Masterton Trophy for perseverance) told Bob McKenzie of the *Toronto Star*.

1993–94
Sergei Fedorov
DETROIT RED WINGS

Stepping up when Detroit captain Steve Yzerman was idled by a back injury, Fedorov, who left his native Russia to join the Wings in 1990, became the first European born and trained Hart winner. He finished second in the Art Ross Trophy race with 56–64–120 totals, including 10 game-winning goals for the Western Conference-leading Wings. "I'm still learning to play in

1994–95 ERIC LINDROS

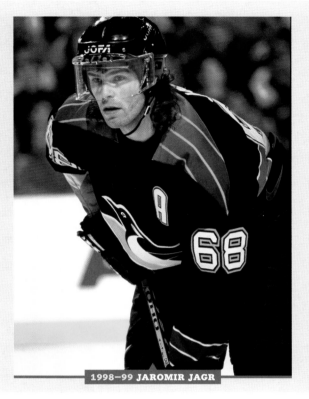

1998–99 JAROMIR JAGR

North America," said Fedorov, who was praised by nine-time Hart winner Wayne Gretzky: "He's a first-class guy, he loves the game, and he cares about the game," Gretzky said. "That's great news for hockey."

1994–95
Eric Lindros
PHILADELPHIA FLYERS

Billed as "The Next One," the hulking center tied for the NHL scoring lead, but lost the Art Ross Trophy because he scored three fewer goals than Pittsburgh's Jaromir Jagr. Lindros led the Flyers to the Atlantic Division title. At 22, he became the youngest Hart winner since Gretzky began his run of eight straight Harts at age 19. "The expectations will never end," Lindros acknowledged to Lance Hornby of the *Toronto Sun*. "It's part of hockey. If you start believing [you're in the same class as Wayne Gretzky], you get satisfied. This is a plateau, but the peak is the Stanley Cup."

1995–96
Mario Lemieux
PITTSBURGH PENGUINS

Returning from a season lost to injury and illness, Lemieux tallied a league-leading 69 goals in 70 games, winning his fifth Art Ross Trophy with an NHL-best 92 assists and 161 points. Lemieux became the sixth player to have won the Hart at least three times. As he accepted his award, Lemieux questioned whether he was done with hockey. "I'll make a decision in a couple or three weeks," he told *The New York Times*. "It will be a very important decision in my life. The big thing was winning the Stanley Cup twice. I think my career would be complete if I retired today." He was inducted into the Hockey Hall of Fame in 1997.

1996–97 · 1997–98 DOMINIK HASEK

1996–97
Dominik Hasek
BUFFALO SABRES

In the midst of the dead-puck era, it was appropriate that a goalie be recognized for the Hart. Hasek posted a league-leading .930 save percentage, earning 37 of Buffalo's 40 wins as the Sabres topped the Northeast Division. He was the first goalie to receive the Hart since Montreal's Jacques Plante in 1961–62. "It was never, never in my wildest dreams," Vezina Trophy winner Hasek said of winning the Hart. "It is a fantastic honor."

1997–98
Dominik Hasek
BUFFALO SABRES

Booed at the start of the season by Buffalo fans, who felt he'd played a role in the departure of Sabres coach Ted Nolan, the Dominator won them over by living up to his nickname. Playing a league-high 72 games, he led the NHL with 13 shutouts and a .932 save percentage to become the first goalie to win back-to-back Harts. "It was a weird, but great season, Hasek told Tim Wharnsby of the *Toronto Sun*. "I heard the fans boo early in the season and it affected my play. But in December it started to turn around."

1998–99
Jaromir Jagr
PITTSBURGH PENGUINS

Jagr ran away with the NHL scoring title by 20 points over his nearest rivals, garnering a league-best 87 assists among his 127 points. "To my parents [Jaromir Sr. and Anna, flown in for the awards show] goes the biggest thanks," Jagr said during his acceptance speech at the first NHL awards show open to the public and televised live. "Without them, I wouldn't be standing here. Hopefully, I'll see you all here next year."

1999–2000 **CHRIS PRONGER**

2000–01 **JOE SAKIC**

1999–2000
Chris Pronger
ST. LOUIS BLUES

It was a big night for the Blues. They took home five awards: the Norris (Pronger), Adams (Joel Quenneville), Jennings (Roman Turek) and Lady Byng (Pavol Demitra), and Chris Pronger captured the Hart in addition to the Norris. In one of the closest votes ever, Pronger bettered the previous season's Hart winner, Jaromir Jagr of Pittsburgh, by a solitary point. "I would probably trade [both trophies] for the Stanley Cup," said Pronger, whose Blues were upset in the first round of the playoffs by the San Jose Sharks. "That's the ultimate team award. But if I had to take nothing or these two, I definitely would take these two." Pronger was the first defenseman to win the Hart since Bobby Orr in 1971–72.

2000–01
Joe Sakic
COLORADO AVALANCHE

The first Hart Trophy winner from the Stanley Cup champions since Edmonton's Mark Messier in 1989–90, Sakic also captained his club to the Cup. The slick Avs center finished second in NHL scoring behind Pittsburgh's Jaromir Jagr, potting 54 goals, second only to Florida's Pavel Bure. He netted an NHL-best 12 game winners. Capturing the award for the first time in his thirteenth NHL season was a record for the longest into a career by a first-time Hart victor. "Joe carried the torch from Day 1," teammate Ray Bourque told the *Ottawa Sun*. "He had his two linemates [Alex Tanguay and Milan Hejduk] going for him and really led the way all year."

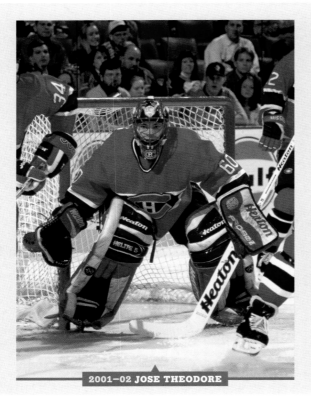

2001–02 JOSE THEODORE

2002–03 PETER FORSBERG

2001–02
Jose Theodore
MONTREAL CANADIENS

For the first time in the history of the Hart Trophy, the voting ended in a deadlock, with both Habs netminder Theodore and Calgary Flames right-winger Iginla garnering 434 points. But Theodore got the nod because he was placed first on 26 of 63 ballots, and Iginla topped just 23 voters' lists. "To get this vote is a big surprise," said Theodore, who won 30 games, posted 7 shutouts, a 2.11 goals-against average and an NHL-best .931 save percentage, backstopping Montreal into the Stanley Cup playoffs for the first time since 1998.

2002–03
Peter Forsberg
COLORADO AVALANCHE

The first Swede to win the Hart Trophy, Forsberg won the NHL scoring race with 106 points, including a league-leading 77 assists as Colorado won its record ninth straight divisional title. His plus-52 rating tied him for the league lead. Forsberg figured in 42 percent of Colorado's 251 goals and beat out childhood friend Markus Naslund of the Vancouver Canucks for the award. The two had been chums since they were eight, growing up in the northern Swedish city of Ornskoldsvik. "I wish we could have shared this," Forsberg said.

2003–04 **MARTIN ST. LOUIS**

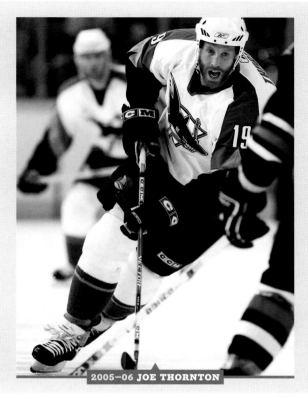

2005–06 **JOE THORNTON**

2003–04
Martin St. Louis
TAMPA BAY LIGHTNING

The first product of NCAA hockey to win the NHL scoring title, St. Louis added the honor as the first U.S. college hockey player to win the Hart. "It's going to be a tough year to top," St. Louis told *The Associated Press* after he became the first player since Wayne Gretzky (in 1987) to win the Hart, Art Ross and Stanley Cup in the same season. He was only the eighth player in NHL history to complete the triple. "I don't know if it means I'm the best player in the NHL. There are a lot of great players and to be considered among them is very flattering."

2005–06
Joe Thornton
SAN JOSE SHARKS

"Jumbo Joe" made history as the first player to win the Hart after being traded during the season. He was dealt by Boston to San Jose 23 games into the campaign, and went on to lead the NHL in scoring with 125 points, including a league-leading 96 assists. "This is a great honor," said Thornton, whose leadership skills were questioned by the Bruins. "It was tough to get traded at first, but I knew, from the minute I walked through the door in San Jose, I was welcome there. It was a great change for me."

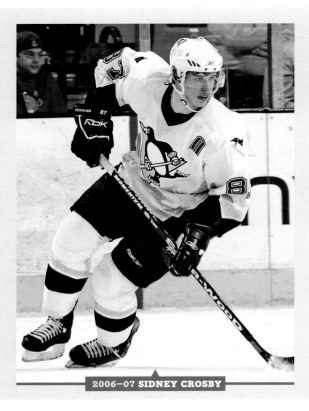

2006–07 **SIDNEY CROSBY**

2007–08 · 2008–09 **ALEXANDER OVECHKIN**

2006–07
Sidney Crosby
PITTSBURGH PENGUINS

The Penguins became the first expansion team to boast three different Hart winners, as Crosby joined Jaromir Jagr and Mario Lemieux with his name on the award. In his second NHL season, Sid the Kid led the league in scoring with 36–84–120 totals and guided the Penguins to their first playoff appearance since 2000–01. At 19, the youngest winner of the award since Wayne Gretzky in 1980–81, Crosby led the Penguins to a 105-point season, second-best in franchise history.

2007–08
Alexander Ovechkin
WASHINGTON CAPITALS

Becoming just the second Russian player to win the Hart, the slick left-winger carried the Capitals on his back from last overall in the league in November to top spot in the Southwest Division,

scoring 51 goals in his final 61 games. Ovechkin won the Rocket Richard and Art Ross Trophies with league-leading 65–47–112 numbers. The beans were spilled the night before the NHL awards when the league inadvertently made "Ovechkin 2007–08 Hart Winner" T-shirts available on its website.

2008–09
Alexander Ovechkin
WASHINGTON CAPITALS

Becoming the first player to win back-to-back Harts since Dominik Hasek and just the eleventh in the history of the award, Ovechkin won the Rocket Richard trophy with 56 goals and was second in NHL scoring with 110 points as the Capitals topped the Southeast Division, winning 50 games. "It's pretty important when people and players give you this," Ovechkin told the *National Post*. "I don't want to stop. I want to be the best next year." Ovechkin's 528 shots on goal were the

2009–10 **HENRIK SEDIN**

2010–11 **COREY PERRY**

second-highest total in NHL history, behind the 550 fired by Boston's Phil Esposito in 1970–71.

2009–10
Henrik Sedin
VANCOUVER CANUCKS

The second Swedish Hart winner and the second to hail from the city of Ornskoldsvik, Sedin won the Art Ross Trophy with career highs in goals (29) assists (83) and points (112), but still seemed stunned to edge Pittsburgh's Sidney Crosby and Washington's Alexander Ovechkin for the award. He received 46 first-place votes to 40 for Ovechkin and 20 for Crosby. "They're the faces of the sport," Sedin said. "Just to watch them play and the things they do, to be standing there next to them and being the old guy, it's a strange feeling."

2010–11
Corey Perry
ANAHEIM DUCKS

The first player from the Anaheim franchise to win the Hart, Perry was also the first right-winger to capture the award since Martin St. Louis of the Tampa Bay Lightning in 2003–04. Perry recorded the first 50-goal season of his career in 2010–11, scoring 19 times in his final 16 games to capture the Maurice "Rocket" Richard Trophy as the NHL's top goal scorer. He finished with 67 first-place Hart votes to 51 for runner-up Daniel Sedin of the Vancouver Canucks. Overall, Perry garnered 1,043 voting points, compared to 960 for Sedin. "I'm an emotional person and it's like when we won the Stanley Cup, I cried after that," Perry said. "You know, it's just personal."

NHLPA MVP

"TERRIBLE TED"

2009-10 RECIPIENT:
ALEXANDER OVECHKIN

The Ted Lindsay Award debuted as the NHLPA MVP award in 2010, replacing the Lester B. Pearson Award, which had been awarded since 1970–71. All past recipients of the Pearson Award are recognized on the Lindsay Award.

"MOST OUTSTANDING PLAYER" AWARD RECIPIENTS:

CHAPTER 6
Creating the NHLPA MVP

CERTAINLY, THE NAME Lester Bowles "Mike" Pearson was no stranger to Canadians. He was the 14th Prime Minister of Canada, serving in office from 1963 to 1968, and world-renowned as an international statesman. So to name an award in his honor was no surprise.

But a hockey award? Now that was a surprising development to those who didn't know Pearson's history that well.

A star hockey player with the Oxford Canadians while studying in England, Pearson was part of the Oxford club that toured Europe in 1922 and 1923, the team going unbeaten on both trips. One of Pearson's teammates at Oxford was Roland Michener, who served as Governor General of Canada from 1967 to 1971, and who became a lifelong friend.

Pearson was invited to play for the British hockey team at the first Winter Olympic Games in 1924, but declined the offer, opting to return to Canada to accept a teaching job in the department of history at the University of Toronto (U of T).

He took charge of the University of Toronto Varsity Blues hockey team from 1924 to 1927. These squads formed the nucleus of the Toronto Varsity Grads team that won the Ontario Senior Hockey Association and Allan Cup titles in 1926–27, and represented Canada at the 1928 Winter Olympics in St. Moritz, Switzerland, winning the gold medal.

Pearson was an all-around athlete who also excelled at football, baseball, lacrosse and rugby. "My interest in sport remained unabated, but began to turn now toward coaching as well as playing," Pearson wrote in his memoirs, of his time as a lecturer at U of T. "Tennis and squash gave me plenty of exercise and competition. I am the proud possessor of a squash cup, and I once had the great honor of getting to the second round in the Canadian national tennis championships, paired with my old Oxford friend Roland Michener. We were eliminated by a Davis Cup pair who eventually won the title."

No matter how busy or hectic his life became, Pearson always gravitated back toward the athletic field, and was especially drawn to the ice rink. "Those were days at the university when the coaches were all amateurs, though a change was soon to come," he wrote. "I was on the athletic association board and found myself becoming actively engaged in teaching football and hockey, as well as history. During my first year, I coached the Victoria College football team to the inter-faculty championship, and helped during the winter with the hockey and basketball teams. Then, in the next year, I moved over to university teams, both in football and hockey. I loved doing this."

After his tenure as prime minister of Canada, Pearson was a board member of both the Canadian Football League's Ottawa Rough Riders and major league baseball's Montreal Expos, and also served as a member of the National Hockey League Players' Association's (NHLPA) board of directors.

On March 11, 1971, the NHLPA held a press conference in Toronto to introduce the new Lester B. Pearson Award, which NHLPA executive director Alan Eagleson announced would be presented to the NHL player who contributed the most to hockey in each season. Eagleson indicated that the winner would be determined by a secret ballot of all NHL players and the name of the recipient would be revealed in late June during the annual NHLPA golf tournament.

The 1970–71 season had belonged to the Boston Bruins. They'd set or equaled 37 NHL records that season. The Boston dominance continued during the NHLPA celebrations when Bruins center Derek Sanderson and goaltender Eddie Johnston combined to capture the American Airlines/NHLPA golf tournament at the Board of Trade Club in Woodbridge, Ontario, each taking home a $2,500 prize. But it was the newly-minted Pearson Award that was the talk of the links that afternoon. Due to be presented the next evening at Toronto's Skyline Hotel following the conclusion of the golf outing, everyone assumed that Bruins defenseman Bobby Orr (who'd already won the Hart Trophy as the player adjudged to be most valuable to his team in the NHL), would be scoring a double.

"At a dinner tomorrow night at the Skyline, the NHLPA will name its player of the year," wrote Ken McKee in the Toronto Star. "Who'll be the first to nominate Orr?" But when the winner was announced, it was Orr's teammate, high-scoring Boston center Phil Esposito who walked away with the award.

His victory in the voting instantly set out that the Pearson would be a different award than the Hart, which the hockey writers had voted to Orr. "I talked this over with Bobby, and we came to the same conclusion," Esposito said. "Although the Hart is an individual thing, its significance is more or less a team thing.

"Bobby deserves it and being second to Bobby Orr is no shame."

After the ceremony, Eagleson presented Pearson with a replica of the award named for him. The Pearson Award was a trailblazing distinction in that it was the first—and remains the only one—among the major North American sports that is voted on exclusively by league players.

Honoring Their Father

It's fair to call Ted Lindsay the granddaddy of the NHLPA, so in a sense, naming an award after the former Detroit Red Wings star who first sought to bring organized labor to the NHL fraternity seems a no-brainer.

At the end of the 2009–10 NHL season, on April 29, 2010, the NHLPA announced that the Lester B. Pearson Award for the most outstanding player in the NHL according to the league's players would in future be known as the Ted Lindsay Award.

"Naming our most outstanding player award after Ted Lindsay is the highest honor our Association can bestow upon him," members of the NHLPA executive board announced in a statement. "We are very proud to honor one of the great players of our game and a true pioneer of our Association."

Clearly, Lindsay was moved by the honor. "It's beautiful," Lindsay said. "I wanted a little character to it, and I think the color in it, the wing and the wheel on the chest is very important to me."

Lindsay also appreciated what the award stood for in NHL circles. "It goes to the best, voted on by his peers," he said. "So that means there's no politics involved. That tells you the whole story. Whoever wins it is entitled to it."

Chicago Blackhawks forward Jamal Mayers, a former member of the NHLPA's executive board, felt it was essential for the NHLPA to preserve Lindsay's legacy to their organization. "It's our job as older players," Mayers said. "This is part of keeping his legacy alive. It's having the younger guys understand and appreciate the history."

That sentiment was echoed by other NHLers. "All NHLPA members, current and former, owe a great deal of gratitude to Ted for his efforts, so it is only fitting that we name our most outstanding player award after him," said Calgary Flames captain Jarome Iginla, the 2001–02 Lester B. Pearson Award recipient. "The Ted Lindsay Award is a prestigious honor that will continue the tradition set forth by the Lester B. Pearson Award."

Hart vs. NHLPA MVP

When talking about the National Hockey League's two most valuable player awards—the Hart Trophy and the Ted Lindsay Award—Detroit Red Wings Pavel Datsyuk is at his glib best. Though he's never won either award, Datsyuk was a 2008–09 finalist for both, and won't put one above the other in terms of significance, at least not in his opinion.

"I'm happy to win any award," said Datsyuk, four-time winner of the Lady Byng Trophy as the NHL player adjudged to have exhibited the best type of sportsmanship and gentlemanly conduct, combined with a high standard of playing ability. "Any award you vote for, I'll take it."

As long as there are two sides, there will be an argument, no matter the issue.

Certainly, the Lindsay (known as the Lester B. Pearson Award from 1971 to 2009) has tended to play second fiddle in terms of attention since it was first inaugurated by the National Hockey League Players' Association (NHLPA). On the surface, it appears distinctly different from the Hart, which is voted on by members of the Professional Hockey Writers' Association and awarded to the player adjudged to be most valuable to his team. The Lindsay Award winner, selected from a ballot of NHLPA members, goes to the most outstanding player in the league.

To some, this debate is moot. "It's pretty much the same award, I'd like to think," suggested San Jose Sharks center Joe Thornton, the 2005–06 Hart Trophy winner. "The wording might be different, but as players, I think that we think it's pretty much the same award."

As to which award means more, that's an entirely different debate. Is it a greater tribute to be recognized by the people who chronicle the game, or by the people who play the game? On this matter, there seems to be almost as many opinions as there are winners of the two awards.

Mark Messier, the only man to captain two different teams to Stanley Cup championships (1989–90 Edmonton Oilers, 1991–92 New York Rangers) is a two-time winner of both the Pearson and the Hart. At his 2007 induction into the Hockey Hall of Fame, Messier, never one to put much stock in individual honors ahead of team accomplishments, still took a moment to reflect upon the personal achievements during his career. When asked which trophy he was most proud of, Messier didn't hesitate. "The Lester B. Pearson Award to me is one of the nicest awards I've ever won," he said. "You get selected by your peers as the top player in the league."

To others, the debate is pointless. Greatness is greatness and should be accepted as so, no matter who decides the outcome. "They're really special awards," said 2009–10 Hart Trophy winner Henrik Sedin of the Vancouver Canucks. "You can ask any guy around the league, and to win either one of those is a really special moment. I don't think it matters which one. It's fun to get rewarded by your peers, for sure, but it's still awfully special to get awarded the Hart."

Clearly, the Hart has tradition on its side, first being presented in 1924, when it was won by center Frank Nighbor of the Ottawa Senators. Through its history, the Hart inscriptions read like a who's who of hockey royalty—Howie Morenz, Eddie Shore, Gordie Howe, Bobby Hull, Maurice Richard, Bobby Orr, Wayne Gretzky, Mario Lemieux, Sidney Crosby, Alexander Ovechkin.

Other sensational players, Hall of Famers such as Marcel Dionne, Jean Ratelle and Steve Yzerman, own only Pearson Awards as recognition of their individual greatness. The first winner of the Pearson, former Boston Bruins center Phil Esposito, owns two of each award, but holds the Pearson closest to his heart. Esposito won the Pearson in 1970–71 and 1973–74. He was a Hart winner in 1968–69 and 1973–74.

Esposito ranks the Pearson ahead of the Hart Trophy. "I do not know why it does not get the recognition," Esposito told Alan Adams of the *National Post*. "As a player, to me, that was the ultimate, that I was voted MVP of the league by the players. That was fantastic.

"There are three things in my career that stand above the rest and one is winning the Pearson. Another is having my number retired [by Boston] and the third is being awarded an [expansion] franchise in Tampa Bay."

That the players' choice for MVP is presented separately during a ceremony at the Hockey Hall of Fame during the afternoon and is not an integral part of the NHL awards show later in the evening might play a role in why the Hart is often looked upon as No. 1 in MVP awards, while the Pearson/Lindsay has always taken a back seat, kind of like a 1A award. Former NHL player and ex-Minnesota Wild general manager Doug Risebrough believes the mentality of the people who play the game has also played a role in the Lindsay Award's perceived inferiority complex.

"The hockey player mentality is not to promote himself," Risebrough said. "Players do not want to make a big deal of it. I do not think it is in our nature as hockey players to be boastful and brash."

Alexander Ovechkin said he appreciates the distinction of the NHLPA MVP more than the Hart a touch more because of who votes for it. "The Pearson, it's a players' award," Ovechkin said. "They know how you play, who you are."

It's a notion that Crosby, the man to whom Ovechkin is so often paralleled, can get on board with as well. "Getting that respect, I guess you could say, from the guys you play against each night, that's probably one of the ultimate

2001–02 Pearson Award winner Jarome Iginla.

compliments you could get," Crosby said. "I'm not downplaying the media's opinion by any means, but it's certainly a huge honor to get that respect."

Veteran center Mike Modano, the leading U.S.-born scorer in NHL history, is another willing to stump for the Lindsay as the more significant of the two honors. "Certainly," Modano said. "I think there's probably no higher honor than being selected by the players you play against and compete against. That's the utmost respect you can get, rather than writers and whoever votes on the other stuff. If the people you're playing against every night feel you're value towards it, that's really great."

Modano believes the Lindsay Award is something his fellow players take very seriously and indicated he puts plenty of time and thought into the matter before filling out his ballot each season. "I think you take a look at it," Modano

said. "You try to see what player has the biggest impact, not only points and production-wise, but just overall. What he does in the scheme of things as far as his team, how he's valuable throughout, not just production-wise."

For Calgary Flames captain Jarome Iginla, a two-time Hart Trophy runner-up and the 2001–02 winner of the Pearson Award, deciding between the two is like choosing between Jessica Alba and Jessica Biel. You're a winner either way. "Both of the awards are tremendous honors and the recognition in either case is truly appreciated," Iginla said. "The Hart Trophy has the prestige. I remember as a kid, watching Wayne Gretzky win it every year and being just in awe of him. Then to be considered for the award myself, that was something very special.

"With the Lindsay Trophy, there is that extra element, because you know it's from the guys you've been battling night after night, and maybe in the heat of action, you've done something or said something to somebody that wasn't exactly in the best light. With the way I play, I end up in a lot of battles, so sometimes, you wonder how that's going to affect other players' views of you. So when you go through those battles on the ice, go hard at it against plenty of other players, it truly is a sign of respect when they vote you this award.

"It really means something in that regard, something that you never forget as a player. I don't know that there's a greater honor than to be recognized by your peers."

Hockey Hall of Famer Bobby Hull, a two-time Hart Trophy winner who was only eligible for the Pearson Award during 3 of his 16 NHL seasons, leans toward the former as the ultimate achievement for a hockey player.

"The Hart Trophy, I believe, is emblematic of the great accomplishment of an individual," Hull said. "Of all the players that you play against and play with, all of a sudden at the end of the year, you're chosen as the most valuable player to a particular team. In the Original Six, there were 125–130 pretty darn good players. Now with 30 teams, you're looking at over 600 players and when you're chosen as the most valuable among a group of men like that, it sure as hell epitomizes what the game is all about and what you're all about.

"I relished those couple of Hart Trophies more so than anything else. They told me that with my play, people thought that I was the most valuable in the league, not only to my team, but the most valuable over all the rest. It's a very prestigious honor to have won the Hart Trophy."

Hull has another reason to embrace the Hart as the ultimate hockey prize. He and his son, fellow Hall of Famer Brett Hull, are the only father-son combination to win the Hart. Brett Hull, then with the St. Louis Blues, also won the Pearson Award during his Hart Trophy-winning campaign of 1990–91.

"It was one thing for me to be able to play 23 years, to make a boyhood dream come true and then to play that long professionally," said Bobby Hull, Hart winner in 1964–65 and 1965–66. "But then to have a kid come along and play the game the way Brett Hull played the game, to do what he did and end up third overall [NHL career] goal scorer just behind Gordon Howe and Wayne Gretzky, argumentatively the greatest player that ever played, that was something else.

"I think that night that Brett Hull was chosen most valuable player, winning the Hart Trophy, that made me feel as though he had reached his pinnacle in the game of hockey. They recognized what a great goal scorer he was, and I don't think there was anybody who could score goals in as many different ways as Brett Hull did. Being there in Toronto as he was awarded the Hart Trophy, it made my chest swell, that's for sure."

The final word on this Hart–Pearson/Lindsay debate is left to two recent winners of each award—Sidney Crosby and Alexander Ovechkin, among eight players to win both trophies, as well as lead the NHL in scoring all in the same season. "You like to win these awards, but you play to win games," Crosby said. "It's just a bonus."

"If I win the Hart and the Lester Pearson, of course I will be happy, but my goal [is always] the Stanley Cup," added Ovechkin.

CHAPTER 7
The Men Behind the Trophies

Lester B. Pearson

CANADIAN PRIME MINISTER Lester B. "Mike" Pearson was a hockey player and a sportsman at heart, whose legacy to Canada is difficult to overlook. One of the most influential Canadians of the 20th century, the country's largest airport, Toronto Pearson International Airport, was named in his honor in 1984. Five Canadian high schools and one college are named for him. Canada's Department of Foreign Affairs and International Trade is housed in the Lester B. Pearson Building, recognizing his contribution to world politics. For four decades, there was also a prominent National Hockey League award named in his honor.

The Lester B. Pearson Trophy was presented by the National Hockey League Players' Association from 1971 to 2009 to the most outstanding player of each NHL season. That it be named in honor of the 14th Prime Minister of Canada might seem puzzling, but take the time to know Pearson's sporting legacy and the reasons for this recognition quickly become clear.

"Sportsman was one of the many lives Pearson led," said Andrew Cohen, author of Pearson's biography in the Significant Canadians Series: *Lester B. Pearson.* "At the end of his life, he said, 'I've had many lives, more lives than a cat. And I've been lucky in all of them.' One was as an athlete and a sportsman. It defined his life, more so than other pursuits."

⋆ ⋆ ⋆

Pearson was born in Newtonbrook, Ontario, on April 23, 1897, the middle of three sons born to Edwin Arthur Pearson, a Methodist minister, and Annie Sarah Bowles. As the offspring of a clergyman, Pearson's childhood was one of constant moving and uprooting as his father was assigned to different parishes.

At 16, he enrolled in the University of Toronto's Victoria College, the same school his father had attended. Pearson quickly made his mark on the school's sporting fields. "Mr. Pearson loved sports and was good at almost all of them except swimming, which he didn't like," Cohen said.

Cohen said Pearson excelled at rugby, lacrosse, hockey and baseball, and later in life, at tennis and squash. "I was very active in athletics," Pearson told Charles Lynch in a 1970 interview printed in the *Montreal Gazette*. "I dropped into college life very quickly, and I loved games."

* * *

Pearson enlisted in the Canadian Army shortly after his 18th birthday in 1915 and was shipped to England to train for combat duty in World War I. Pearson began his tour as a hospital orderly in France and stretchered the wounded from the front lines to hospital. He would try to take his mind off the horrors of war by partaking with other soldiers in games of soccer and field hockey.

Pearson became a quartermaster, but in 1916, was returned to England and sent to Oxford to train as an infantry officer. However, instead of joining the ground war, Pearson was asked to join the Royal Flying Corps, which was in desperate need of pilots. While in training, his flight commander decided Lester wasn't a suitable name for a flier, and nicknamed him "Mike," a handle he carried proudly the rest of his life.

A crash-landing in another training exercise mildly injured Pearson, and he was sent to London for a few days to recuperate. Out on the town one night, Pearson got off a bus on Edgeware Road and didn't see another bus

Lester B. Pearson addresses the crowd before awarding the Lester B. Pearson Award to Jean Ratelle, the player's choice for MVP in 1971–72. NHLPA executive director Alan Eagleson is in the background.

without headlights coming in the opposite direction, and was struck, suffering leg and head injuries. After a brief hospitalization, he was shipped home to Canada.

Oxford Blues

In 1921, Pearson opted to resume his education and landed a coveted scholarship to attend St. John's College at Oxford, the famous British university. A huge development in his tenure there came on October 23, 1921, when the Oxford University Ice Hockey Club was organized, with Ken Taylor as secretary. "The team was formed from American and Canadian students, including Pearson, after trials at the Manchester ice rink, the only one in England and nearly 200 miles north of Oxford," noted British hockey historian Martin Harris, a member of the Society for International Hockey Research.

"He played hockey at Oxford—most famously, he played at Oxford," biographer Andrew Cohen said.

Pearson fondly recalled to Charles Lynch his time on the ice at Oxford. "I played defense on the hockey team, on the Oxford team," Pearson said. "I didn't skate like Bobby Orr, but nobody ever did."

The Oxford squad toured Europe during the 1921–22 season, routing all of its opposition.

Pearson's own account of that hockey season is one filled with happy memories. "We had to call it ice hockey at Oxford to distinguish it from the ground variety which for climatic reasons was naturally more widely played."

Back Bencher

Pearson returned to the University of Toronto (U of T) in the fall of 1923, to accept a position as a lecturer at the school. He also intended to keep his feet firmly planted in the sporting world, though.

"I coached the hockey team and a football team," he told Lynch. "This was great fun, after teaching, to go out on the campus with the boys and run up and down.

"Coaching university teams was very energetic and interesting—I got in close touch with a lot of undergraduates through sports."

The U of T hockey team he coached from 1924–27 iced a loaded roster. They included future NHLers Hugh Plaxton and Dave Trottier, the latter later a Stanley Cup winner with the Montreal Maroons in 1934–35. In 1928, they formed the nucleus of the gold medal-winning Canadian Olympic team at the Winter Games in St. Moritz, Switzerland. The coaches for that team were Conn Smythe and Harold Ballard.

"I loved doing this," Pearson said of coaching. "It took up only two or three hours a day, and I had some talent in getting the most out of my players."

Pearson, who also played two years of inter-collegiate basketball and coached the lacrosse team, was among the 12 in the inaugural class inducted into the University of Toronto Sports Hall of Fame in 1987.

International Man of History

In 1928, Pearson entered the political arena for the first time, accepting a position with Canada's External Affairs office. It all could have been scuttled before it ever started, had Pearson given in to his sporting urges. Shortly after accepting the External Affairs position, Pearson was offered the athletic directorship at the University of Toronto. In his memoirs, he admits he was sorely tempted to return and accept the university's offer.

Working in Canada's diplomatic service, Pearson advanced to a position with the High Commission in London, England, in the mid-1930s. His persistent warnings that war in Europe was imminent went unheeded by his superiors, and he returned home to Canada just six days before Britain declared war on Germany in 1939. During the war, he worked as chief aide to High Commissioner Vincent Massey in London. By 1945, he was serving as Canada's Ambassador to the United States.

Pearson served with Canada's delegation at the United Nations for seven years, including a stint as head of the General Assembly from 1952 to 1953. Twice he was nominated for the secretary general's post. He came closest to winning the position in 1953, but was vetoed as the choice by the Soviet Union, who opposed Pearson's work as one of the architects of the North Atlantic Treaty Organization. Pearson was offered the post as NATO secretary-general in 1952, but turned it down to remain in the Canadian cabinet, where he was serving as external affairs minister.

Nobel Cause

Pearson was awarded the Nobel Peace Prize in 1957 for the dominant role he'd played a year earlier in creating the United Nations Emergency Force that helped avert war in the Middle East, following the combined British-French-Israeli attack on Egypt over the nationalization of the Suez Canal. The force served in a peacekeeping role, providing a buffer zone between the Egyptian defenders and the invaders, and establishing Canada's long-held reputation as international keepers of the peace. Barely a month after he received his Nobel Prize in 1957, Pearson won the leadership of the Canadian Liberal Party. Though his party was routed in the 1958 federal election, it narrowly lost four years later, and was able to overtake the Conservative minority government in 1963, making Pearson prime minister of Canada.

Canadian Icon

Pearson's legacies as Canada's leader are many. He is responsible for the introduction of medicare and the Canada Pension Plan. Under his watch, Canada created its own flag and national anthem. He also introduced the Order of Canada.

On April 20, 1968, when he officially retired as prime minister and handed the reigns of the country over to Pierre Elliott Trudeau, Pearson said he intended to "go home, put my feet up and watch the hockey game."

"He loved watching hockey," Cohen said. "He far preferred to watch a hockey game than to do other things political that were obligations of his life. It was a big part of his life."

When Pearson's time did come—he succumbed to cancer at age 75 on December 28, 1972—even then, sports was at the forefront of his mind.

He called for his good friend, Liberal Senator and party strategist Keith Davey to visit him one final time, a tale Davey related in a 1986 *Toronto Star* article he penned.

"Almost as often as I saw the prime minister we would engage in some hockey or baseball banter," Davey wrote. "I saw Pearson for the final time at his home about three weeks before he died.

"He greeted me by saying, 'Keith, I have some bad news for you. The Leafs are not going to make the playoffs.' He was dreadfully ill and to cheer him I said, 'Oh, come on. Sure they will.' Then he added, 'It's a little worse than that. It's a crisis you're going to have to face alone.' It was his way of telling me it was over.

"A few weeks later, on the last day of 1972—a windy, sleety, rain-driven December 31 afternoon—I marched in his lengthy funeral procession in Ottawa as an honorary pallbearer."

Ted Lindsay

THERE WERE MANY game nights when forward Tomas Holmstrom, a rookie with the Detroit Red Wings during the 1996–97 National Hockey League season, didn't find his sweater hanging in his dressing-room stall, meaning he'd spend the evening in the press box as a healthy scratch.

The lack of regular playing time made it imperative that Holmstrom maintain a rigorous off-ice conditioning regimen, and fortunately for him, he found a willing training partner on those long, lonely days he'd spend pumping iron.

Little did he know at the time that his workout buddy was in fact, a Detroit hockey legend.

It was Hockey Hall of Famer Ted Lindsay.

"We'd get there at the same time, and he helped me out while we were working out," Holmstrom remembered, while admitting much time passed before he was clued into the identity and legend of the old fellow spotting for him while he pumped iron.

"No, not really," Holmstrom said as to whether he knew then who Lindsay was. "I had just got here [from Sweden]. As time went on, I started hearing the stories and I'd see the banner [recognizing the retirement of Lindsay's No. 7 sweater] up there [in the Joe Louis Arena rafters]."

Lindsay remembers those days well. "When Tomas Holmstrom came over from Sweden, I was working out in the back room where the weights are, three or four times a week," said Lindsay, still such a regular in the Detroit dressing room that the Wings continue to issue him his own stall. "When they came off the ice, Tomas would come in and work out with me. That's where I became friends with him. It's nice to see him grow from a nice kid just hoping to make it, into what he's become, an established star in the league."

These days, Holmstrom, a veteran of over 900 NHL games and like Lindsay, a four-time Stanley Cup winner, recognizes not only what Lindsay means to the Red Wings, but to all hockey players.

He was the man who put his career on the line in order to put the players in a better earning position.

On February 11, 1957, Lindsay, then captain of the Red Wings, was named president of the first NHL Players' Association, whose goals at the time were hardly radical.

"Actually, we don't have many grievances," Lindsay explained to *The Canadian Press*. "We just felt we should have an organization of this kind."

Lindsay listed as the main goal of the organization to "promote, foster and protect the best interests of NHL players," the No. 1 priority on that list of goals being an improved pension plan for NHLers. "We just want to make playing in the league more attractive for Canadian and American players. We're not looking for any trouble."

Regardless, Lindsay would find it.

The bid was defeated and despite posting a career-high 85 points during the 1956–57 season, the Wings shunted Lindsay off to Chicago.

Although his attempt to organize the players eventually failed, it paved the way for the birth of the NHLPA a decade later. "Don't ask me why I did it," Lindsay said. "I was one of the better hockey players in the world and I was having one of my best years as a Red Wing at the time. I felt a responsibility, because I saw fellows being sent down. The clubs could send you home—they could send me home—and they didn't owe you five cents. That's not right."

The 1944 Memorial Cup champion Oshawa Generals. Ted Lindsay is the second uniformed player from the left in the top row.

It's also why the NHLPA moved in 2010 to rename the Lester B. Pearson Award—the trophy it has presented annually to the league's most outstanding player by virtue of a players-only ballot since 1970–71. The award is now known as the Ted Lindsay Trophy.

"This is a great honor to have bestowed upon me," Lindsay said. "I took great pride in my hockey career, both on the ice competing towards a championship with my teammates, and off of the ice for the work that we did to ensure our fellow players enjoyed proper rights and benefits."

NHL players, even those far too young to have ever witnessed the man they called Terrible Ted in action, realize the price he paid so that their earning power would increase. "All NHLPA members, current and former, owe a great deal of gratitude to Ted for his efforts, so it is only fitting that we name our most outstanding player award after him," said Calgary Flames captain Jarome Iginla, the 2001–02 Lester B. Pearson Award recipient.

"I see Ted Lindsay one or two times a week and I love to hear the stories of when he played and what he went through with the players' association," former NHL defenseman Chris Chelios said. "He was all about doing the right thing. Every player that has played owes him a lot for the sacrifices that he made."

"I would tip my hat to him," Holmstrom added. "He's a first-class man."

A man who was born with hockey pulsating through his veins.

* * *

Lindsay broke into the NHL with Detroit in 1944, after helping the Oshawa Generals capture the Memorial Cup. He jumped right from the junior ranks into the big leagues, a rarity in the days of the six-team NHL.

Lindsay was also following a path first carved out by his father's skates. When he took the ice for his NHL debut October 29, 1944, against the Boston Bruins, Lindsay made league history. He was the first son of an original NHLer to skate in the league.

Bert Lindsay was nearing the end of a lengthy pro career when he donned the pads for the Montreal Wanderers and skated out between the pipes for a December 19, 1917, game against the Toronto Arenas, the opening night in NHL history. The Wanderers won that night by a 10–9 count, but it would be their only NHL victory. The team's home rink, the Westmount Arena, burned to the ground on January 2, 1918, and the club folded a few days later.

The following season, Bert Lindsay stopped pucks for the Arenas, then hung up his pads for good, ending a career that saw him play for the Edmonton Pros against the Ottawa Senators in the 1908–09 Stanley Cup final. He was also the netminder for the Pacific Coast Hockey Association's Victoria Aristocrats in the 1913–14 Stanley Cup final.

Mining the Talent

Ted Lindsay was born in Renfrew on July 29, 1925, and if his hockey bloodlines were in his genes, then perhaps his take-no-prisoners brand of hockey emanated from the skates he wore as a youngster.

Bert Lindsay spent $4.75 to purchase a pair of Red Horner model skates for his son. Toronto Maple Leafs defenseman Horner was a legendary NHL tough guy in the 1930s. He led the league in penalty minutes for a record eight seasons from 1932–33 to 1939–40 and held forth as the NHL's career penalty-minute leader until 1957, when he relinquished the title to Lindsay.

When the Great Depression hit in the 1930s,

Bert Lindsay relocated his family to Kirkland Lake so that he could work in the gold mines there. This is the town that Ted considers to be his home, and it's where he played all his youth hockey, winning an Ontario Minor Hockey Association title with the Kirkland Lake juveniles in 1941–42.

The next year, he and teammate Gus Mortson left home for Toronto, to play with the St. Michael's Majors of the Ontario Hockey Association's Junior A Series. During this era in Memorial Cup play, teams could add players to the roster from clubs they'd eliminated along the playdown road. When Oshawa bounced St. Mike's from the 1944 playoffs, the Generals collected both left-winger Lindsay, defenseman Mortson and forward David Bauer (later to become Father David Bauer and gain fame as creator of Canada's national team program) to aid their cause.

In seven games with Oshawa, Lindsay scored seven goals and dished out two assists. He was extremely productive in clutch situations. He scored twice in the Generals' 3–1 win over the Montreal Royals to clinch the Eastern final, then tallied two more goals in the 11–4 victory over the Trail Smoke Eaters that clinched the Memorial Cup and the Canadian junior crown.

An antagonist on the ice, the young Lindsay was an anomaly off the ice. Most Ontario boys saved their NHL love for one team, the Leafs. But Lindsay was quite fond of another franchise, the Red Wings.

The strong signal from Detroit radio station WJR–AM carried all the way to Kirkland Lake and Lindsay could listen to the Wings' games. "They played my kind of hockey and that's how I became a Red Wing fan, not ever thinking I'd play for them," Lindsay said. He was especially fond of tough-as-nails defenseman "Black Jack" Stewart, later Lindsay's teammate in Detroit.

Making the Jump

Lindsay's path to Detroit was paved with miscommunication on the part of the hockey operations staff of the rival Maple Leafs. Told there was a talented prospect skating at forward for St. Mike's, Toronto dispatched a scout to check the kid out. But when he arrived that night, what the scout failed to recognize was that Lindsay, the object of their affection, missed the game through injury and instead, the Leafs added his teammate Joe Sadler to their protected list. Detroit scout Carson Cooper quickly swooped in to acquire Lindsay's pro rights for the Red Wings.

Though he was 19 and still left with a year of junior eligibility, Wings coach/general manager Jack Adams signed Lindsay to a pro contract on October 18, 1944, just prior to the start of the 1944–45 regular season, but it wasn't easy. Even as a teenager, Lindsay proved a tough negotiator.

In fact, at first, Lindsay was convinced he'd be better served by returning to play his last junior campaign with St. Mike's. "My rationale was that if I went back to St. Mike's, I was going to play 40 minutes a game," Lindsay explained. St. Mike's coach Paul McNamara convinced Lindsay otherwise, pointing out how rare chances to skate in the NHL were for players in the days of the six-team NHL.

"Adams guaranteed me that I would play in 45 (of 50 regular-season) games and not have to sit on the bench," said Lindsay, whose resistance to blindly following the orders of management were also revealed early when Adams asked him to go to Detroit's American Hockey League farm club in Indianapolis because of a player shortage and play in a game against Hershey.

"I told him no, and he was pissed," Lindsay recalled. "But there was no sense in making him mad at the start of my career." Lindsay reported

and played, but was later ruled an ineligible player by the AHL and the official record of his appearance was expunged.

His first NHL goal was tallied against New York Rangers netminder Ken McAuley and Lindsay's first of many fistic bouts left veteran Montreal defenseman Glen Harmon suffering from a broken hand. As the two were escorted to the penalty box, Harmon grinned at Lindsay and said, "Nice going, kid."

Others quickly took notice of the kid from Kirkland Lake. "He's going to be a real hockey player or I miss my guess," Montreal defenseman Leo Lamoureux told the *Windsor Star*. Adams wasn't afraid to give the teenager significant responsibility on the ice, asking him to shadow Montreal sniper Maurice "Rocket" Richard. Richard, who became the NHL's first 50-goal scorer that season, was impressed. "[Lindsay] is almost impossible to shake," he said.

Adams busied himself stumping for Lindsay, seeking to garner the Calder Memorial Trophy as the NHL's top rookie for his prize pupil. "Ted is only a kid of 19 who a year ago was playing junior hockey," Adams explained to Doug Vaughan of the *Windsor Star*. "I've used him against all the top right-wingers in the league and he has never given a bad performance. He hasn't scored as many goals as [Ken] Smith of Boston, but he's got his share against the best forward lines, while the Boston player has been doing his chores against second- and third-rate lines.

"Unless I'm very much mistaken, Ted will be a National Leaguer long after fellows like [Toronto goalie Frank] McCool, Smith and [New York Rangers right-winger Walt] Atanas are gone and forgotten."

Though Adams would be proven correct in the long run, Lindsay finished third in the Calder voting that season, behind McCool and Smith.

A Stir Is Born

Lindsay didn't take long to establish a reputation around the league. Two reputations, actually.

He was surfacing rapidly as both an NHL star, and someone who was not to be taken lightly on the ice, whether or not the puck belonged to him. During the 1947–48 season, Lindsay led the NHL with 33 goals.

Adams, who'd coached Detroit since 1927, elevated Lindsay to a place among Detroit's all-time greats. "I have no hesitation in naming Ted Lindsay the best left-winger we have ever had," Adams told the *Windsor Star*. "He's better than [former NHL All-Star] Herbie Lewis."

In terms of all-around play, Adams saw another Detroit legend when he watched Lindsay in action. "Lindsay in many ways reminds me of the best player we ever had, Larry Aurie," Adams said. "Larry, despite his size, never backed down from anyone."

Like Lindsay, who stood five-foot-eight and weighed 163 pounds, Aurie was a gritty five-foot-six, 148-pounder who led the NHL with 23 goals in 1936–37. "Pound for pound, he was as good a hockey player as you ever saw," Adams said of Aurie.

Lindsay was in the process of usurping that title. "No one was more competitive," teammate Marcel Pronovost said of Lindsay, a fact Lindsay does not dispute.

"I hated everybody I played against and they hated me," Lindsay said. "I had the idea that I should beat up every player I tangled with and nothing ever convinced me it wasn't a good idea.

"You had to play tough in those days, or they'd run you out of the building."

He would fight for every inch of the inch, but once he gained it, Lindsay made things happen. In 1949–50, he led the NHL in scoring as Detroit won the Stanley Cup, playing a starring role on Detroit's famed Production Line. Lindsay, center Sid Abel and right-winger Gordie Howe finished 1–2–3 in the Art Ross Trophy race that season, the first time a championship team iced the league's top three point producers.

"My job on the Production Line was just being a good left-winger," Lindsay said. "The three of us were all greatly talented. We all knew to put the puck where the hole was. Nobody could ever figure out what we were doing, but we all knew what each other was doing."

Detroit dominated the NHL during the late 1940s through the mid-1950s, finishing first seven times between 1948–49 and 1954–55, an NHL record that remains on the books today.

"It was a unit," said Lindsay, captain of Detroit's Cup winners in 1954 and 1955. "To win seven league championships in a row, nobody's ever going to defeat that record in hockey. Nobody will ever win it seven years in a row. Not with 30 teams."

The Wings wouldn't win it all again until 1997 and while those teams of the 1950s are now just a memory, Lindsay would stack them up against any of the NHL's great dynasties.

"We had great skaters," he said. "We had great puckhandlers.

"It was puck control, but our game was a defensive game. A lot of people think we were all old fogies back in those days who couldn't skate. We had guys who could skate with anybody today."

When the Wings won the Cup in 1954–55, Lindsay inadvertently launched a Stanley Cup tradition by scooping up Lord Stanley's mug and skated around the ice with it. "When they presented the Cup, I just went over and picked it up," Lindsay said. "I wanted the fans to see what we were playing for. Apparently, I started a tradition."

Terrible Ted

Lindsay made no friends between the boards and even those he was close with away from the rink would incur his wrath. During a 1947 playoff game against Toronto, Lindsay touched off a near riot when he cranked Toronto defenseman Gus Mortson, one of his closest pals, across the head with his stick. "I checked Lindsay and I guess he didn't like it," Mortson told *The Canadian Press.* "He turned and let me have it."

There was no remorse on Lindsay's part. "I don't know anybody when a hockey game starts," he said.

They called him Scarface, due to the more than 600 stitches needed to repair facial damage. Lindsay suffered so many broken noses during his career, he claims to have lost count. "I used to be homely when I was younger, but then I had all this involuntary plastic surgery," Lindsay said. But the nickname he is more commonly known by is "Terrible Ted."

"The Toronto writers called me Scarface, because it seemed like I always either had a black eye or a cut," Lindsay said. "It was always a compliment, as far as I was concerned."

* * *

Lindsay won the NHL scoring title in 1949–50, and led the league in penalty minutes in 1958–59. He and former Montreal Maroons star Nels Stewart are the only players to turn this unique double in the history of the NHL.

During his career, Lindsay garnered five so-called Gordie Howe hat tricks—a goal, an assist and a fighting major in the same game. Always a man with an opinion during his NHL career, Lindsay was assessed 52 misconducts of the 10-minute variety and eight game misconduct penalties.

Lindsay was the first Red Wing to reach the 200-goal plateau. His career-high 55 assists, first registered in 1949–50 and equaled in 1956–57, remain the club's single-season mark for helpers by a left-winger. Lindsay also established a club record that's never been surpassed by potting three power-play goals March 20, 1955, against the Montreal Canadiens.

Union Activist

On the surface, the last person who figured to spearhead organized labor among NHL players was Lindsay. "You'd get to the [NHL] All-Star Game and Ted Lindsay would walk by and grunt," recalled New York Rangers star Andy Bathgate. "That's the only words you'd get out of him."

To this day, Lindsay isn't even sure how he became the point man on this power play. "The Lord didn't come down and say, 'Ted, you're one of the better players in hockey today,'" Lindsay said. " 'Somebody like you has to do this.' "

Truth be told, Lindsay led the way for one reason—because deep down, he knew it was the right thing to do. "When I did it, [the NHL] was a dictatorship," he said. "I just wanted to give us a voice. We had no voice."

Lindsay enjoyed his best statistical season with the Wings during that 1956–57 campaign, leading the NHL with 55 assists while collecting 85 points, but it was his work behind the scenes that was making the most headlines. That's when Lindsay launched his crusade to form the first NHL players' association.

"I made $5,500 my first year," Lindsay said. "During most of my career, I made between seven and ten thousand dollars. When we signed our contract, you couldn't take it out of the manager's office. It was against the bylaws—at least that's what they told us.

"If you brought a lawyer or an agent into the room, they'd say, 'Son, good luck to you. We won't need you. We hope you have a good life.' That was their feeling. Edmonton was our farm club in the Western League and Indianapolis was our farm club in the American League and they had players in both those places who were as good as we were, so they didn't have to worry about personnel."

His biggest challenge would be to unite opponents who sought to destroy each other on the ice to a common cause that would ultimately benefit all involved. "Things were different back then," Lindsay said. "Hockey players were so competitive. They hated every member of every other team."

They held clandestine meetings, putting an end run on the NHL's no-fraternization policy that prohibited rival players from speaking to each other. Lindsay convinced top players such as his close friend Gus Mortson of the Chicago Black Hawks, Bill Gadsby of the New York Rangers, Jim Thomson of the Toronto Maple Leafs and Montreal Canadiens star Doug Harvey that there was merit in forming a players' association. "We had to have Toronto or Montreal on board," Lindsay said. "If you didn't have Toronto or Montreal, it wouldn't work."

Lindsay also knew better than to label his group as a union. "I couldn't sell the word 'union,'" he said. "In the 1950s, unionists were considered communists. The word had negative connotations. I never advocated collective bargaining. We were supposed to be an association of professionals who could negotiate our own fees."

Out of his own pocket, Lindsay hired the same New York lawyers who helped baseball players negotiate their first collective agreement. He consulted with Cleveland Indians pitcher Bob Feller, who'd help organize the Major League Baseball Players' Association. The owners of the six NHL teams saw his plan as a threat to their

Bill Juzda attempts to take out Ted Lindsay in early 1950s NHL action.

monopoly and put their own plan into place to scuttle the players' association.

Thomson was traded to Chicago and shockingly, in the summer of 1957, Lindsay was also dealt to the lowly Black Hawks, who hadn't won a playoff series since 1944.

"I had my best year ever as a Red Wing the year I was traded," Lindsay said. "I was traded because of the union. I know Jack Adams turned every player on the team against me, one by one.

"A series of rumors about my attitude, as well as derogatory remarks about myself and my family showed me that the personal resentment of the Detroit general manager toward me would make it impossible for me to continue playing hockey here in Detroit," Lindsay told Matt Dennis of the *Windsor Star*.

Slowly, the owners turned the players against the idea of forming an association and in

February 1957, the NHLPA was defeated in its bid for certification. Lindsay's dream had been sidelined, but he remained undeterred.

"I'd do it again," Lindsay said. "I was not a crusader, I wasn't trying to change hockey. It was just something we as players needed as a vehicle to be able to discuss things. The effort was not a failure, because we did make a few small gains, and we paved the way for [NHL players] down the road to form a union [in 1967]."

Lindsay also immediately noticed a difference in the game upon his arrival in the Windy City. "When I was traded to Chicago, I was able to negotiate a contract there, which we could never do in Detroit," he said.

Motown Revival

Lindsay played three seasons in Chicago, helping the Blackhawks earn their first playoff position in seven seasons before retiring following the 1959–60 season. But hockey wasn't done with him just yet.

In the fall of 1964, Lindsay announced he would attempt a comeback at the age of 39 with the Red Wings. "It wasn't tough for me," Lindsay said. "It was something I wanted to do. I wanted to end up a Red Wing, and I wanted to end up maybe doing color on television."

"[Former linemate] Sid [Abel], he was the GM and the coach and he says, 'Come back and play. I think you can help us.' I'm 39, I haven't played for four years and I laughed at him. But he was serious. 'No, I think you can help us.' So I said, 'I'll go to training camp and see how I feel.'

"I was working my [manufacturing] business with [former teammate] Marty Pavelich. They were training at Olympia in Detroit. The only favor I asked was that I go on with the first shift at 8 o'clock in the morning. He said, 'We can arrange that.' I'd be on the ice from 8 to 9:30,

shower, get dressed in a shirt and tie and go to lunch with a customer, then take my old body home to bed at about 3 o'clock in the afternoon and try to get some sleep and a dinner. And get ready for the next morning and see if I'm able to get out of bed. That's the way we did it."

The day before the season opener, the Wings signed Lindsay. "Ted signed a year's contract, but if he doesn't feel he can take it, he'll quit," Abel said. "And if we don't feel he can do the job, we'll let him go."

Not only could Lindsay take it, old Scarface could still dish it out, too. He collected a misconduct in the season opener against Toronto and in January, blasted the NHL after referee Vern Buffey assessed Lindsay a misconduct and game misconduct and accompanying $25 and $50 fines. "I'm going to tell Sid not to pay the money," Lindsay told *The Canadian Press.* "And I'm not going to sit for [NHL president Clarence] Campbell's kangaroo court, either."

Lindsay was suspended indefinitely and after initially threatening to take the NHL to court, he wrote a letter of apology to Campbell, as well as a personal check for $75 to cover his fines, though he insisted he'd written the letter under protest.

Overall, Lindsay's season was a success. He scored 14 goals and helped Detroit to a first-place finish.

"When you're doing something you love, it's never hard," he said of his comeback. "You're doing it because you want to do it.

"I knew for sure I could play. They picked us for fifth or sixth spot in the league, but after we went once around the league, I said, 'Who's any better than us?' We ended up winning the league championship and should have won the Stanley Cup if it wasn't for those jackass referees."

By season's end, Lindsay had won over Campbell, so often his foe and one of his harshest critics. "I know I was among the knowledgeable hockey people who expressed skepticism when it was first announced that Lindsay would try a comeback after being away from the game for four years," Campbell announced in an official NHL press release in late February of 1965. But now I know I was wrong.

"Lindsay has done what I thought was next to impossible. He is an amazing athlete."

Man of Principle

When Detroit left Lindsay unprotected in the 1965 NHL Intra-League draft, the rival Leafs threatened to claim him, so this time, he retired for good.

When Lindsay was inducted into the Hockey Hall of Fame in 1966, he was just the third player to have the mandatory three-year waiting period waived, following Boston's Aubrey "Dit" Clapper (1947) and Montreal's Maurice "Rocket" Richard (1961). But when the August 27, 1966, enshrinement date arrived, Lindsay was a no-show. Told the induction ceremony was an all-male affair and wives and children weren't welcome, Lindsay stayed home. "If my family can't share in this, I won't go," he said. "They sacrificed a lot through my career and went through a lot of inconvenience. They deserve it as much as I do."

Apparently, Lindsay opened a few eyes and some minds, because it wasn't long after that the Hall of Fame changed its policy and welcomed family members to attend the annual day of enshrinement.

Ever the non-conformist, in 1955 Lindsay was the first NHL to player to appeal a league suspension. He lost his case, but made his point, that he would forever question authority if he felt they were in the wrong.

The man who first sought to launch the NHLPA was no fan of Alan Eagleson, the man the players put in charge of the association when the NHLPA was officially formed in 1967. "Get rid of Eagleson," Lindsay advised NHL players in 1970. "He's more interested in exploiting the players for his own good."

Today, Lindsay, 85, is still employed by a Michigan-based stamping firm. "I'm still working five days a week, sometimes six," he said. "I love my game and I still love people. I'm lucky to have good health."

He's a regular presence around the Red Wings dressing room at Joe Louis Arena, some 45 years after his last NHL game. "I get into the Red Wings dressing room 3–4 times a week," Lindsay said. "I know all the guys.

"When I come into the room, it's always Mr. Lindsay. I'm not looking for that, but they respect me, probably for my age, I guess, but I think it's because of what I did for the players' association."

Most understand the price Lindsay paid so that they could earn the big money. "The unfortunate thing is that a lot of the European players don't know who Ted Lindsay is and aren't aware of what his battles and struggles were," suggested former Wings defenseman Chris Chelios, now a club executive.

Holmstrom isn't among them. "He comes around once or twice a week, talks to the guys," Holmstrom said. "It's good. He has all his charity work and he's very involved in hockey.

"He's been retired for a long time. I've never seen him play, but I've heard the legend. It's too bad I couldn't see him play. It would be fun to see some tapes."

Jaromir Jagr sits in the Founders' Room at the Hockey Hall of Fame after being awarded the Lester B. Pearson Award for the 1999–2000 season.

CHAPTER 8
Controversies and Surprises

WHEN ST. LOUIS Blues defenseman Chris Pronger nipped Pittsburgh Penguins right-winger Jaromir Jagr by one vote to capture the 1999–2000 Hart Trophy, he was thrilled. When Pronger finished third behind Jagr and Florida Panthers right-winger Pavel Bure for the Lester B. Pearson Trophy, he was philosophical. "This proves the writers know more about hockey than the players," Pronger said after the Hart and Pearson winners were different players for the first time since 1989.

Jagr, considered by many to be the favorite to win the Hart that season, received the 30th annual Lester B. Pearson Trophy earlier on the day of the awards banquet. He garnered 192 votes, while Bure was listed on 159 votes and Pronger was tabbed 129 times, which was the closest voting in the history of the award. It was the second time that Jagr had won the Pearson, but lost the Hart, the only player to have this happen to him twice in the history of the award. In accepting the Pearson, Jagr displayed that he knew a thing or two about philosophy as well. "I think this might even be a bit more special than the [Hart] because it is voted on by your peers," Jagr said. "It's a trophy voted on

by the players you play against, the players you face every night."

He was certainly a worthy winner, though a solid case could be made for both of his fellow finalists. Jagr led the NHL in scoring with 42–54–96 totals, despite missing 19 games due to a variety of injuries, joining fellow Penguin Mario Lemieux as the only players to win an NHL scoring title while missing more than seven games during the season. Jagr posted a league-leading points-per-game average of 1.52. Bure led the NHL with 58 goals, 14 more than any other player, while Pronger topped the NHL in plus-minus, led the league in average ice time and won the Norris Trophy as the

NHL's most valuable defenseman.

Handicapping the race, Jagr felt it more likely that Bure would be the one to upset him than Pronger. "I didn't have a chance to look at Pronger much during the season," Jagr told the *Pittsburgh Post-Gazette*. "I paid more attention to Bure because he's a forward. He scored 58 goals. That's a lot of goals. And he had a lot of game winners [an NHL-leading 14]. That always helps."

There may have been surprise in Florida, or the suggestion of controversy in St. Louis as a result of the Pearson decision, but in Pittsburgh, the only thought was that Jagr's peers got it right. "We have the best player in the world," Penguins player-owner Lemieux told the *Pittsburgh Post-Gazette* of Jagr. "He had a great year."

"Everyone here is biased, of course," admitted Penguins general manager Craig Patrick, "but we think he had an outstanding year. We feel he deserves to be MVP."

In 2005–06, Jagr, by then a member of the New York Rangers, was the Pearson winner, while San Jose Sharks center Joe Thornton captured the Hart Trophy. "He was my vote for the Pearson," Thornton said of Jagr. "He was my MVP. He's the full package."

In his first season with the Rangers, Jagr produced franchise records for goals (54) and points (123), finishing second only to Thornton in overall NHL scoring. "I'm glad I got at least one trophy," Jagr told *The Canadian Press*, pointing out his long trek from Europe to attend the awards.

Jagr was bitter with the perception that he rediscovered his game as a Ranger, and also seemed miffed to be runner-up for the Hart yet again. "I thought I was still pretty good before," Jagr told Ken Campbell of the *Toronto Star*. "Hey, I was a finalist for this award [Hart] five times. I've only won it once, but that's still pretty good isn't it?"

Since the Pearson, which was renamed the Ted Lindsay Award in 2010, was first presented in 1971, there have been 17 instances in which the writers and the players disagreed on who they felt was the most valuable player in the National Hockey League.

Early on, players and writers appeared to be from different planets when it came to assessing the MVP of the NHL. They differentiated on the first 6 winners and 9 of the first 11 selections.

The players recognized Phil Esposito's record 76-goal, 152-point season in 1970–71 and named him the first winner of their most outstanding player award, while the writers went with Esposito's teammate, defenseman Bobby Orr, who'd recorded an NHL-record 102 assists, as the Hart Trophy winner.

"There is a difference," Esposito, a two-time winner of both the Pearson and the Hart sought to explain to Alan Adams of the *National Post* in 2000, when discussing the merits of the two awards, and why there can logically be different winners in the same season. "One is the most valuable player in the league [Pearson/Lindsay] and the other is the most valuable player to his team [Hart]."

Some veterans of the game saw Esposito's offensive outburst as more good fortune than great accomplishment. Buddy O'Connor, the 1947–48 Hart Trophy winner with the New York Rangers, was of the opinion that Esposito lucked into his success with the Bruins after he was dealt to Boston by the Chicago Black Hawks in 1967. "In a way, yes," O'Connor told Dink Carroll of the *Montreal Gazette*. "But you need a little luck as well as talent in hockey.

"The best thing that ever happened to Esposito was the trade. He always had the ability to score, but with Chicago, his job was to throw the puck to Bobby Hull. Boston didn't have a scoring ace, and when Esposito showed he could put the puck in the net, it became the job of the other guys to throw the puck to him."

Bruins general manager Milt Schmidt, who engineered the trade for Esposito, naturally saw it differently, in that Esposito solved a problem for the Bruins upon his arrival in Boston. "There was a role for him with our club," said Schmidt, the 1950–51 Hart Trophy winner with the Bruins. "He found that out and he assumed the responsibility. Some guys don't want responsibility of any kind. Give Espo credit. He's been great for us, and we've been good for him."

One of the most controversial Pearson/Hart discrepancies occurred during the 1971–72 season, the second year that the NHLPA presented the Pearson Award. That spring, the players voted their honor to New York Rangers center Jean Ratelle, who was battling for the NHL scoring lead when he went down for the season with a fractured ankle. Despite being limited to 63 games by his injury, Ratelle collected club-records with 63 assists and 109 points, good for third overall in the NHL and 31 more points than he'd ever previously recorded during a single season.

Working between left-winger Vic Hadfield and right-winger Rod Gilbert on New York's vaunted GAG (goal-a-game) line, Ratelle's passes helped make Hadfield the first 50-goal scorer in Rangers' history. They were the first line in NHL history on which all three players enjoyed a 40-goal season. "This has been our big year because of Ratelle's consistent strength," Gilbert told Ted Blackman of the *Montreal Gazette*.

A smooth skater and an accomplished playmaker armed with an accurate wrist shot, and a player capable of also filling a checking role, Ratelle collected just four penalty minutes all season and was also presented with the Lady

Jean Ratelle, the 1971–72 NHLPA MVP.

Byng Trophy as the NHL's best combination of productivity and sportsmanship. The only other Pearson winner to also be presented the Lady Byng would be Joe Sakic of the Colorado Avalanche in 2000–01.

"That Ratelle has developed into a great hockey player," Toronto Maple Leafs assistant GM Frank "King" Clancy told Dink Carroll of the *Montreal Gazette*. "In my book, he's the best center in the league today. He can do everything."

Even though Esposito eventually won his second straight scoring title and third in four seasons, and Orr, who finished second in the scoring race, skated away with his third straight Hart Trophy, Rangers coach-GM Emile Francis was ready and willing to go to bat for his man. "Has Esposito done as much for Boston as Ratelle did for New York?" Francis asked *The Canadian Press*. "[Ratelle] is superb at faceoffs, does an awful lot of work on defense and passes like

Mike Liut, the 1980–81 Pearson Award winner, was the first goalie to ever win the prize.

[two-time Hart winner Jean] Beliveau. He has made his line great, and this has turned the race around."

Look at the data and Francis may have a valid point. With Ratelle, the Rangers were challenging the Bruins for first overall in the NHL. Without him, they slumped to 10 points in arrears of Boston. And minus the injured Ratelle in the playoffs, the Rangers fell in a six-game Stanley Cup final against the Bruins. And while neither of Esposito's linemates (Ken Hodge or Wayne Cashman) cracked the top-10 scorers, Hadfield (fourth) and Gilbert (fifth) ran right behind Ratelle in the scoring chase.

Nearly four decades after Ratelle's win, Thornton, who won the Hart in 2005–06 but lost the Pearson to Jagr, put forth another theory as to why the slick Rangers center, who was never a Hart Trophy finalist during his career, might

have won the players over during the 1971–72 campaign.

"I think that's kind of voted probably about a month before the season ends," Thornton said of the Pearson/Lindsay ballot conducted by the NHLPA. "It's not like the Hart, where the season's done and you can kind of reflect. The Pearson, guys tend to check out who's doing good at that time."

At the time of his March 2 injury, when his right ankle was shattered after being struck by a shot from teammate Dale Rolfe in a game against the California Golden Seals, it was easy to argue that Ratelle was that guy. He trailed Esposito 110–109 in the points race when his ankle was fractured and was riding a 13-game point-scoring streak.

* * *

It's hard to imagine Orr being selected for an award to be deemed controversial, yet his choice as the 1974–75 winner of the Pearson Award raised eyebrows, not so much because he won, but more so because he didn't even come close to winning the Hart Trophy.

Orr won his second NHL scoring title that season—he remains the only defenseman ever to lead the league in scoring—and captured his record eighth straight Norris Trophy as the NHL's best defender. But the Hart was a contest between Philadelphia Flyers center Bobby Clarke and Los Angeles Kings goalie Rogatien Vachon, with Clarke outpointing Vachon 127–113 in the writers' poll.

With 135 points, Orr, the only defenseman ever voted the Pearson Award, had a hand in 42 percent of Boston's 345 goals that season. "Bobby Orr is the best hockey player in the league," Bruins GM Harry Sinden told the *Montreal Gazette*. "He does so many spectacular things and so much is expected of him."

Naturally, Clarke's camp begged to differ. "Bobby Clarke is the most valuable player in hockey, by miles" insisted Flyers GM Keith Allen to the *Rock Hill Herald*. "I've given the matter a lot of thought, and I don't know any player in hockey who means more to his team than Bobby Clarke does to the Philadelphia Flyers. Take Orr away from Boston and they'd still be in virtually the same place in the standings."

Another legend who didn't immediately garner the love of his peer group until he'd been on the scene for a few years was Wayne Gretzky of the Edmonton Oilers. Surprisingly, his fellow players were slow to board the Great Gretzky train. While hockey writers voted Gretzky every Hart Trophy from his first NHL season in 1979–80 through 1986–87, it wasn't until 1981–82, when the Oilers center recorded new NHL standards for goals (92), assists (120) and points (212), that his peers viewed Gretzky as their most outstanding performer and voted him the Pearson Award.

Los Angeles Kings center Marcel Dionne, who'd tied with Gretzky for the scoring lead in 1979–80, but won the Art Ross Trophy because he'd scored more goals than The Great One, was the Pearson winner that season, repeating his win of the prior season. In each campaign Dionne was bettered for the Hart—by Gretzky in 1979–80 and by New York Islanders center Bryan Trottier in 1978–79.

"I was fortunate to get nominated for anything," said Dionne, the Hart Trophy runner-up in 1979–80. "It was great." Clearly, though, he treasures his two Pearson Awards. "I think personally, it's the greatest award individually for a player, because it's your peers. As players, you see more of what's going on."

The following season (1980–81) saw Gretzky shatter Esposito's single-season points mark of 152, collecting 164 points, but it was a stopper that the players decided was the NHL's show stopper. The players selected St. Louis Blues goalie Mike Liut as the Pearson winner. "Liut was to the 1980–81 Blues what [pitcher] Bob Gibson was to the 1968 [St. Louis] Cardinals," wrote Dan O'Neill in the *St. Louis Post-Dispatch*. "He played 61 games and got points in 46 of them. He was the foundation of one of the best seasons in franchise history, a team that finished with 107 points and a Smythe Division title."

Through the 1980s, two centers dominated the NHL, Gretzky and Lemieux. But there was a third superstar center on the horizon, playing in the shadows of The Great One and Super Mario—Stevie Y. The Detroit Red Wings captain Steve Yzerman blossomed during the 1988–89 season. Rebounding from a serious, season-ending knee injury late in the 1987–88 campaign, Yzerman finished third in NHL scoring and established Detroit franchise records with 65–90–155 totals.

This sensational trio were nominated as finalists for both the Hart Trophy and Pearson Awards, and from the outside, both races were viewed as close ones. "Whether it's myself, or Mario, or Steve Yzerman, there's going to be controversy," Gretzky told Jim Matheson of the *Edmonton Journal*. "I'll be thrilled to death if I win, but it's not like those guys didn't have great years. It's sort of like choosing between Magic [Johnson] and Michael Jordan."

Gretzky did note the distinction between the Hart and Pearson, though. "The problem with the MVP award is it doesn't mean most outstanding player," he said. When the voting was done on both sides, it was Lemieux, the Art Ross Trophy winner with 199 points, who was left empty-handed. Gretzky won the Hart Trophy for the ninth time, and in a huge upset, the players handed the Pearson to Yzerman.

"I don't consider myself in the same class as a Wayne Gretzky and a Mario Lemieux," Yzerman said after his win. "Wayne, and now Mario, have really dominated the game and I don't ever want to put myself in their category. I don't feel I have done the things they have done on the same magnitude. I'm not playing second fiddle, but I am comfortable with where I am."

* * *

The players and writers were left with an unusual conundrum during the 2002–03 season. The choice for the Hart and Pearson came down to a pair of sensational forwards from Ornskoldsvik, Sweden—Colorado Avalanche center Peter Forsberg and Vancouver Canucks left-winger Markus Naslund.

Forsberg, who nipped Naslund on the last day of the season to wear the NHL scoring crown, got the Hart nod, while the players went for Naslund as their most outstanding player. "If you've got an ounce of brains, and Markus Naslund has the puck, I think you are afraid," Canucks GM Brian Burke told Joe O'Connor of *The (Vancouver) Province*.

"Even though [the Pearson Award] does not get the publicity that the Hart Trophy gets, it is still a neat thing when your peers vote for you," said Naslund, the Canucks captain and the first Vancouver player ever to be a finalist for either award.

In 2010, the first year of the Ted Lindsay Award, the vote was again split, and it was a Vancouver player who once more caused the surprise. Canucks center Henrik Sedin had won the Art Ross Trophy as NHL scoring leader for the first time in his career, but the smart money was on the other two finalists for both awards—Pittsburgh center Sidney Crosby and Washington left-winger Alexander Ovechkin—to take either the Hart, or Lindsay, or both.

Instead, it was a shocked Sedin who captured the writers' nod for the Hart. "They're the faces of the sport," Sedin said of Crosby and Ovechkin. "They have been since they joined the league. Those players are second to none. I mean, I thought the Hart was going to be really, really tough. I thought that was going to be out of the question. But maybe the other one [Lindsay], but I'm happy. I'll take this."

Ovechkin was equally thrilled earlier in the day when he was named first winner of the Lindsay, giving him an NHLPA hat trick to go with the Pearson Awards he'd won in 2007–08 and 2008–09. He's the only player to have won the Lindsay, Pearson and Hart. "It's pretty important when people and players give you this [recognition]," Ovechkin said. "I don't want to stop. I want to be the best again next year."

CHAPTER 9
Seminal Seasons

Esposito Gets His Fill

Milt Schmidt was just minding his own business in his office at the Boston Garden the afternoon of May 15, 1967, when the phone rang. "It was a long-distance call from Key Biscayne, Florida," recalled Schmidt, 93, and enjoying retirement in Westwood, Massachusetts. "I thought, 'Who the heck would be calling me from Key Biscayne, Florida?'"

In fact, it was Tommy Ivan, general manager of the Chicago Blackhawks and the two men were about to embark on a journey which would ultimately consummate one of hockey's most memorable blockbuster trades.

"We started talking at 3 p.m.," said Schmidt, who was Boston's assistant GM, "and to make a long story short, by 8 p.m., we came to an agreement about the players who would be involved."

The Bruins sent goalie Jack Norris, defenseman Gilles Marotte and center Pit Martin to Chicago for centers Phil Esposito and Fred Stanfield and right-winger Ken Hodge, a move that would dramatically change the future of both clubs.

Even though Esposito would become the record-setting gain from the deal, he wasn't the key to Boston making the move. "We didn't know much about Hodge or Esposito, but we sure liked Stanfield," Schmidt said. "He was a strong skater and puckhandler."

Bruins coach Tom Johnson put Esposito and Hodge on a line with Wayne Cashman to start the 1970–71 season and they became the NHL's most formidable forward unit. "Esposito got Hodge to go in the corners," Schmidt said. "Cashman and Hodge would go in the corner and get the puck and you knew where Esposito would be."

Esposito would be in front of the net, the place from where he scored a then-NHL-record 76 goals and 152 points during the 1970–71 season, a seminal season in league history that earned him the first Lester B. Pearson Award

Alan Eagleson and Lester B. Pearson present Phil Esposito the first ever NHLPA MVP award.

as the NHLPA's most outstanding player of the regular season.

Schmidt smiles when thinking about the good fortune that smiled on him the day of the Esposito trade. "We'd finished out of the playoffs for eight straight years, so I figured no matter what deal I made, I couldn't make us worse," Schmidt reasoned. "But I never expected what came of it. We went from the bottom of the league to what was basically a dynasty."

The linchpins of that dynasty were Esposito, the 1970–71 Pearson winner, and defenseman Bobby Orr, the 1970–71 Hart Trophy winner. "In Boston, I played 35–40 minutes a game and Bobby Orr played over 40 minutes a game," Esposito recalled. "The more you play, the more you're into the game."

No one was into the game more than Esposito and Orr during Boston's amazing 1970–71

campaign. The entire season was a 1–2 run for glory between Esposito and Orr. "It will be a close race, but we don't ever worry about it," Esposito said at the time.

Esposito had won the Art Ross Trophy as NHL scoring champion in 1968–69, producing a league-record 126 points, becoming the first player ever to top the 100-point plateau during an NHL season. Orr took charge in 1969–70. He set an NHL mark with 87 assists and became the first defenseman in league history to lead the NHL in scoring, posting 120 points, 21 better than second-place finisher Esposito.

They'd also divided individual honors at each season's end: Esposito won the Hart Trophy in 1968-69, Orr in 1969–70. They'd both contend for that award again in 1970–71, along with a new trophy, the Pearson Award, which would be decided by a ballot of NHL players and would determine in their mind who was the most outstanding player in the league during regular-season play.

Each player recognized his value to the other. "If they're bothering Orr, they're not bothering me," Esposito told *The Associated Press*.

He was matter-of-fact about his uncanny ability to find the back of the net from his regular position camped out in the slot on the edge of the opposition's goal crease. "Some nights they go in and some nights, they don't," Esposito said. "You just have to keep shooting. The goals come eventually."

After netting a modern-day NHL-record fifth hat trick of the season during a 9–5 shootout with the Los Angeles Kings on January 15, 1971, Esposito had netted 41 goals on the season—eight shy of the NHL record for centers he'd set two seasons earlier—and talk heated up about his chances of shattering Bobby Hull's NHL single-season mark of 58 goals, set with the

Chicago Black Hawks in 1968–69. "What if I get hurt?" snarled Esposito, a superstitious sort. "I don't really like to think about records. If I start thinking about them, I'll start fussing. I'm still knocking on wood, though. No predictions. We have a long way to go."

By the end of February, as the goals kept coming, even the usually low-key Esposito was throwing caution to the wind. Sitting with 51 goals and 18 games left to play, Esposito, who'd joined Hull and the Montreal Canadiens duo of Maurice "Rocket" Richard and Bernie "Boom Boom" Geoffrion as the only players in NHL history to register 50-goal seasons, was ready to go out on a limb. "Sure I have a good chance," he told *The Associated Press*. "I need less than a goal every two games to break it, and that's well below the pace I've been going at all season.

"Unless I completely collapse, I should get nine goals in 18 games. But I'm not thinking about any figure in particular. I take it game-by-game, goal-by-goal."

Nothing, it seemed, could stop Espo. Not the opposition, not the grind of the schedule, not even surgery. After netting his 52nd goal of the season February 28, 1971, in a 4–3 win over the Toronto Maple Leafs, Esposito revealed he'd undergone surgery to remove an aneurysm from his forehead, a lump that had developed after a collision with teammate Johnny Bucyk earlier in the month. "It had been bothering me, and I'd lost some of my sharpness," Esposito told *United Press International*.

That was news to the other 13 teams in the league. Esposito tied Hull's single-season goal record with his 58th tally on March 8, 1971, late in the second period of an 8–1 rout of the California Golden Seals before 10,411 fans in Oakland, and his Boston teammates wore Esposito out as they continuously sought to set him up for third-period chances. "They didn't feed me any more than usual until the last period," Esposito explained to *The Associated Press*. "I finally told them, 'Listen, buzz off me.' I was pressing a little and I shouldn't have been. I've got a lot of time left."

Esposito thought he'd tied the record earlier in the frame when he rifled a 30-foot shot past Seals goalie Gary Smith, but referee Ron Wicks waved the tally off, signaling a penalty against Wayne Cashman, Esposito's linemate. "I was really happy—for a second," Esposito said.

His happiness wouldn't have long to wait. In a 7–2 drubbing of the Los Angeles Kings on March 12, 1971, Esposito pushed two pucks past Kings goalie Denis DeJordy, giving him 60 goals on the season and a new NHL standard. "I'm glad it's over," Esposito said. "With 11 games left after this one, I knew that sooner or later, I'd get it. But I've been fortunate against Los Angeles and I like playing here. I'm just glad the pressure's off." The Kings fans afforded Esposito a standing ovation after his record-breaking marker.

The 60-goal total also shattered another little-known NHL mark, that one for combined regular-season and playoff goals. Jean Beliveau had netted 59 goals for the Canadiens over the course of the regular-season and post-season during the 1955–56 campaign. And with an assist for a three-point night, Esposito reached 128 points for the season, surpassing his record 126-point total of two seasons earlier.

Even though he'd toppled Hull, Chicago's Golden Jet, the burly Boston center tipped his hat to Hull, his old Chicago teammate and linemate: "To me, Bobby is still the greatest goal scorer that ever lived—that ever will live. I don't think anybody else will ever score the way he has."

Hull proved it was an equal admiration society, offering up his own bon mots to Esposito.

"Anything Phil gets he deserves and I say more power to him," Hull told *The Canadian Press.* "Boston put it all together and Phil fit in perfectly. All the Boston players seem to complement each other. They have a great team."

Esposito closed out his outstanding, one-of-a-kind campaign with nine goals in his last five games, including a hat trick in the final game of the season, a 7–2 rout of Montreal, finishing with 76 goals and 152 points.

He proved to be an equal-opportunity scorer. Statistics released at the end of the season showed that Esposito scored 30 goals in 30 games against the Original Six franchises, and 46 goals in 48 games versus the eight post-1967 expansion franchises. The Kings were his most frequent victim, surrendering 11 goals, followed by the Pittsburgh Penguins with 9 and Detroit Red Wings and Montreal, with 8 apiece. Esposito scored 42 of his goals at Boston and tallied 34 times in road games.

Esposito set nine records himself. Besides the marks for goals and points, he also established new standards for overall regular-season and playoff goals (79), most three-goal games (seven), most power-play goals (25), most goals and points by a center, most game-winning goals (16), and most shots on goal (550). The Esposito-Cashman-Hodge line established new standards for goals (140) and points (336) by a unit.

Those achievements were among the 37 NHL records shattered by the Bruins. Boston players finished 1-2-3-4 in NHL scoring. Orr was second with 37–102–139 totals, all new standards for a defenseman. Johnny Bucyk, with 51, gave Boston two 50-goal scorers—an NHL first; and Bucyk (116) and Hodge (105) gave the club a record four 100-point scorers. Cashman, Esposito's left-winger, finished seventh in league scoring with 79 points.

"Give those guys all the credit in the world,"

Esposito said of his linemates. "They get the puck to me and all I have to do is let it go. It takes three to tango in my business. If a center hasn't got good wings, he won't do much. And if the wings haven't got a good centerman, they won't do much.

"I give a lot of the credit for my points to Kenny and Cash. We suit each other to a T."

Shockingly eliminated by Montreal in their seven-game 1971 Stanley Cup quarterfinal, Esposito felt it put a significant damper on his one-of-a-kind campaign. "What good are all those goals if you don't win the Cup?" he asked. When the awards were meted out at season's end, the writers went with Orr as the Hart Trophy winner, while balloting among the players for the first time resulted in Esposito capturing the inaugural Pearson Award.

Esposito found it easy to share the stage with Orr. "I never thought I was capable of scoring 60 goals, or that Bobby Orr was capable of 100 assists," Esposito said, before reconsidering: "Well, Orr is capable of anything."

As he accepted his Pearson Award, Esposito also paused to deal with rumors that an unnamed NHL team had offered the Bruins $2 million for his services. "Yeah, I've heard about the offer, all right," he said in the *Regina Leader-Post.* "Maybe it's only a rumor, but I keep hearing about it."

NHL president Clarence Campbell suggested there were three clubs capable of coming up with that kind of cash. Toronto and the New York Rangers were two of them. The Black Hawks, the team that had foolishly let him go in 1967, were the third.

A Dominating Performance

As baffling as he was brilliant. As irrational as he was ingenious. As unbelievable as he was unbeatable.

Dominik Hasek won back-to-back Pearson Awards in 1996–97 and 1997–98. He was the second goalie to ever win the award, and no goalie has been named the NHLPA MVP since.

There was only one Dominik Hasek—"The Dominator" who dominated NHL shooters like no other goaltender.

Employing a style which is part butterfly, part Baryshnikov and part Gumby, Hasek captured two Pearson Awards, won six Vezina Trophies and back-to-back Hart Trophies as NHL MVP. "He's second to none in the game as far as goalies are concerned," said Hall of Famer and former teammate Brett Hull, himself a Pearson winner.

In an era when goal-scoring was stymied, Hasek was the leader of the pack in breaking the hearts of the shooters, the reason why he earned back-to-back Lester B. Pearson Awards.

Hasek's wide array of puckstopping habits—whether it was laying across the goal line, rushing to the blue line to beat an attacker to the biscuit, or discarding his goal stick to scoop up a loose puck with his blocker hand—may have looked nothing like a conventional netminder, especially in the era of butterfly clones between the posts—but it was the nothing he so often left on the scoreboard under his team's name that made his coaches smile.

"Dominik Hasek has 60,000 bad habits," former NHL coach Pat Burns once said. "He loses his stick, he stays on his knees, he's on his back. Sometimes he's like a dead perch in the bottom of the boat, but he stops the puck."

Sweden's Pelle Lindbergh, the 1984–85 Vezina Trophy winner and the first European netminder to play in the Stanley Cup final that spring with the Philadelphia Flyers, was the first goalie from across the Atlantic Ocean to enjoy success in the NHL. After Lindbergh, it wasn't until Hasek's arrival in Buffalo following an August 7, 1992, trade with the Chicago Blackhawks that another European goaltender would make it in the NHL. And once he got into the flow, Hasek would take the league by storm.

He was the first European netminder to not only win the Hart Trophy (and he did it two seasons in a row—1996–97, 1997–98), but also the first to win the Stanley Cup (2001–02 with the Detroit Red Wings). And he was the second European player and second goaltender of any nationality to win the Lester B. Pearson Award. Only his future Detroit teammate Sergei Fedorov (1993–94) had preceded him in accepting the Hart; and former St. Louis Blues netminder Mike Liut (1980–81) and Hasek remain the only goaltenders to win the Pearson/Lindsay Award. Additionally, Hasek is the only netminder in NHL history to win the Pearson, Hart and Vezina in the same season, and he did it two seasons in succession.

What makes these results even more fascinating is that three different branches of the game viewed Hasek as the best—the writers, who voted on the Hart, the league's general managers, who voted on the Vezina, and the members of the NHLPA, who picked the Pearson winner. "This is something I cannot describe in words," Hasek said of his unique achievement. "It's a fantastic honor for me."

Hasek's six Vezina Trophies are second only to the seven won by Hall of Famer Jacques Plante.

And that isn't the only parallel between these two legendary puckstoppers. Both were eccentric in personality, obsessive perfectionists between the posts and frequently embroiled in the midst of controversy.

"They're different styles of goalies, but very similar in that they're both perfectionists, dedicated to fitness and determined to always find ways to improve," said Hall of Famer Scotty Bowman, who coached both Plante and Hasek. "They're definitely unique individuals, but both men played the game with a lot of confidence."

The Dominator knew individual glory long before any fans of the NHL knew his name. Prior to signing as a free agent with the Blackhawks in 1990, Hasek was a three-time winner of the Golden Stick Award as top player in the Czech Extraliga. He was also recognized five times as the top goaltender in the league while playing for Pardubice and Dukla Jihlava. So famous is he in his homeland that two Czech astronomers named a newly-discovered asteroid in his honor.

Hasek backstopped the Czech Republic to a gold medal in the 1998 Winter Olympics, the first Winter Games in which there was full participation by NHL players. The only bauble missing from his résumé is a world championship gold medal.

It took time for that greatness to emerge in NHL rinks. He idled as back-up in Chicago behind Vezina winner Ed Belfour, but opportunity knocked for Hasek when he moved to Buffalo. "When I first came to the NHL [with Chicago], it was frustrating because I never played, so I can't show them that I was good enough," Hasek said.

Hasek's work ethic allowed him to stand out in the crowd. Even in practice, he strove to be unbeatable. "Hockey is supposed to be fun," Hasek explained. "For me, fun is stopping all the shots."

It wasn't much fun for anybody else on the ice. *Hockey Night in Canada* put a shot clock on Hasek one night for the pre-game warm-up, counting how many pucks made it past him during the 20-minute session. Final tally? Three goals on upwards of 160 shots. "In practice, nobody scores on The Dominator," two-time Pearson winner Jaromir Jagr said.

During the 1996–97 season, Hasek won a career-high 37 games, posted five shutouts and a 2.27 goals-against average and led the league in save percentage for the fourth straight season at .930, as he backstopped a bunch of overachieving Sabres to the Northeast Division title, the first time the team had finished atop their division since 1980–81.

The other side of Hasek's personality came out in the playoffs. He was suspended by the league after an altercation with a Buffalo sportswriter and feuded with coach Ted Nolan, insisting he didn't want him to return as Buffalo's coach. Nolan, who won the Jack Adams Trophy as NHL coach of the year, was not rehired by the team and Sabres general manager John Muckler also left the club.

Buffalo fans, excited by the team's turnaround the previous season, began the 1997–98 campaign angry over the changes at the top, and like NHL forwards, aimed their most potent shots directly at Hasek. Even teammates joined the fray, with Sabres tough guy Matthew Barnaby suggesting he might run his own goalie during training camp. New Sabres coach Lindy Ruff made it a moot point, placing Barnaby and Hasek on the same team for training-camp scrimmages. "Every player understands the value of Dominik Hasek to the hockey team," Ruff told Larry Sicinski of the *Hamilton Spectator*. "If they don't, they're very foolish."

Not that anyone believed it would have actually happened. "Are you telling me that somebody is going to run the NHL's MVP and maybe prevent his team from winning?" Hasek's agent Ritch Winter told Jim Matheson of the *Edmonton Journal*.

During Buffalo's home opener of 1997–98, fans booed Hasek incessantly during pre-game ceremonies and throughout the game itself, a 4–2 loss to the Dallas Stars. "I'm baffled," Sabres forward Dixon Ward said to *The Associated Press*. "Dom brought this team from nowhere to somewhere in an awfully big hurry. He deserves a little more respect."

By the end of November, Hasek was pulling the fans back over to his side. "Winning goes hand in hand with forgiving," noted Ruff after Hasek received a rousing ovation following a 6–1 victory over the New York Islanders. "I feel more comfortable when people are cheering for me," Hasek said. "I know the organization and my teammates are behind me, but it's also important to have the fans."

While the Olympic Games were not officially part of the criteria for determining the 1997–98 Pearson winner, it's hard to imagine that NHL players didn't take Hasek's other-worldly performance into account when casting their ballots. The Czechs weren't the best team at the 1998 Nagano Games, but they were the team with the best goalie.

"We felt comfortable because of him," Czech forward Martin Rucinsky told Jim Kelley of *Sports Illustrated*. "I've tried to score on him in practice every day and I can't do it. Usually in a situation like that [breakaway] I score about 50 percent of the time, but I couldn't beat him. Not once."

In the semifinals against Canada, Hasek backstopped the Czech Republic to a 2–1 shootout win, foiling all five Canadian shooters—Theoren

Fleury, Ray Bourque, Joe Nieuwendyk, Eric Lindros and Brendan Shanahan. "It couldn't have been a good feeling for them [the Canadians] going into a shootout and facing Dominik Hasek, I can tell you that," Rucinsky said.

"You've got Dom behind you and you're going into a shootout," added Czech forward Robert Reichel, who beat Canada's Patrick Roy with the only goal of the shootout for the win. "He's the best breakaway goalie in the world. I'm so happy for him. He was there for us and he deserves to be in the finals."

Hasek ramped it up one more time, stopping all 20 shots in the gold-medal game, making Petr Svoboda's third-period goal stand up as the Czechs blanked their long-time rivals Russia 1–0. "He's our god," Svoboda said of Hasek.

"For sure it was the biggest pressure ever in my hockey career," Hasek said of the Olympic format. "I don't like shootouts, but I understand them. I would prefer the NHL style with overtime, but this is the Olympic way."

Hasek's second Pearson–Hart–Vezina trifecta was founded in his 13-shutout, 2.09 GAA, .932 save percentage performance for a Buffalo team that overcame it's early-season crisis to reach the Stanley Cup final four for the first spring since 1980.

"When you've got a goalie that gets into people's heads and you're actually thinking about that, rather than just going about playing hockey, it makes a difference," Dallas Stars left-winger Brenden Morrow said of playing against Hasek. "He can get into people's heads."

Others shared Morrow's view of the mental games Hasek played on shooter's psyches. "Sometimes in our sport, one individual can make a huge difference," Toronto Maple Leafs coach Ron Wilson told *The Associated Press.*

Four times during the season, Hasek posted shutouts in consecutive games. His six shutouts in December equaled the NHL record for shutouts in a month, established by George Hainsworth of the Montreal Canadiens in January and February of 1929. "He had one of the best years a goalie has ever had," Detroit Red Wings goalie Chris Osgood said of Hasek. "He's the best player, bar none … the best player in the league for what he does."

While others outside of Buffalo often chose to focus on Hasek's unorthodox style and personal idiosyncracies, Sabres players—who jokingly nicknamed Hasek "Kramer," after the oddball Seinfeld character—felt that people who didn't get a steady diet of Hasek's performance couldn't possibly appreciate the magnificence of his mastery in the art of puckstopping. "I think what people don't realize is that he makes saves over and over that other goalies only make one in a million," Sabres captain Michael Peca told the *New York Daily News* during the 1998 Stanley Cup playoffs.

The list of players who've won back-to-back Pearson/Lindsay Awards is as short as it is legendary—Wayne Gretzky, Marcel Dionne, Jaromir Jagr, Alexander Ovechkin, Guy Lafleur and Hasek. The Dominator is the lone member of the group who didn't play forward, the lone stopper among the show stoppers.

A Gordie Howe in goalie pads, Hasek has come out of retirement twice and played the 2010–11 season between the pipes for Spartak Moscow of Russia's Kontinental Hockey League at the age of 46.

Ovie's Opus

The seemingly ever-present, devilish-looking gap-toothed grin. The seemingly never-ending run of highlight-reel goals that leave spectators with mouths agape.

From the moment Alexander Ovechkin first pulled on a Washington Capitals sweater for the 2005–06 National Hockey League season, it was apparent he was a difference-maker, just as it was evident that he was a different sort of dude.

"He brings a new era to the league," Washington defenseman Mike Green told Dan Barnes of the *Edmonton Journal*. "The NHL is really old school and he brings a new idea to the fans. He celebrates like it's the last goal he's going to score every time and he makes it exciting."

Ovechkin was a Lester B. Pearson Award finalist as a rookie, the first time that had ever happened. And he won the award in 2007–08 and 2008–09, and then, after it underwent its metamorphosis to the Ted Lindsay Award, Ovechkin was the inaugural winner of the newly-minted trophy in 2009–10.

With that triumph, he made history as the first player to have his name engraved on both awards doled out by the NHLPA to its most outstanding regular-season player. Ovechkin also joined Wayne Gretzky and Guy Lafleur as the only players to be voted the honor a minimum of three successive seasons.

"I have I think [it's the] most hard trophy to get and the players vote, so I'm very happy," Ovechkin said after his 2009–10 Lindsay Award recognition. "I feel like it's okay. I'm happy."

When something excites Ovechkin, it's never hard to tell. No NHL player wears his emotions on the sleeve of his jersey the way he does. When he's happy, you know it. "[Ovechkin] scores goals, he makes plays, he's exciting to watch, he's got a smile on his face, he's excited when his teammates score, and that's being the whole package of a hockey player," former Carolina Hurricanes forward Cory Stillman told the *Washington Post*, a sentiment most everyone in hockey shares.

Ovechkin brings unparalleled talent to the ice,

Three-time NHLPA MVP Alex Ovechkin is the only player to have won both the Pearson Award and the Lindsay Award.

but with it he arrives ready to share an unbridled passion and love for the game. Watching the way his eyes light up when he scores is an unforgettable moment. "When I score goals, I'm very happy," Ovechkin said. "When we win the game I'm happy, too. I like making nice plays and I just don't keep my emotions. I just give my emotions."

He's endeared himself to the hockey public with his uncanny ability to light red lamps. Ovechkin set an NHL-record for left-wingers for goals in a season (65) during the 2007–08 campaign, the first of his Pearson triumphs. But it's more than just the highlight-film plays that make Ovechkin a great asset to the game: his enthusiastic attitude and his willingness to embrace off-the-wall ideas help sell hockey to those who generally might not gravitate to the game.

When it came to the Q factor—the measurement marketing types utilize to estimate an athlete's celebrity status—Ovechkin was well behind Crosby when both made their NHL debuts in the fall of 2006. "When I just come here, nobody knows me," Ovechkin said. "Everybody knows Crosby, Crosby, on television, on radio. Whole hockey world, Crosby, Crosby."

Ovechkin's ability to not take himself seriously, whether it be rapping out some rhymes to sell cars for a Washington dealership, or have his floating head appear on the shelf of a high-school kid's locker to hawk a national brand of skates, have separated him, at least in terms of personality, from the super-serious Crosby.

"His electrifying play and charismatic personality ... make him one of the most sought after athletes for companies and brands to grow their business," said IMG senior vice president David Abrutyn, whose company represents Ovechkin.

Ovechkin takes the constant parallels with Crosby in stride, comparing it to another legendary sporting rivalry of two great teams. "It's like in soccer, when Real Madrid and Barcelona play," Ovechkin told Dan Rosen of NHL.com. "They play against each other and everybody says, 'Wow, this is going to be a sick game,' and they can't wait for it."

They are different people, and different players, though both are different in a very good way.

"He's a great player," Crosby said of Ovechkin. "He's got good speed. He's got a great shot, too. He can do it all I think. He's definitely dangerous when he's out there. He's someone I'm sure other teams have to watch."

Asked to pick the one aspect of Ovechkin's game he admires the most, like Ovechkin with the puck on his stick, Sid the Kid doesn't hesitate. "I'd say his goal-scoring ability," Crosby noted. "I don't think you can really teach anyone that. It's just a knack. It's an ability. You know, he definitely has that. So it's exciting to watch when someone can score goals like that."

Followers of the game see the Ovechkin–Crosby rivalry on a par with other great sporting duels, whether it be Rocket Richard–Gordie Howe or Mario Lemieux–Wayne Gretzky on the ice, Magic Johnson–Larry Bird on the hardwood, or Rafael Nadal–Roger Federer on the tennis court.

In every one of these legendary showdowns, the rivalry was created as much by their talent, drive and determination as it was by the unique styles of each player that identified them as great, yet distinct.

"I don't compare me and Sidney because I think we are different players," Ovechkin said. "He's a great passer and like Gretzky, he sees the ice real well."

When it comes to NHL players and the Pearson/Lindsay Award, they've mostly had eyes for Ovechkin. He's won it three times in a row, and been a finalist four times. Crosby owns just one Pearson Award and was a finalist on one other occasion. Clearly, the fact that his peers see him as the man resonates with Ovechkin. "Every player thinks that [being voted the best] by the players is the most important thing," Ovechkin said. "You play against the guys, and when they vote for you, it's the most important thing."

Ovechkin's first Pearson win following the 2007–08 season was a no-brainer for his fellow players. Not only did Ovechkin (just 22 at the time) shatter Luc Robitaille's NHL goal-scoring record for left-wingers, but he also finished with 112 points to win both the Art Ross Trophy as the league's leading scorer and the Maurice Richard Trophy as the league's top goal scorer. Ovechkin's 65 goals were the most in the league since Lemieux scored 69 times for Pittsburgh in 1995–96.

Ovechkin led his team back from 30th overall in the NHL in November to a Southeast Division title for the first time since the 2000–01 season and also Washington's first playoff appearance in four seasons. "I always think about my personal statistics," Ovechkin admitted. "I always want to be the best. But right now, the time you know, I don't care about different team, I care about my team and myself. I just want to help my team to win the game and bring points."

Ovechkin again led the NHL in goals with 56 in 2008–09, finishing second in scoring behind Pittsburgh's Evgeni Malkin, but once more, his peers saw him as the league's most outstanding player and voted him the Pearson Award over fellow Russians Malkin and Detroit's Pavel Datsyuk. "I think every year is going to be his best season," Capitals coach Bruce Boudreau said. "He just seems to get better. He hasn't reached his prime as far as age goes. As far as the numbers go, it's not just the numbers."

Ovechkin's third straight honor—receiving the inaugural Ted Lindsay Award—came as a bit of a surprise. He finished behind Rocket Richard Trophy winners Crosby and Tampa Bay's Steve Stamkos in goals (51–50) and was third in NHL scoring with 109 points, but perhaps his peers took into account that Ovechkin missed 10 games due to injury. "He's trying to be the difference in the game, he wants to be the star, and he's going do whatever he can, whether it's hitting or scoring," Cory Stillman told the *Washington Post*. "You look at his stats, you look at his hits, his shots, everything, he's doing that."

Whether it's delivering a sensational goal or a devastating hit, his teammates are never surprised when Ovechkin does something that no one else appears to have ever done on the ice. "In the biggest moments, usually your biggest guys step to the front," Capitals forward Brooks Laich said. "That's what Alex does."

"He's the leader on the ice and off the ice," Boudreau added. "He's the best player."

Ovechkin's passion, performance and all-around game has even won him fans in an unusual corner—Coach's Corner. "He's good. He's exciting. There's no doubt about it," Don Cherry of *Hockey Night in Canada* said of Ovechkin.

To the man himself, it comes down to a simple philosophy. Live life, love life, leave nothing in the tank. Ovechkin said on arriving in the NHL as a rookie in 2005: "You go to the team and you know this is the NHL and probably all the young guys dream to play in NHL, and it's hard to realize that you're in the NHL. It's no more little kids, no more take the puck, beat five guys and the goalie and put it in the net.

"It's hard work here, and nobody gives you easy ways. You have to fight. You have to live for this, you know."

2007–08 • 2008–09 • 2009–10
ALEXANDER OVECHKIN

CHAPTER 10
NHLPA MVP Winners

1970–71
Phil Esposito
BOSTON BRUINS

The Bruins set or tied 37 National Hockey League individual records en route to a league-best 57–14–7 record, and their burly center etched his name all over those marks. Esposito's goals (76) and points (152) totals obliterated the previous NHL standards. Esposito also set new single-season marks for hat tricks (7), power-play goals (25), shots on goal (550), and game-winning goals (16). He and linemates Wayne Cashman and Ken Hodge combined to establish new totals for goals (140) and points (336) collected by a forward unit. And to those who suggested he'd padded his stats against weak expansion franchises, Esposito scored 30 goals in 30 games against the Original Six teams and 46 goals in 48 games against the eight newer clubs. Esposito was inducted into the Hockey Hall of Fame in 1984.

1971–72
Jean Ratelle
NEW YORK RANGERS

The Pearson vote is held a month before season's end, which may explain why Ratelle defeated Boston stars Bobby Orr and Phil Esposito in the player balloting even though he missed the last month after suffering a cracked right ankle when hit by teammate Dale Rolfe's shot during a 4–1 victory on March 1 over the California Golden Seals. At the time, Ratelle had recorded a Rangers-record 109 points and was one back of Esposito in the Art Ross Trophy race. Ratelle missed the last 15 games, but even at that, only Esposito, Orr and John Bucyk had scored as many points in a single season in league history as Ratelle had managed in his shortened season. His 109 points remained the club scoring mark until Jaromir Jagr collected 123 points in 2005–06. Ratelle was elected to the Hockey Hall of Fame in 1985.

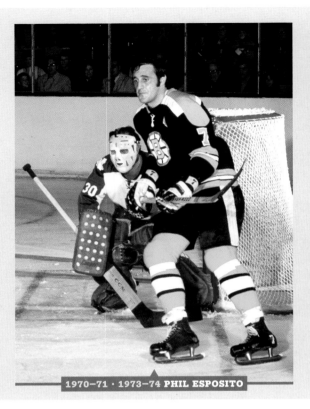

1970–71 · 1973–74 **PHIL ESPOSITO**

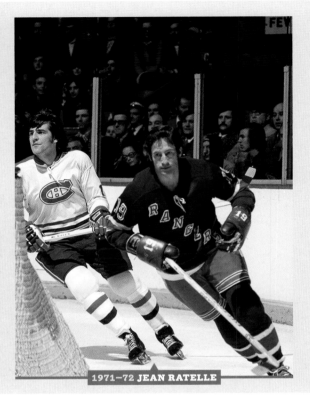

1971–72 **JEAN RATELLE**

1972–73
Bobby Clarke
PHILADELPHIA FLYERS

The Flyers center broke the four-year stranglehold Boston's Phil Esposito and Bobby Orr held on the top two spots in the Art Ross Trophy race, finishing second to Esposito with 37–67–104 totals, becoming the first player from an expansion franchise to top the 100-point plateau. Clarke was also the first player to win both the Pearson and Hart Trophies in the same season, but was modest in victory. "I don't even know how they picked me most valuable on our club," Clarke told *The Canadian Press.* "We had Rick MacLeish with 50 goals and Bill Flett with 43." Though he won both the Pearson and Hart, Clarke, a Hall of Famer in 1987, was named to the NHL's Second All-Star Team, the first Hart winner not to be selected to the First All-Star Team since Jean Beliveau in 1963–64.

1973–74
Phil Esposito
BOSTON BRUINS

Winning his fourth scoring title and fifth in six years, the Bruins center topped the 100-point plateau for the fifth time in six seasons, collecting 68–77–145 totals for the NHL-leading Bruins. Esposito turned the MVP double, also capturing the Hart Trophy. Esposito joined Gordie Howe (1950–51 to 1953–54) as the only players to win four successive Art Ross Trophies. Esposito also became the first player to top the NHL in goals for five straight seasons. His goals and points totals were second only to his NHL-record 76 goals and 152 points in 1970–71. "Actually, I'm never really sure of where I am at in the individual scoring race," Esposito told Frank Brown of *The Associated Press.* Esposito also collected his 1,000th NHL point February 15, 1974, against the Vancouver Canucks in just his 745th game, which was the fastest anyone had done it.

1974–75 **BOBBY ORR**

1975–76 · 1976–77 · 1977–78 **GUY LAFLEUR**

1974–75
Bobby Orr
BOSTON BRUINS

The only defenseman to ever win an NHL scoring title, Orr grabbed his second Art Ross Trophy this season, setting NHL marks for rearguards with 46 goals and 135 points. In doing so, Orr became the first—and only—defenseman to win the Lester B. Pearson Award. Orr set a record by being named to the NHL First All-Star Team for the eighth consecutive season. He also set a league mark by winning the Norris Trophy for the eighth season in succession. A Hall of Fame enshrinee in 1979, Orr reached the 100-point barrier for the sixth time and figured in 42 percent of the 345 goals the Bruins scored during the regular season. In the summer, *Boston Globe* readers voted Orr Boston's greatest athlete ever, ahead of Ted Williams of the Boston Red Sox and Bill Russell of the Boston Celtics.

1975–76
Guy Lafleur
MONTREAL CANADIENS

The Flower was a late bloomer, but once he blossomed, he carried the Montreal Canadiens back to the top of the NHL. "I have a lot more confidence now," Lafleur told the *Montreal Gazette* after posting his second consecutive 50-goal season and winning the Art Ross Trophy for the first time with 56–69–125 numbers. "He has more stamina than any player on our team," Montreal coach Scotty Bowman said. "He can play a long shift, rest for 30 seconds and go right back on again." Becoming the first Pearson winner from a Stanley Cup championship team, as well as the first right-winger to win the award, Lafleur, who finished third in the Hart Trophy voting, was selected to the NHL's First All-Star Team.

1976–77
Guy Lafleur
MONTREAL CANADIENS

Becoming the first player to win back-to-back Pearsons and joining Phil Esposito as the only two-time winner of the award, the Canadiens right-winger potted 56 goals and collected 136 points to win his second consecutive Art Ross Trophy. Leading Montreal to a first-overall finish in the regular-season standings, Lafleur set NHL records for assists (80) and consecutive games with a point (28) by a right-winger. "He's a hockey player's hockey player," NHLPA executive director Alan Eagleson told *The Canadian Press*. "He's the guy the players think deserve it." Lafleur collected 138 votes, edging out Los Angeles Kings center Marcel Dionne, second with 111 votes. Toronto Maple Leafs defenseman Borje Salming was third in the voting with 43, followed by Montreal defenseman Larry Robinson with 35.

1977–78
Guy Lafleur
MONTREAL CANADIENS

In leading Montreal to its third successive Stanley Cup and winning his third Art Ross Trophy in as many seasons, Lafleur fired a hat trick against the Minnesota North Stars in the span of 6:19 during a 5–2 Canadiens victory on March 13, 1978. "I'm sure that's the fastest three goals I've ever scored," Lafleur said. All these threes added up to another hat trick for Lafleur. He became the first player to win the Pearson three times, and he'd captured the award three years in a row, making it a natural hat trick of hardware. Lafleur also led Montreal to its third straight first overall finish during regular-season play, which included an NHL-record 28-game unbeaten streak. He became a Hall of Famer in 1988.

1978–79
Marcel Dionne
LOS ANGELES KINGS

Finishing second in the Art Ross Trophy race for the second time in three seasons, the Kings slick center collected 130 points, four less than Hart Trophy winner Bryan Trottier of the New York Islanders. By winning the Pearson, Dionne became the first player from a Pacific Time Zone to win an NHL MVP award. "Playing in L.A. is different," Dionne admitted to Wayne Lockwood of the *Copley News Service*. "But I like it. As long as you discipline yourself, L.A. is a good place to play. There's a lot less pressure. You can get away from hockey when you need to. People don't bother you as much if you're losing or things are going bad." Dionne became a Hall of Famer in 1992.

1979–80
Marcel Dionne
LOS ANGELES KINGS

Twice runner-up in the Art Ross Trophy race, Dionne won the scoring title this season. Though his 137-point total left him tied with Wayne Gretzky of the Edmonton Oilers, Dionne took the tie breaker because he'd scored 53 goals to Gretzky's 51. "Marcel Dionne is the best center in hockey," Kings coach Bob Berry said. In Pearson balloting, Dionne received 147 votes, 33 more than second-place finisher Gretzky, who'd won the Hart Trophy. Three-time Pearson winner Guy Lafleur of the Montreal Canadiens and Chicago Black Hawks goaltender Tony Esposito tied for third with 35 points apiece. Dionne also beat out Gretzky in the voting for the center position on the NHL's First All-Star Team, edging Gretzky 250–238. Dionne joined Guy Lafleur (three) and Phil Esposito (two) as multiple Pearson winners.

1978–79 · 1979–80 **MARCEL DIONNE**

1980–81 **MIKE LIUT**

1980–81
Mike Liut
ST. LOUIS BLUES

The key reason the Blues jumped from 80 to a Smythe-Division-leading 107 points, Liut won 33 games, becoming the first goaltender to be voted the Pearson Award. The lanky netminder was being compared to Montreal legend Ken Dryden. "It's flattering to be compared to Ken Dryden, but I guess it's part of hockey for a current player to be always compared to a predecessor, the way Denis Potvin was to Bobby Orr," Liut said. He even earned the MVP nod in the NHL All-Star Game, a first for a goaltender, after stopping all 25 shots he faced during his 31:43 of work. A second-year NHLer, Liut felt his performance was simply a carryover from the success he had enjoyed in the WHA. "I was just being more recognized because of the larger audience," Liut told the *Regina Leader-Post*.

1981–82
Wayne Gretzky
EDMONTON OILERS

One season after shattering Phil Esposito's NHL mark of 152 points, Gretzky obliterated Esposito's single-season standard of 76 goals, potting 92 tallies as part of a record 212-point campaign, easily winning the Pearson Award for the first time in his career. "He'll be the first player, if he plays long enough, and doesn't get hurt, who'll get 2,000 points," Esposito told *The Associated Press*. "If he plays as long as I did, 18 years, he'll score 1,000 goals." Bobby Hull, who'd held the NHL single-season goals record before Esposito, marveled at the way Gretzky understood his responsibility to the fans. "He knows people have paid good money to watch him perform," Hull said. "He has a fantastic style and is about four steps ahead of everybody."

1982–83
Wayne Gretzky
EDMONTON OILERS

It sounds silly to suggest someone only scored 71 goals and collected 196 points, but Gretzky himself had raised the bar so high with his unparalleled ability, that such was the case. He did rewrite the single-season assists mark for the third straight season, garnering 125 helpers. That was five better than his NHL mark of the previous season and far ahead of the then-record 109 assists he dished out in 1980–81. Gretzky won his second straight Pearson, and praise from his boss. "He's talented, but he also works at it," Oilers coach Glen Sather told *The Associated Press*. "Bobby Orr and Gordie Howe were great players, but what makes Wayne the best is that I don't think over his career I've seen him take two or three games off. Every game he has more determination than anybody. That's what makes him great."

1983–84
Wayne Gretzky
EDMONTON OILERS

Only 23, there were already 37 records etched next to Gretzky's name inside the pages of the NHL record book. Among those he established while winning his fourth successive Art Ross Trophy and claiming his third Pearson Award in a row was to become the fastest player in league history to garner 1,000 points. Gretzky ascended to that plateau in 424 games, obliterating Guy Lafleur's previous mark of 724 games. "I remember what some high-profile people said when I first broke in, that I was too small, too slow—and well, we've heard other things," Gretzky told *The Associated Press*. "I felt if I kept playing the way I did, then over a period of time, I would prove them wrong."

1984–85
Wayne Gretzky
EDMONTON OILERS

The Great One took his fourth successive Pearson, bettering Guy Lafleur's previous mark of three in a row. Gretzky won the Art Ross Trophy, topping 200 points for the third time in four seasons, including an NHL-record 135 assists. "[Gretzky's] the kind of hockey player who plays from inside," Oilers coach Glen Sather told *The Associated Press*. "He's self-motivated, which is what makes him so great." Gretzky, 24, was savoring every moment of the unparalleled success he was achieving, and then suggested to the *Montreal Gazette* something that must have scared every NHL opponent. "I'd like to think I'll peak in six years," Gretzky said. "But if I'm at my peak now, I think I'll be satisfied."

1985–86
Mario Lemieux
PITTSBURGH PENGUINS

The Magnificent One ended The Great One's four-year stranglehold on the Pearson. The Penguins center polled 137 votes from his peers to 107 for Gretzky, who was followed in the voting by Edmonton Oilers defenseman Paul Coffey and Montreal Canadiens defenseman Larry Robinson. Lemieux, the NHL's rookie of the year in 1984–85, collected 48 goals and 93 assists for 141 points, finishing second in scoring to Gretzky's NHL-record 215 points on 52 goals and 163 assists. Lemieux was the first player from a non-playoff team to earn the Pearson nod, and not everyone agreed with the choice. "It's astounding that Mario Lemieux, after refusing to join Team Canada at the world championships, would get the Lester B. Pearson Award for his contributions to hockey," wrote Jim Proudfoot in the *Toronto Star*. "The late Mike Pearson, a patriot, would have been revolted by the way Lemieux conducted himself when he was needed overseas." Lemieux became a Hall of Famer in 1997.

1986–87
Wayne Gretzky
EDMONTON OILERS

Winning his seventh successive Art Ross Trophy and taking the Oilers back to the top of the NHL standings for the second straight campaign, Gretzky recaptured the Pearson for the fifth time in six years, making the award part of his private domain. No one else had won it more than three times. In making the announcement, NHLPA executive director Alan Eagleson said, "Everyone in hockey owes Wayne Gretzky a great debt for his contributions." Gretzky, who had previously won the award four years in a row (1982–85), outpointed Boston Bruins defenseman Ray Bourque in voting by the players. Gretzky received 254 votes to 60 for runner-up Bourque. Gretzky was inducted into the Hockey Hall of Fame in 1999.

1987–88
Mario Lemieux
PITTSBURGH PENGUINS

Winning his first Art Ross Trophy after producing 70–98–168 totals, Lemieux earned his second Pearson nod in three seasons. Lemieux was the runaway winner, polling 182 votes. Five-time Pearson winner Wayne Gretzky of the Edmonton Oilers was second with 56 votes and Steve Yzerman of the Detroit Red Wings followed with 45 votes. Pittsburgh's 36–35–9 slate was the Penguins' best since the 1979–80 season, but wasn't good enough to earn a playoff spot. Lemieux joined Marcel Dionne and Phil Esposito as two-time winners of the award. Guy Lafleur was a three-time Pearson honoree. "When things

1981–82 · 1982–83 · 1983–84
1984–85 · 1986–87 **WAYNE GRETZKY**

happen that have happened to me, it's always good," Lemieux told the *Toronto Star's* Frank Orr. "I am very proud of the honors I've received. When you finish ahead of Wayne Gretzky and Mark Messier and the other players like them in anything, it's very satisfying."

1988–89 STEVE YZERMAN

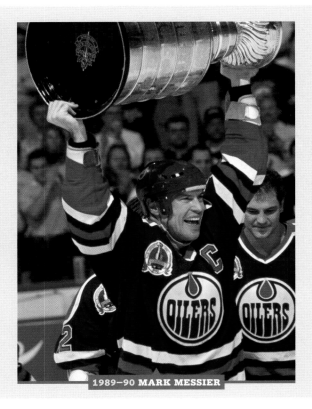
1989–90 MARK MESSIER

1988–89
Steve Yzerman
DETROIT RED WINGS

Yzerman had been working on a prepared speech all week, but not for this moment. "The only lines I know right now are my wedding vows and I don't think they're the appropriate ones for this occasion," Yzerman grinned. (The Detroit Red Wing center wed his high school sweetheart, Lisa Brennan, a few days later in Ottawa.) Yzerman gained the nod by a close margin over Pittsburgh Penguins center Mario Lemieux in a fan ballot, with Wayne Gretzky of the Los Angeles Kings finishing third. "This is a thrill for me," the Wings captain said. "One thing that's very important to me is how my colleagues and other players think of me." Yzerman said. Rebounding from a serious knee injury suffered late in the 1987–88 campaign, Yzerman finished third in the NHL scoring race with 65–90–155 totals, all career highs. He became a Hall of Fame enshrinee in 2009.

1989–90
Mark Messier
EDMONTON OILERS

Emerging from Wayne Gretzky's shadow, Messier led the Oilers to second overall in the NHL standings and finished second behind Gretzky in the Art Ross Trophy race with a career-best 129 points. "If I was a general manager and had a new franchise, over anybody, he'd probably be the guy I'd pick to start a new franchise," said Boston Bruins defenseman Ray Bourque, who was second in the Pearson balloting. St. Louis Blues right-winger Brett Hull placed third. The Oilers won the Stanley Cup just two years after the trade which sent Gretzky to Los Angeles. "I don't think anybody had anything to prove to Gretzky," Messier said. Others felt Messier was the one who made the Oilers whole again. "This is no longer Wayne Gretzky's team," Edmonton coach John Muckler told the *Toronto Star*. Messier was inducted into the Hockey Hall of Fame in 2007.

1985–86 · 1987–88
1992–93 · 1995–96
MARIO LEMIEUX

1990–91 BRETT HULL

1991–92 MARK MESSIER

1990–91
Brett Hull
ST. LOUIS BLUES

Scoring 86 goals, an NHL record for a right-winger, and becoming the fifth player in league history to collect 50 goals in 50 games or less (he did it in 49), Brett Hull established that he could illuminate red lamps at a pace equal to, or better than, that of his famous father, Chicago's Bobby Hull, the legendary Golden Jet. The younger Hull joined Wayne Gretzky, Mario Lemieux, Mike Bossy and Maurice Richard as part of the exclusive 50-in-50 club. "When you look at who has done this, and who hasn't, it is some pretty amazing company to be in," he said. Hull was named on 294 of the 432 ballots cast. Five-time Pearson winner Wayne Gretzky of Los Angeles was second in the voting and Chicago Blackhawks goaltender Ed Belfour finished third. Brett Hull became a Hall of Famer in 2009.

1991–92
Mark Messier
NEW YORK RANGERS

Mark "The Moose" Messier, the Rangers captain, had previously won the Pearson as Edmonton's captain in 1989–90. "To be back here two years later means that I played with a lot of great players this season and I firmly believe we have an outstanding nucleus, that we're going to win the Stanley Cup," Messier said of the Rangers. "I keep telling the fans to be patient, but I don't think they like that patient part too much." The Moose led the Rangers in scoring with 107 points, leading New York to a 50–25–5 record, the best in franchise history. "I never imagined in my wildest dreams that I'd win it once, and to do it again in New York is such a great feeling," Messier said. "I thought I felt good when I was 29 and won it, but I can honestly say I feel better at 31."

1993–94 SERGEI FEDOROV

1993–94
Sergei Fedorov
DETROIT RED WINGS

The first European-born and -trained player to capture the Pearson, Fedorov also won the Hart and Selke Trophies after finishing second in NHL scoring with 128 points and posting a plus-48 rating. "This means a lot to me," Fedorov said. He scored 10 game-winning goals and collected 11 shorthanded points, but admitted that in his fourth NHL season, he was still adapting to the North American brand of hockey. "I'm still learning to play in North America," Fedorov said. "It's different. European players play differently than North American players. But every year, the two styles are getting closer together." Praised by five-time Pearson winner Wayne Gretzky as "the future of our game," Fedorov indicated he'd try to live up to the high standards set by The Great One. "I want to learn more about the league, and how I can support hockey," Fedorov said.

1994–95
Eric Lindros
PHILADELPHIA FLYERS

While tying for the NHL scoring lead and capturing the Hart Trophy to go with his Pearson Award, the hulking Philadelphia center was also winning fans throughout the league. "After his first year in the league, I felt it was just a matter of time before he emerged as one of the top players," Chicago defenseman Chris Chelios said of Lindros. "He did it pretty quick. Real quick. He's going to be a great ambassador for hockey in the years to come." Lindros donated his $10,000 prize money to two minor hockey associations. The money was to be split between Red Circle and the Toronto Nats Peewee Hockey Club, two organizations he'd played youth hockey with. Lindros finished as the top NHLer in plus/minus with a plus-27 rating.

1992–93
Mario Lemieux
PITTSBURGH PENGUINS

Super Mario won his third Pearson in a fashion befitting his nickname. On January 5, 1993, he tearfully announced that he would be forced to leave the game, having been diagnosed with Hodgkin's Disease (a form of cancer). He returned to action two months later and chased down Buffalo's Pat LaFontaine to win his fourth Art Ross Trophy with 69–91–160 totals from only 60 games. "He's a once-in-a-lifetime player," Philadelphia Flyers coach Bill Dineen said. The Penguins finished atop the NHL with a 56–21–7 record, but were a .500 club at 11–11–2 without Lemieux. "He's got a presence like no other player in the league," Pittsburgh teammate Rick Tocchet said. Lemieux's agent Tom Reich accepted the Pearson Award on his client's behalf, as Lemieux was busy helping his bride-to-be Nathalie make final plans for their upcoming wedding.

1995—96
Mario Lemieux
PITTSBURGH PENGUINS

The Penguins captain sat out the 1994–95 lockout-shortened season to recuperate from his battle with cancer and to allow his wonky back time to heal, but came back with a vengeance. He led the NHL with 69 goals and won his fifth Art Ross Trophy, collecting 161 points in just 61 games, an average of 2.3 points per game. In victory, Lemieux talked about what he'd lost as a player due to injury and illness, admitting he had "lost a half a step" due to the ailments. "When you're not able to challenge players with your speed like you have in the past, it's frustrating," he said. Lemieux finished ahead of Mark Messier of the New York Rangers and Eric Lindros of the Philadelphia Flyers in the voting. It was the first time in the history of the award that all three finalists were past Pearson winners.

1996—97
Dominik Hasek
BUFFALO SABRES

Only the second netminder to win the Pearson, The Dominator was both stunned and honored by his selection. "To be recognized by my peers as the best, I was more surprised than when I won my first Vezina Trophy," Hasek said, and added that he'd cast his Pearson ballot for a shooter. "I always vote for the players that I didn't want to face, the really best players." That season, Hasek also won the Hart and Vezina Trophies, an NHL first. He led the NHL in save percentage for the fourth straight season. Four-time Pearson winner Mario Lemieux of the Pittsburgh Penguins was runner-up in the voting, while Anaheim Ducks left-winger Paul Kariya finished third.

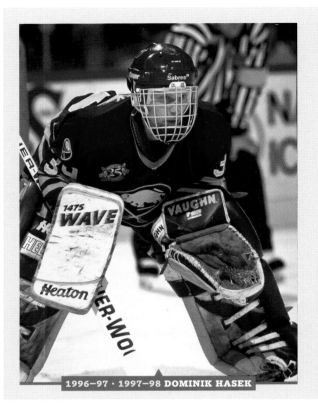

1996–97 · 1997–98 DOMINIK HASEK

1997—98
Dominik Hasek
BUFFALO SABRES

The Dominator repeated his dominance of the NHL awards, winning his second straight Pearson Award and Hart Trophy, as well as picking up another Vezina Trophy. Hasek was 33–23–13 with a 2.09 goals-against average and a league-leading 13 shutouts, the most since Chicago's Tony Esposito recorded 15 whitewashes in 1969–70. Hasek also led the NHL in save percentage for the fifth straight season. "It was a good year, but I believe I can play better," Hasek said. "Lots of players—like [Jacques] Plante and [Terry] Sawchuk—didn't win the Hart and Pearson twice, but they won one trophy that I didn't—the Stanley Cup. So, until I win that one, I don't think I am as good as they are. I'm missing one trophy, and that's the one I want the most."

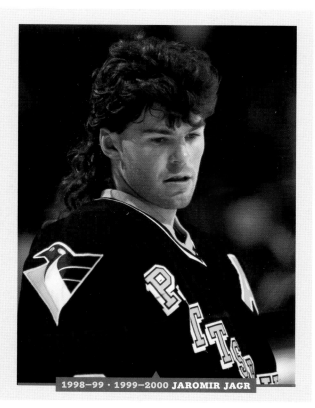

1998-99 · 1999-2000 **JAROMIR JAGR**

1999—2000
Jaromir Jagr
PITTSBURGH PENGUINS

Jagr beat out Pavel Bure of the Florida Panthers and St. Louis Blues defenseman Chris Pronger for his second straight Pearson. The result was the closest in the award's 30-year history. Jagr received 192 votes to 159 for Bure and 129 for Pronger, and seemed genuinely surprised by his triumph. "You guys deserved to be here, but I was more lucky, I guess," said Jagr, who captured his third straight scoring title with 42 goals and 54 assists despite missing 19 games due to injury. He averaged a league-best 1.52 points per game. "I said it last year and I'm going to say it again" Jagr said. "This trophy is very special to me because it's voted by the players."

1998—99
Jaromir Jagr
PITTSBURGH PENGUINS

Winning his first Pearson Award, Jagr led the NHL with 127 points, figured in more than half of the Penguins' goals and picked up his third Art Ross Trophy as leading scorer. Jagr's 20-point cushion over Anaheim's Teemu Selanne was the biggest victory margin in the NHL scoring race since 1990–91. "This is probably the best thing that has happened to me since 1991 when we won the Stanley Cup in Pittsburgh," Jagr said. Named captain of the Penguins at the start of the season, Jagr grew into the role. "He's more mature than before, but he's still the same person he always was," Pittsburgh GM Craig Patrick told Mike Ulmer of the *National Post*. "He never had to lead, now he has to."

2000—01
Joe Sakic
COLORADO AVALANCHE

"Gentleman Joe" captained the Avs to the President's Trophy, leading all NHLers in power-play points (46) and game-winning goals (12), and tied for first in the league with a plus-45 rating. Sakic finished second by three points to Pittsburgh's Jaromir Jagr in the Art Ross Trophy race, posting 54–65–118 totals. "It is just a thrill," Sakic told *USA Today*'s Alan Adams during the NHL awards ceremony at the Air Canada Centre. "It feels real good. This is a moment I will cherish. It is not every day you get this opportunity." Sakic garnered 585 voting points. Pittsburgh center Mario Lemieux, a four-time Pearson winner, was runner-up with 272 points. "He never down-shifted at all," Dallas Stars GM Bob Gainey said of Sakic. "He kept it in high gear all season."

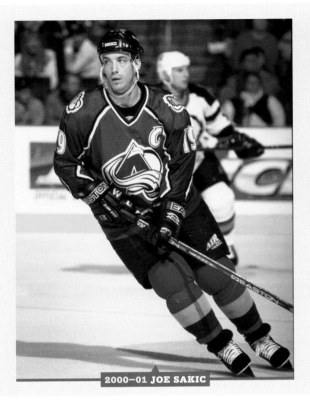

2000–01 JOE SAKIC

2001–02 JAROME IGINLA

2001–02
Jarome Iginla
CALGARY FLAMES

The first thing the rugged Flames right-winger did upon accepting his Pearson Award was apologize to his fellow NHLers. "I want to say that for all those accidental slashes and face-washes and the trash-talking that I did this season, now I feel a little bad," Iginla said after receiving the award at the Hockey Hall of Fame. Iginla, whose father is from Nigeria and whose mother is from the United States, was the first black player to win the Pearson Award. Iginla won the NHL scoring title with 96 points, including a league-high 52 goals, earning him the Art Ross Trophy as the league's top scorer and the Maurice Richard Trophy as the top goal scorer. Two goaltenders, Sean Burke of the Phoenix Coyotes and Patrick Roy of the Colorado Avalanche, finished as runners-up behind Iginla in the player voting.

2002–03
Markus Naslund
VANCOUVER CANUCKS

The first Canuck and the first Swede ever to capture the Pearson Award, Naslund finished with 48–56–104 totals and was nipped on the last day of the season for the goal-scoring crown by Colorado's Milan Hejduk and for the scoring title by Peter Forsberg of the Avalanche. Still, Naslund led the league with 12 game-winning goals and his 24 power-play goals were second only to the 25 scored by linemate Todd Bertuzzi. Ten-year veteran Naslund also led all NHLers with 54 power-play points. "Even though [the Pearson award] does not get the publicity that the Hart Trophy gets, it is still a neat thing when your peers vote for you," Naslund, the Canucks captain, told Joe O'Connor of the *Vancouver Province*. Forsberg and Boston Bruins center Joe Thornton were the other finalists for the Pearson. "It is a big day for Sweden," said Forsberg, who won the Hart Trophy.

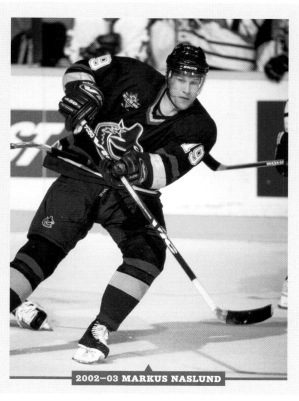

2002–03 **MARKUS NASLUND**

2003–04 **MARTIN ST. LOUIS**

2003–04
Martin St. Louis
TAMPA BAY LIGHTNING

A graduate of the University of Vermont, St. Louis became the first NCAA-trained winner of the Pearson, after leading the NHL in scoring with 94 points and helping the Lightning finish atop the Southeast Division standings. He beat out Colorado captain Joe Sakic and Florida goalie Roberto Luongo for the Pearson. Sakic was the last player (2000–01) before St. Louis to win the Pearson and the Hart in the same year. "Besides the Stanley Cup, this is probably the trophy I will remember and cherish for the rest of my life," St. Louis said. He was the first player in 17 years to win the Pearson, Hart, Art Ross and Stanley Cup in the same season. "Individually, I'm proud of the way things have gone, but I can't do it without the support of my teammates," he said. "Win or lose, I'm not going to be a different player."

2005–06
Jaromir Jagr
NEW YORK RANGERS

Even the Hart Trophy winner knew who deserved the Pearson, and he insisted it wasn't him. "He was my pick for the Lester B. Pearson," Hart winner Joe Thornton of the San Jose Sharks said of Jagr, the Rangers right-winger who wound up second to Thornton in NHL scoring with 123 points. "I've been telling everybody he was my MVP all year long. I love watching him play. He has so much size, so much skill. He's the full package." Jagr was also second in goals with 54. The Rangers became the first team to boast three Pearson winners, as Jagr joined Mark Messier (1991–92) and Jean Ratelle (1971–72). Thornton and Washington's Alexander Ovechkin were runners-up in the balloting.

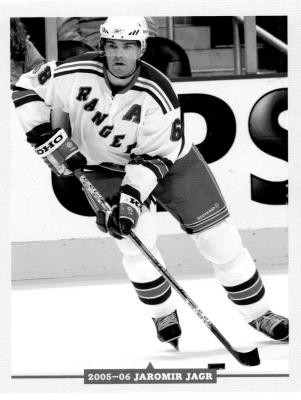

2005–06 **JAROMIR JAGR**

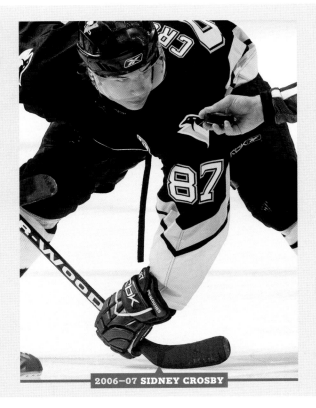

2006–07 **SIDNEY CROSBY**

2006–07
Sidney Crosby
PITTSBURGH PENGUINS

Sid the Kid's status as hockey's next greatest star was firmly established as he led the NHL in scoring with 120 points, was voted the Hart Trophy as NHL MVP by the writers, and awarded the Pearson as the most outstanding player in a vote of his peers. "Each one is a privilege, but to rank them, I don't think I could do it," Crosby said of his hardware collection. There is really no right answer to that question. However, to be recognized by the guys you play with is something I'm proud of." He did note that the most important bauble remained an elusive one. "That is something I want to achieve above and beyond this," Crosby said, pointing toward the Stanley Cup. (Pittsburgh did win the Cup two years later.) He joined Jaromir Jagr and Mario Lemieux as Penguins who'd won the Pearson and at the age of 19, supplanted Wayne Gretzky (21)

as the youngest winner of the award. Tampa Bay's Vincent Lecavalier and Vancouver's Roberto Luongo were also Pearson finalists.

2007–08
Alexander Ovechkin
WASHINGTON CAPITALS

Ovechkin brought the same enthusiasm he carries with him on the ice to the podium as he accepted his first Pearson Award. "I think it's huge for a player to win this award," Ovechkin said. "It tells a lot about the way you are viewed around the league. I think all players want to win this trophy." Rallying Washington from 30th overall in the NHL in November to a Southeast Division title, Ovechkin led the NHL with 65 goals and 112 points, becoming the first NHLer to score 60 times in a season since Pittsburgh's Mario Lemieux netted 69 goals in 1995–96. A finalist for the award in 2005–06, Ovechkin joined Sergei Fedorov as the only Russians to win the Pearson.

2010–11 DANIEL SEDIN

2008–09
Alexander Ovechkin
WASHINGTON CAPITALS

Ovechkin captured the Maurice Richard Trophy by netting 56 goals and finished second in the NHL scoring race with 110 points, as the Capitals won their second successive Southeast Division title. "The Pearson, it's a players' award," said Ovechkin, the sixth player to win the Pearson back-to-back and the first since Jaromir Jagr in 1999–2000. "They know how you play, who you are." Ovechkin dedicated the win to his grandfather Nikolay Kabayev, who died in November. "This year was a really hard year for my family," Ovechkin said. "This award, I give it to him and all my family." All three finalists were Russians, with Detroit's Pavel Datsyuk and Pittsburgh's Evgeni Malkin also up for the Pearson.

2009–10
Alexander Ovechkin
WASHINGTON CAPITALS

Renamed the Ted Lindsay Award by the NHLPA on April 29, 2010, the trophy's name was new, but its winner was a familiar face. Ovechkin captured the player vote for the third successive season, joining Wayne Gretzky and Guy Lafleur as the only players to win the award at least three years in a row. Vancouver Canucks forward Henrik Sedin and Pittsburgh Penguins center Sidney Crosby (2006–07 Pearson winner), were the other finalists for the award. Ovechkin finished third in goals (50) and tied for second in points (109), and factored in a league-high 43.3 percent of Washington's goals. "I have, I think, the most hardest trophy to get and the players vote for it, so I'm very happy," Ovechkin said. "Every player thinks that [being voted] by the players is the most important thing. You play against the guys, and when they vote for you, it's the most important thing."

2010–11
Daniel Sedin
VANCOUVER CANUCKS

Sedin led the NHL in scoring with 104 points and tied for fourth in goals with 41, while placing third in both assists (63) and game-winning goals (10), as Vancouver won its first Presidents' Trophy and reached the Stanley Cup final. "I think we should be happy, we should be proud of the team and our players," Sedin said. "We're going to have a lot of years going forward and we're going to be a good team." Daniel followed his brother and linemate Henrik in winning the Art Ross Trophy, but couldn't duplicate his twin sibling's 2010 Hart Trophy win, finishing second in the voting to Anaheim's Corey Perry. Sedin was the first Canuck since Marcus Naslund in 2002–03, and only the second in history, to be named the NHLPA's MVP.

Conn Smythe Trophy

3

The Conn Smythe Trophy, designed to represent Maple Leaf Gardens, is named after former Toronto Maple Leafs owner Conn Smythe.

CHAPTER 11
The Conn Smythe Trophy and the Man Behind It

The Trophy

THERE MAY BE no trophy in contention more contentious than the National Hockey League's Conn Smythe Trophy, awarded each spring to the most valuable player in the playoffs.

Does a voter choose a dominant player from the Stanley Cup-winning team—a player who has endured four rounds of high-octane action to help lead his team to the Promised Land? And if so, who is to say that certain players contributed more significantly than others? A team is comprised of many different parts, working together for a common goal, so is a goal scorer more valuable than a checker who contained the opponents' best scorers? And what about a goaltender who kept his team in the series by making miraculous saves? Or a defenseman who does everything in his ability to keep the other teams from getting good scoring chances and moves the puck efficiently out of his end? Okay then, what about a player who has excelled throughout the post-season but ended up on the losing end of the Stanley Cup series? And let's extend it further. What about a player whose team does not succeed in reaching the final but who has performed at such an exceptional level that his name cannot be dismissed from discussion? Rhetorical questions all, but ones debated each spring toward the completion of the playoffs.

Others might ask whether there shouldn't, indeed, be two separate trophies—one for the best player in the Stanley Cup final and another for the player who was best through the entire post-season. At times, the winner may be one and the same, but that would not always be the case.

What is especially exciting about the Conn Smythe Trophy is that from the time hockey began, certain players have emerged as invaluable to their team during championship series. Sometimes, it was the star of the team, but just as often, it was a lesser light who got hot at just the right moment and helped his team to victory.

Origins of the Conn Smythe Trophy

On April 16, 1964, just prior to Game 3 of that year's Stanley Cup final, National Hockey League president Clarence Campbell introduced the concept of adding a trophy for the most valuable player of the playoffs. "Baseball picks the best player in the World Series and gives him a car. The National Football League awards an automobile to the top man in its final. Canadian football used to similarly recognize the outstanding performer in the Grey Cup. It would be a good idea for the NHL to do the same thing." Campbell suggested that the NHL should reward the outstanding player in the post-season each spring with a cash award, possibly $2,000.

The idea was greeted with great enthusiasm. "The offer is valid," stated Dick Beddoes of *The Globe and Mail*. "Very often, the stars of the regular season are monumental busts in the playoffs. Secondary performers occasionally respond in resolute fashion to Stanley Cup competition."

Campbell intended to present the idea of a playoff MVP at the next meeting of the NHL Board of Directors. Rumors immediately swirled that Campbell was going to propose that the trophy be named to honor Conn Smythe. Campbell denied that idea, stating that the concept was in the formative stage at that point. "It will be up to [the league governors] to decide on whom to name it after," he stated. Stafford Smythe commented, "I will put Dad's name up

[for nomination] and don't think there will be any difficulty. I'm sure other hockey men recognize what he has done for hockey and will be anxious to honor him in this way." Frank Selke agreed. "I can think of nothing more appropriate than to name a trophy after Conn." Even the senior Smythe added his remarks. "I would be pleased if this one had my name on it," he said. "I've always admired the best in hockey—the best team and the best players. No one stars in the Stanley Cup finals without being a dandy."

On June 11, 1964, the 47th annual meeting of the NHL's board of governors took place, with the league governors—Walter Brown of the Boston Bruins, James Norris of the Chicago Black Hawks, Bruce Norris of the Detroit Red Wings, David Molson of the Montreal Canadiens, William Jennings of the New York Rangers and Stafford Smythe of the Toronto Maple Leafs—voting unanimously to introduce a new trophy that would honor the most valuable player of the NHL playoffs. Unlike other professional sports leagues who honored the MVP of the championship series or championship game, this award would be bestowed upon the best player through the entire post-season. All agreed that the award would be named after Conn Smythe, an honorary NHL governor and the founder and former general manager of the Toronto Maple Leafs. His son Stafford offered to supply the trophy as a gift to the league from his hockey club. The trophy was designed to look like Maple Leaf Gardens, the famous locale where the Leafs played (from November 12, 1931, until February 13, 1999), and the physical legacy of Conn Smythe's tenure as team owner. The trophy is also adorned with a large maple leaf that acts as a backdrop for the model of Maple Leaf Gardens. The league governors also decided to bestow a $1,000 cash reward to the recipient each spring.

The Grandest of Thefts

After the Hockey Hall of Fame was locked and secured for the night on December 5, 1970, thieves removed the lock from the front door of the building without triggering the alarm system and got away with the Stanley Cup, the Masterton Trophy and the Conn Smythe Trophy. Curator Lefty Reid was frantic. "One day, a mouse set [the alarm] off, yet it doesn't work when the trophies are taken!"

Not long afterwards, Detective Wally Harkness received the first in a series of phone calls from a woman who wanted to negotiate the return of the trophies in exchange for the release of a suspect in a serious robbery charge. In one of six calls, the woman stated that her accomplices would dump the trophies into Lake Ontario if the police didn't cooperate. Harkness did not budge at her desperate negotiation.

On December 23, Detective Harkness went outside to find out why his dog was barking and found the trophies on the driveway of his East York home. The Stanley Cup and the Smythe Trophy were found in good condition but the Masterton Trophy had been slightly damaged.

Selecting the Winner

At the semiannual meeting of the NHL's governors held on October 9, 1964, the day prior to the annual NHL All-Star Game, the board decided that selection for the newly-minted Conn Smythe Trophy would be conducted by the six National Hockey League governors who would submit a confidential vote. The winner would be announced just prior to the awarding of the Stanley Cup, with the recipient presented with the trophy at center ice.

In 1967, the governors decided to add more drama to the announcement, and made the decision to award the Conn Smythe Trophy at a reception the day after the Stanley Cup presentation. This short-lived idea lasted but one year. Word of the winner leaked out during the final contest, and while the trophy was awarded the next day, there wasn't a sports writer or fan who didn't know who the winner was going to be.

In January 1971, *SPORT* magazine announced that it wanted to take over the awarding of the Conn Smythe Trophy from the league governors, using a committee of hockey experts selected by the magazine, and then award a car to the winner.

However, the NHL refused to allow the magazine to hijack the Conn Smythe Trophy. *SPORT* magazine then stated that it would present a Dodge Charger to the most valuable player of the NHL playoffs, using members of the Professional Hockey Writers' Association to select its winner. The NHL balked, uncomfortable with the increasing number of awards being distributed to NHL members and teams, and with a realization that a trophy and car presentation would upstage the Conn Smythe Trophy, which was by then accompanied by a bonus of $1,500. Instead, concessions were made. Beginning in 1971, winners of the Conn Smythe Trophy were selected by the Professional Hockey Writers' Association, and the recipient was awarded a car. That spring, Ken Dryden won the Conn Smythe Trophy, and was presented with the award and a Dodge Charger.

Today, like most of the NHL merit awards, the Conn Smythe Trophy is voted on by members of the Professional Hockey Writers' Association. Where the Smythe differs from the other individual NHL trophies awarded is that there is but one name announced, whereas with other awards, the three finalists are announced in advance and the winner awarded the trophy at the annual NHL Awards ceremony.

The Man

CONSTANCE FALKLAND SMYTHE was born in Toronto on February 1, 1895. The Smythe family home was located on McMillan Street (later re-named Mutual Street). In 1927, the newly-purchased Maple Leafs played at the Arena Gardens (often known as the Mutual Street Arena), just down the street from where he was born. And that Smythe home was also just a wrist shot away from where Maple Leaf Gardens would be built under Smythe's direction in 1931.

The patriotic Smythe served in World War I, winning a Military Cross for bravery, but in October 1917, he was captured and became a prisoner of war until the Armistice. When he returned from the war, he began a sand and gravel business, as well as going back to the University of Toronto to earn a civil engineering degree.

Before the war, Smythe had been a fine hockey player, but by the time the war ended and he returned to Canada, his involvement with hockey was in coaching and managing. Between 1923 and 1926, Smythe was so successful coaching the University of Toronto Varsity team, including winning an intercollegiate championship and a berth in the Allan Cup senior hockey final, that he was recommended for a position with a new NHL franchise being created in New York. Colonel John Hammond had observed the success of the New York Americans in 1925–26 and had secured a franchise that would become the New York Rangers. He hired Smythe to create a team that would begin playing out of Madison Square Garden for the 1926–27 season.

"I knew every hockey player in the world right then," boasted Smythe in his autobiography. "I'd been going to Toronto St. Patricks games for years and was familiar with players on the seven teams then in the NHL. Also, I had a pretty good line on players in the Western Hockey League, which was very close to NHL caliber. The Western League was folding. A lot of those players were on the loose."

Smythe assembled a dynamic team, but never enjoyed the fruits of his efforts. Before the season began, Smythe was replaced by Lester Patrick. "To say I was shattered was putting it mildly," he admitted. But he took his severance pay ($10,000), made a bet on a football game that paid off, and used his winnings to invest in the Toronto St. Patricks, who were considering a move to Philadelphia. Using a consortium of investors to finance the purchase, Smythe bought the franchise, and on February 14, 1927, the Toronto Maple Leafs were born. Ironically, the New York Rangers, the team Smythe created, won the Stanley Cup in 1927–28, while the Maple Leafs, the team he assumed, finished last.

Slowly … very slowly … Smythe added components to the Maple Leafs that made them competitive. He added goaltender Lorne Chabot, Harold Cotton, Andy Blair, Francis "King" Clancy and summoned Red Horner, Charlie Conacher and Harvey Jackson from the Toronto Marlboros, the Leafs' junior affiliate. Soon, the 8,000-seat Arena Gardens, their home rink, was determined to be too small for the overflow crowds attending games, and as a result, revenues were being lost. Smythe decided that a new arena was required.

A feat such as constructing a new arena would be a monumental task at the best of times, but the 1930s were the worst of times. The Depression had left most businesses scrambling to make their payroll, and saw many individuals scrambling to find work. And yet, Smythe found a way to circumvent those obstacles in order to create his hockey palace.

After investigating a site on the waterfront and another near College and Spadina, Smythe was offered the opportunity to purchase land owned by the T. Eaton Company, and after negotiating both the location and price, completed a negotiation that would give him property for an arena at the corner of Carlton and Church Streets for a price of $350,000. In order to help finance construction, Smythe and his colleague, Frank Selke, devised a plan that would pay workers approximately 20 percent of their pay in Gardens' shares.

It took the contractors (Thomson Brothers) but five months to build Maple Leaf Gardens, a monumental task exacerbated by the fact they went into the project knowing they'd lose money. Miraculously, after the first shovel plunged into the ground on June 1, 1931, the Gardens opened later that year on November 12 with the Leafs hosting the Chicago Black Hawks. That season concluded on April 9, 1932, when Maple Leaf Gardens was the site of the first Stanley Cup championship won by the Toronto Maple Leafs.

Smythe was legendary in his dealings with the other general managers. Although diminutive in stature, Smythe's battles with Art Ross of the Boston Bruins and Jack Adams of the Detroit Red Wings were anything but short. They were intense, and on occasion, resulted in fisticuffs. Yet, he was a fine judge of talent and the Leafs were always competitive during his tenure.

When World War II erupted in the fall of 1939, the 45-year-old Smythe was ready to bear arms for Canada, much to his wife's chagrin. Conn encouraged all the players in the Leafs' system to enlist in the war effort. At first, Smythe

Turk Broda is hugged by Conn Smythe in the Maple Leafs dressing room after Game 4 of the Stanley Cup final on April 16, 1949, at Maple Leaf Gardens. Toronto swept Detroit to win the Stanley Cup.

himself was rejected because of his age, but he used his influence to form a Sportsmen's Battery, and in September 1941, Smythe was named the Commanding Officer of the 30th Battery, part of the Armed Forces 7th Toronto Regiment, Royal Canadian Artillery. Shortly afterwards, Smythe was named acting Major.

After the attack on Pearl Harbor, Smythe's battery was sent to Vancouver Island to protect Canada from a possible attack from the Japanese. Later, they were sent to England, where Conn spent more than twenty months. During a particularly gruesome attack by the Germans, Smythe was badly wounded in the back by what was likely a bomb fragment, an injury with which he would suffer for the rest of his life.

While serving in the war effort, Smythe had delegated responsibility for Maple Leaf Gardens and the team to a committee that included coach Hap Day and assistant general manager, Frank Selke. And while recuperating from his war injury, Smythe was offered the NHL presidency, which he quickly declined. "I've got a lovely wife, family and sand and gravel business plus my work at the Gardens. Damned if I'll give up all that to be president of the NHL," he said.

He returned to his role as managing director (a title that seemed to constantly shift through his tenure) in the spring of 1945, just in time to see his Maple Leafs defeat the Red Wings for the Stanley Cup.

The Leafs, under Smythe's command, were re-tooled and won four more championships later that decade, collecting Lord Stanley's Cup in 1947, 1948, 1949 and again in 1951. For three decades, there was no man more powerful in hockey than Conn Smythe.

In February 1955, Smythe relinquished the role of general manager of the Maple Leafs to long-time employee, Hap Day. Day had predated the Maple Leafs, playing with the St. Pats beginning in 1924–25, served as the first captain of the Maple Leafs and, after retiring as a player, was hired as coach in 1940–41 and stayed in that position until the spring of 1950. During his time as coach, Day guided the Leafs to five Stanley Cup championships. In 1950, Day was promoted to assistant general manager under Smythe, but truth be told, really was the team's general manager in everything but name.

Preparing his succession plan, Conn encouraged his son Stafford to create a hockey committee and in March 1957, the "Silver Seven" was formed to consult on hockey matters in Toronto. "Good hockey men in many ways," sighed Smythe in his autobiography, "but it just seemed that once the bunch of them got together, a certain amount of good sense went out the window."

Conn's son Stafford, chairman of the hockey committee, pushed for control of Maple Leaf Gardens. In November 1961, Conn was prepared to sell his shares in the Gardens to his son. "Stafford and I talked for three days over various aspects of the deal, and finally reached an agreement," wrote Conn. "At the time, I thought I was selling only to him, and [he] gave me the assurance that the honesty and class I had tried to bring to the place would continue. A few days later, when he told me he was selling part of my shares to [Harold] Ballard and [John] Bassett, I exploded. 'That's a lousy deal! That's the worst business mistake you could ever make! You have the whole pot and now you're going to get a third instead, so that every time this place makes a million dollars, you're going to give two-thirds away!'"

Stafford didn't have the finances to buy the Gardens' shares on his own, but Harold Ballard believed he could raise the $2 million required to purchase the shares. The two spent several nights poring over the Maple Leaf Gardens' financial records to analyze how successful the organization could be. Harold Ballard arranged a loan to make the purchase, but insisted that John Bassett Sr. be included, in spite of Stafford's belief that he and Ballard could make the purchase on their own. The three arranged the financing to offer Conn $2.3 million, or approximately $40 per share (the shares were trading at $33 each at the time), giving them almost 60 percent of the team and Maple Leaf Gardens. Each of the three partners would own approximately 20 percent of the shares.

On November 23, 1961, the deal was consummated, begrudgingly by Conn, who tendered his resignation as president and managing director.

Bassett's *Toronto Telegram* broke the story with a front-page headline that blurted: "Change of Control for The Gardens." Conn was rewarded with a retiring salary of $15,000 per year for life, an office, secretary, car, driver and seats to home games. Conn was also retained as a member of the board of directors.

Conn Smythe's relationship with Maple Leaf Gardens came to a tumultuous end on March 29, 1966. With 13,919 fans shoehorned into Maple Leaf Gardens, Cassius Clay and George Chuvalo slugged it out in a monumental heavyweight boxing match. The battle had come under immense scrutiny because Clay, the World Heavyweight champion, refused to be drafted into the United States Army. "I ain't got no quarrel with the Viet Cong," he stated. And as a result, many boxing commissions refused to approve any defense of his belt. But Harold Ballard managed to have the Ontario Minister of Labour, who controlled boxing in the province, approve the match and he booked it into Maple Leaf Gardens.

While the match went the distance, one man was seething in the background. Smythe, who served in both World Wars, detested the fact that Ballard had allowed a draft dodger to use the Gardens' stage to ply his trade. "Cash before class," he spat. While Cassius Clay (later to be known as Muhammad Ali) retained the heavyweight championship, Smythe resigned his position as a director of Maple Leaf Gardens and, in disgust, sold the last of his shares in the building and team he had built. "The Gardens was founded by men—sportsmen—who fought for their country," he stated in his autobiography. "It is no place for those who want to evade conscription."

The boxing match of March 29, 1966, severed the last official connection to the Toronto Maple Leafs and Maple Leaf Gardens by Smythe, who had purchased the franchise in 1927, renamed it the Toronto Maple Leafs and miraculously, in the depth of the Great Depression, orchestrated the construction of Maple Leaf Gardens in 1931.

But while the Toronto Maple Leafs, Maple Leaf Gardens, his sand and gravel business and his investments in horseracing had been very profitable for Conn Smythe, he also used his considerable influence for philanthropic ventures. From the time of building Maple Leaf Gardens, Smythe had provided space for the Ontario Society for Crippled Children, managed by a friend from public school. Following the war, Smythe got actively involved in the organization. In 1948, he used his influence to secure land owned by the province for the Ontario Society for Crippled Children. The property, at the junction of Kingston Road and Danforth Avenue in the Scarborough area of Toronto, houses what is now called Variety Village, which offers specialized programs and services, regardless of ability.

Smythe was actively involved in helping Reverend Bob Rumball build the Ontario Community Centre for the Deaf. With Conn as honorary chairman of the fundraising campaign in 1973, and using his contacts of high-worth individuals, the campaign was able to raise the purchase price of $900,000 to purchase an estate on Bayview Avenue in Toronto, and in April 1979, having raised more than $7 million, the Ontario Community Centre for the Deaf (now re-named as the Bob Rumball Centre for the Deaf) was opened. "We could not have done this without Conn Smythe," Rumball said at the time.

Earlier, in 1960, Smythe had set up the Conn Smythe Charitable Foundation, which distributes money to charities in the Toronto area. During his lifetime, Smythe administered funds from the foundation with the assistance of his children and Hap Day. Just prior to his death in 1980,

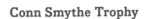

Conn Smythe, Ted Kennedy and Turk Broda visit hospital patients with the Stanley Cup.

The Hockey Hall of Fame was officially opened on August 26, 1961. Canadian Prime Minister John Diefenbaker and United States Ambassador Livingston T. Merchant presided over the opening. "There is nothing greater than hockey to bring about national unity and a closer relationship between the United States and Canada," stated Prime Minister Diefenbaker at that time.

After serving as the Hall's chairman for several years, Conn Smythe resigned in June 1971 when Busher Jackson was posthumously inducted into the Hockey Hall of Fame. Smythe had fought bitterly to keep Jackson out of the Hall, in spite of the fact that Jackson had helped Smythe's Leafs win the Stanley Cup in 1932. Jackson had been a notorious womanizer and had battled alcoholism through much of his life. Smythe stated, "If the standards are going to be lowered, I'll get out as chairman of the board."

Conn Smythe died November 18, 1980. During his 85 years, he had accomplished much, both in the hockey world and for charities. In 1981, to honor Smythe's legacy, the annual Sports Celebrities Dinner in Toronto, which had been raising funds for the Ontario Society for Crippled Children since 1952, was re-named the Conn Smythe Sports Celebrities Dinner, with proceeds channeled to the same charity, which by then had been renamed Easter Seals Ontario. The fundraising dinner, which features some of the highest profile athletes from various disciplines, has raised more than $6 million to date.

But Conn Smythe's most enduring legacy may very well be the trophy awarded to the most valuable player of each spring's playoffs—the Conn Smythe Trophy.

Conn appointed his grandson, Tom Smythe, to continue the foundation after his death.

Smythe was also instrumental in securing a permanent home for the Hockey Hall of Fame. Although the Hall of Fame had been established in 1943, with the first Honored Members inducted in 1945, it was still a virtual museum, after plans to build in Kingston failed to materialize. But in 1960, Smythe, who was chairman of the NHL owners' committee, successfully lobbied the NHL and the other team owners to finance a Hockey Hall of Fame building on land secured from the City of Toronto on the grounds of the Canadian National Exhibition. Smythe then personally supervised construction, and on May 1, 1961, the building was completed.

CHAPTER 12
Multiple Winners

THE CONN SMYTHE Trophy has been awarded 46 times, and at 35 of those announcements, the award has gone to a new recipient. Five players have the distinction of winning the trophy more than once, a truly remarkable feat, and one that has helped all five players become inducted to the Hockey Hall of Fame.

Patrick Roy
1986, 1993, 2001

At a media conference held on May 28, 2003, Patrick Roy announced his retirement. His legacy as one of the greatest goaltenders in hockey history is unarguable. At the conclusion of his playing career, Patrick had won the Vezina Trophy three times (1989, 1990 and 1992), the Jennings Trophy five times (1987, 1988, 1989, 1992 and 2002), the Stanley Cup on four occasions (1986, 1993, 1996 and 2001) and is the sole player to have received the Conn Smythe Trophy three times.

Roy joined the Montreal Canadiens as their principal goaltender in 1985–86, usurping the role from Steve Penney and Doug Soetaert. The Canadiens decided to ride the rookie's strong season into the 1985–86 playoffs.

There was nothing easy about the route taken to the Stanley Cup final by Roy and his Canadiens. Although they brushed aside the Bruins in three straight in the best-of-five opening series, the Hartford Whalers pushed Montreal to seven games before the Canadiens triumphed. Then, on a roll, Montreal defeated the New York Rangers to earn a berth in the Stanley Cup final series.

Meantime, they caught a break when the favored Edmonton Oilers, who had won the Stanley Cup the previous two seasons, were eliminated in shocking fashion by the Calgary Flames in the second round of the playoffs.

So it was the Canadiens versus Calgary challenging each other for the Stanley Cup in 1986,

Patrick Roy as a rookie facing the Calgary Flames in the 1986 Stanley Cup final. Montreal won the series in five games.

the first time two Canadian teams had faced each other for hockey supremacy since Toronto and Montreal in 1967.

Calgary opened the 1986 series with a convincing 5–2 win, but the Habs took the next four games straight: Brian Skrudland scored a goal nine seconds into overtime to give Montreal a 3–2 win in Game 2. The Canadiens outscored the Flames 5–3 at home in Montreal to collect a win in Game 3, and then Patrick Roy slammed the door shut on Calgary to earn a 1–0 win for Montreal in Game 4. Then in the fifth game in Calgary on May 24, the Montreal Canadiens

edged the Flames 4–3 to win the Stanley Cup.

Without rookie netminder Roy, the Canadiens would never have won this Stanley Cup championship, and he was named recipient of the Conn Smythe Trophy for his stellar goaltending. "I had always dreamed about it [winning the Stanley Cup] but never believed it would happen to me," he said amidst the excitement.

In 1992–93, the Canadiens finished third in the powerful Adams Division, behind Boston and Quebec. The first playoff series saw Montreal spank their archrivals, the Nordiques, four games to two. The juggernaut had begun. They then swept the Buffalo Sabres and defeated the New York Islanders in five games. This set up an unlikely final—the Canadiens versus the Los Angeles Kings. For Montreal, it was their first return to the final since 1989. For Los Angeles, it was their first-ever visit to a Stanley Cup final.

L.A. had also finished third in their division, but led by Wayne Gretzky, you never knew just how dangerous the Kings might be. Patrick Roy surrendered just twelve goals in five games in that final to lead the Habs to a Stanley Cup victory, their last at the Montreal Forum. The Canadiens set an NHL record by winning ten of the requisite sixteen games in overtime, including three in the final.

Patrick Roy had been superb again in net and was chosen by the Professional Hockey Writers' Association as the winner of the Conn Smythe Trophy. He joined Wayne Gretzky, Bernie Parent and Bobby Orr as the only multiple winners of the prestigious award.

By 2000–01, Roy was a member of the Colorado Avalanche. His team had finished first overall during the regular season and was back in the Stanley Cup final. They beat the Vancouver Canucks in four games, took seven to edge the L.A. Kings and then dumped the St. Louis Blues four games to one. That set up a final against the reigning Stanley Cup champions, the New Jersey Devils.

The Avalanche's Roy and the Devils' Brodeur are regarded as two of the greatest goaltenders in hockey's history, and it was a landmark series. The Devils desperately wanted to repeat, while the Avalanche wanted to reward veteran Raymond Bourque with his first-ever Stanley Cup win.

Patrick Roy was on a mission, and played brilliantly. He earned shutouts in Games 1 and 6, and allowed just eleven goals in the hotly contested seven-game series to guide his Avalanche past the Devils.

Roy had a shutout streak of 227 minutes and 41 seconds finally snapped in Game 2, just 1:41 shy of a record held by Clint Benedict. "I didn't know what the shutout record was," Patrick admitted. "It didn't mean anything to me. What means [something] to me is winning at the end!"

The awarding of the Smythe was overshadowed by the Stanley Cup celebration with Bourque, but Patrick Roy became the first player, and only one to date, to win three playoff MVP awards. "For a little boy from Quebec, I never thought that [winning the Conn Smythe Trophy three times] would happen. These individual honors are always fun, don't get me wrong, but there's nothing better than winning." He added, "Overall, just to be remembered as a champion, that's what it's all about to me."

Bobby Orr
1970, 1972

Bobby Orr's exploits in 1969–70 are extraordinary. As he continued to revolutionize how defensemen could play the game, he set NHL records that will be marveled at for years to come. Scoring 33 goals from his blue-line position (seventh highest total in the NHL that season) was only part of the story. His 87 assists were 31 more than second-place Phil Esposito, and for the first time in NHL history, a defenseman won the scoring race. Orr's 120 points were 21 more than teammate Esposito, and earned Orr the Art Ross Trophy. His dominant play also earned Bobby the Hart Trophy as the NHL's most valuable player through the regular season, and he also laid claim to the Norris Trophy for the third consecutive season. But the show wasn't over for Bobby Orr or his Boston Bruins.

For the third straight spring, the St. Louis Blues emerged from the Western Division to compete in the Stanley Cup final, and for the

Two-time Conn Smythe winner Bobby Orr.

third straight spring, they were swept by their opponents.

Boston feasted on the Blues, scoring twenty goals in the four-game final. Bobby Orr scored but one in the final, but it was the pivotal tally. After sixty minutes of play, the Bruins and the Blues were deadlocked at three goals apiece. But forty seconds into overtime on that Mother's Day in Boston, Bobby Orr scored one of the most famous goals in NHL history, putting the puck past Glenn Hall as Blues' blueliner Noel Picard sent him hurtling through the air.

"It wasn't me who scored the winning goal," he shrugged with undue modesty. "The credit belongs to the team! These guys I play with are unbelievable. Just unbelievable!"

But it was Orr who was unbelievable. His timely goal, the ninth of the post-season, had earned the Bruins the Stanley Cup, their first since 1941, and confirmed his name as the winner

of the Conn Smythe Trophy.

Two years later, the Boston Bruins returned to the Stanley Cup final, this time challenged by the New York Rangers. Through the 1950s and 1960s, these two franchises had been the picture of futility. In the two decades stretching from 1951–52 to 1971–72, the Rangers had missed the playoffs eleven times, while Boston missed post-season play on nine occasions. But the two teams now were as powerful as any in the NHL. They had finished one–two in the league standings—Boston with 119 points and the Rangers with 109.

The Stanley Cup final of 1972 was the first Bruins-Rangers final since 1929. Boston took an immediate lead, winning the first two games of the series, but the Rangers battled back with a 5–2 win in Game 3. The teams traded wins in Games 4 and 5 before Boston wrapped up the series with a 3–0 victory in Game 6 to win the Stanley Cup.

After the game, Vic Hadfield of the New York Rangers simply shook his head. "The two clubs were even in faceoffs, even in power plays, even in penalty kills, even in everything…except they had Bobby Orr."

Orr had again enjoyed a prodigious season of productivity, finishing with 117 points, second in NHL scoring to teammate Phil Esposito. Orr's 80 assists led the league by a wide margin, and continued into the post-season when he led in the playoffs with 19 assists. In the final alone, Bobby scored four goals and matched it with four assists. Despite nursing a damaged knee that required off-season surgery, Bobby Orr became the first two-time Conn Smythe Trophy recipient, recognizing his productivity and all-around dominating play in the spring of 1972.

Bernie Parent
1974, 1975

The second player to earn the Conn Smythe Trophy twice was Bernie Parent, goaltender for the Philadelphia Flyers.

The 1973–74 NHL regular season concluded with the Boston Bruins and Philadelphia Flyers finishing first and second respectively. Both were fuelled by strong offense, intimidating skaters and a Hall of Fame netminder. And it was only fitting, therefore, that the two dominant teams would emerge as opponents in the Stanley Cup final.

Flyers' coach Fred Shero drilled into his team that no one player—read "Bobby Orr"—could defeat an entire team. The Big Bad Bruins and the Broad Street Bullies went to war in the spring of 1974. The series was intense, but the spirited contests provided great entertainment for fans. Going into Game 6 on May 19, the Flyers led three games to Boston's two. Fred Shero delivered a resonating pre-game speech to his charges: "Win tonight and we will walk together forever." That night, Kate Smith surprised fans in the Philadelphia Spectrum by appearing to sing "God Bless America" prior to the opening faceoff.

Perhaps it was the rousing talk from Shero. Maybe it was the luck of Kate Smith's performance. More likely, it was the play of Bernie Parent that earned the Stanley Cup for the Flyers. Parent had been sensational enough against the high-flying Bruins throughout the playoffs, but slammed the door shut in Game 6, earning a 1–0 shutout that gave Philadelphia renown as the first of the 1967–68 expansion teams to claim Lord Stanley's silverware. Bernie Parent was awarded the Conn Smythe Trophy, which joined the Vezina Trophy and a First All-Star Team selection on his mantel that year.

But Parent wasn't done. In 1974–75, for a second straight season, Parent recorded twelve shutouts through the regular season, he again was named a First Team All-Star and again won both the Vezina and Conn Smythe trophies. This time, the Flyers (who ended the season in a three-way tie for first-place overall with the Montreal Canadiens and Buffalo Sabres) met the Sabres in the Stanley Cup final. The curious series featured a fog-shrouded contest in Buffalo and an on-ice bat-killing by the Sabres' Jim Lorentz.

The 1975 series went six games, and each home team won in the first five games, and as the series progressed, fans at the Spectrum in Philadelphia chanted Parent's name with every save. When the dust had settled (or rather, the fog lifted), the Philadelphia Flyers had once again won the Stanley Cup, and the hero of the series once again was Bernie Parent.

Wayne Gretzky
1985, 1988

Arguably the greatest player ever to pull on a pair of skates, Wayne Gretzky is another multiple Conn Smythe Trophy winner, named twice during the Oilers' dynasty of the 1980s.

The day after winning the Stanley Cup in 1985, police told Wayne Gretzky that two people had threatened his life. It could very easily have been any of his opponents—that season, Wayne had once again monopolized the National Hockey League. His league-best 73 goals were two more than teammate Jari Kurri, but his Art Ross-winning 208 points bettered second-place Kurri by 73 points! In fact, Gretzky's assist total alone would have tied him with Kurri for the league's scoring championship.

The Oilers, with 109 points, had secured second place overall, with first going to the Philadelphia Flyers with 113. It seemed appropriate that the NHL's two best teams should meet in the Stanley Cup final.

The Flyers had owned Edmonton at home during the regular season, winning the last eight straight games at the Spectrum. And, in Game 1 of the final, Philadelphia thumped the Oilers 4–1. "We stunk up the Spectrum the first night," Gretzky stated in *Gretzky,* his autobiography. "Philadelphia never admitted it, but I think they purposely made the ice choppy to slow us down. It was like playing on a lake."

The Oilers quietly fumed, and came ready for bear in Game 2, which reversed the trend of Philadelphia winning at home against Edmonton, as the Oilers took the second contest by a 3–1 score.

Edmonton then took the next three games, all played at their home rink, the Northlands Coliseum, to capture Lord Stanley's Mug: in Game 3, the Oilers edged the Flyers 4–3; Grant Fuhr stoned the Flyers' Ron Sutter on a penalty shot to give the Oilers great momentum in Game 4, which Edmonton won by a 5–3 count. The Stanley Cup was presented to the Edmonton Oilers on May 30, 1985, after the home team destroyed the visitors, 8–3 in Game 5. "We came out flying and squashed Philly," Gretzky recalled.

Wayne Gretzky led the playoffs with a record 47 points and was named winner of the Conn Smythe Trophy. But there is an argument that can be made that Paul Coffey deserved consideration, which he surely got, and even Gretzky would have given his teammate the award. Coffey set several playoff records for defensemen, including most goals (12), most assists (25), most points (37). Both Coffey and Gretzky had 11 points in the final against the Flyers. "I won the Conn Smythe, but Cof deserved it," Wayne admitted in *Gretzky.* "To this day, I wished they'd given it to him. He was the true superstar of those playoffs."

In 1988, Gretzky was at it again. It was during the second round of the 1988 playoffs, in a series against Calgary, that he learned that he was going to be a father, his fiancée Janet Jones pregnant with their first child. "I was so pumped up they had to tie me down. I knew I was going to play great that night," he stated in his autobiography.

That night, the Oilers beat the Calgary Flames in overtime to win Game 2. Gretzky scored the winner on a slapshot from the blueline to give Edmonton a two games to none lead.

After eliminating Detroit, the Oilers faced the Boston Bruins for the Stanley Cup. The Bruins had an old friend of the Oilers in goal—Andy Moog, who had won three Stanley Cup championships playing with Edmonton.

In each of the first three games, the Oilers had doubled the Bruins: 2–1 in Game 1, 4–2 in Game 2 and 6–3 in Game 3. And then, one of the more curious occurrences took place in Game 4.

At 16:37 of the second period, with the score knotted at three, the power went out in the old Boston Garden. The perplexed players were escorted to their respective dressing rooms by police officers using flashlights. While the players kibitzed, waiting for the lights to come back on, workers labored to find the problem. Fifteen minutes later, with no solution, NHL officials entered both dressing rooms and pronounced that the game was over. The statistics would still count, but the game would be replayed, this time in Edmonton.

This time, the Oilers shot the lights out against Boston with a convincing 6–3 victory, and won the fourth Stanley Cup in franchise history in a sweep of the Bruins. Gretzky again set playoff records, collecting 31 assists in the 18 post-season contests, and 13 in the final. Wayne again led all competitors in scoring with 43 points. While netminder Grant Fuhr had played well, there was no doubt that the voters would award the Conn Smythe to Wayne Gretzky.

In his autobiography, Gretzky had a sentimental pick for his Conn Smythe Trophy choice. "I wish they'd given it to Steve [Smith], the kid who got blamed for the 1986 playoff loss. [Smith had put the puck into his own net, banking a pass off the back of Grant Fuhr's skates in Game 7 of the 1986 Conference final against Calgary.] Nobody on the ice was better during those playoffs than Steve Smith."

After accepting both the Conn Smythe Trophy and the Stanley Cup, Wayne Gretzky gathered his teammates on the ice around him and the Cup for a team portrait. This tradition, started on May 26, 1988, by Gretzky with the Oilers, was prophetic for Gretzky. That summer, after getting married, he was traded from Edmonton to the Los Angeles Kings. "I had no idea it was to be my last moment as an Oiler. What better way to end it? 'Destiny,' my Dad would say."

Although the Edmonton Oilers would win another Stanley Cup without Gretzky, it was the beginning of the erosion of the Oilers' dynasty.

Mario Lemieux
1991, 1992

Prior to Mario Lemieux's arrival in Pittsburgh, the Penguins struggled with attendance, averaging fewer than 7,000 fans per game in 1983–84, but the arrival of "Mario the Magnificent" changed that concern substantially.

The league's top rookie in 1984–85, Lemieux's exciting play and dominant style earned Mario the Hart Trophy in 1988, and he led the league in scoring in both 1987–88 and 1988–89.

During the 1989–90 season, Lemieux missed 21 games to injury, yet still finished fourth in NHL scoring with 123 points, but it was all in vain, as the Penguins failed to qualify for the playoffs.

Mario's back problems carried over for fifty

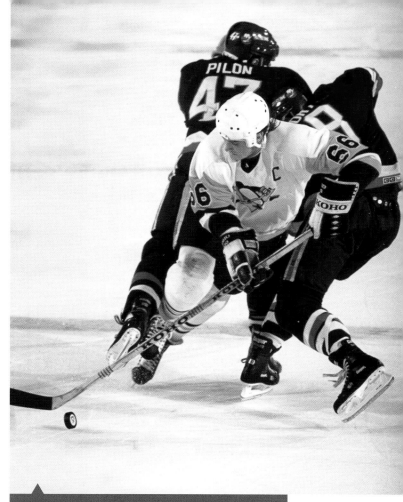

Two-time Conn Smythe winner Mario Lemieux splits the New York Islander defense.

games into the 1990–91 season, and trainer Skip Thayer had to tie Lemieux's skates in order for the star to play. Yet, in 26 games, he still collected 45 points.

The Penguins took seven games to move past New Jersey in the opening round of the playoffs, but then systematically eliminated the Washington Capitals four games to one, Boston's Bruins in six games and proceeded to the Stanley Cup final against the Minnesota North Stars.

Minnesota struck first, edging the Penguins 5–4, but Mario and his mates struck back in Game 2, a contest that featured one of the most viewed games in hockey history. During the second period, Mario picked up the puck just outside his own blue line, skated through center avoiding all green sweaters, undressed defenseman Shawn Chambers by tucking the puck between his legs and skating around him and then forced Jon Casey in goal to commit to his left before switching the puck to his backhand and tucking the puck into the open net as he crashed into the net. The goal (and a re-creation) is used to start each broadcast of *Hockey Night in Canada*. The game ended in a 4–1 win for the Penguins.

The series took six games, but with a convincing 8–0 win in the final game (the widest margin of victory in a Stanley Cup-deciding game), Mario Lemieux and the Pittsburgh Penguins won the franchise's first championship.

In spite of his back woes, Lemieux connected for 44 points through the playoffs (second only to Wayne Gretzky's 47 in 1984–85), including 12 points in the five games he played in the final, to outdistance all others in winning the Conn Smythe Trophy.

The Penguins lost head coach Bob Johnson to cancer in October 1991, and while he would be all but impossible to replace, Scotty Bowman stepped in to handle the team. Lemieux's back problems also continued and restricted him to 64 games in 1991–92. Nevertheless, he still won the Art Ross Trophy as the league's scoring champion for the third time, collecting 131 points.

In the 1992 playoffs, the Penguins faced Washington in the opening round, and eliminated them in seven games. Pittsburgh next faced the Patrick Division-winning New York Rangers. During the second game, a slash by Adam Graves broke Mario's left hand, eliminating him from playoff action for five games, but the Penguins still dumped New York in six games. Then in the third round, with Mario back in the lineup, Pittsburgh blanked Boston to earn a second consecutive berth in the Stanley Cup final, this time challenged by the Chicago Blackhawks.

Mario again was dominant as the Pittsburgh Penguins swept the Hawks in four straight games to claim their second straight Stanley Cup championship. Lemieux scored five goals and had eight points in the final, giving him a playoff-best 16 goals and 34 points to top all others in the 1991–92 post-season. The Conn Smythe Trophy was again awarded to Mario Lemieux by NHL president John Ziegler, making the Penguins' star the first player to win back-to-back playoff MVP awards since Bernie Parent of the Philadelphia Flyers in 1974 and 1975.

CHAPTER 13
Seminal Seasons

Jean Beliveau

1965

The inaugural recipient of the Conn Smythe Trophy was Jean Beliveau, the star center of the Montreal Canadiens. In 1965, Beliveau's Habs eliminated the reigning Stanley Cup champions, the Toronto Maple Leafs, in five semifinal contests, with captain Beliveau matching three goals with three assists to help power the Habs past the stunned Leafs.

The series' victory gave Montreal the right to face the powerful Chicago Black Hawks in the Stanley Cup final. The Habs' captain led his charges past Bobby Hull and the Black Hawks. Beliveau monopolized the offense for the Canadiens, scoring five goals and adding five assists in the seven-game series to give Montreal the Stanley Cup championship, its thirteenth in franchise history. In fact, Jean scored the winning goal, a tally at the 14-second mark of the first period in Game 7 that led to the 4–0 win for Montreal.

On May 1, 1965, following Montreal's win over Chicago, two trophies were carried to center ice for presentation by National Hockey League President Clarence Campbell. With a hushed Forum crowd listening intently to Campbell, fans heard the NHL president announce that the newly-minted Conn Smythe Trophy for the most valuable player in the 1965 playoffs was going to none other than Jean Beliveau. After accepting the award, Beliveau then placed the trophy back on the table as Campbell then presented the Stanley Cup to him, who accepted it on behalf of the victorious Canadiens.

An argument could be made that Montreal's netminder, Gump Worsley, might also have been considered for the prestigious award. Worsley earned two shutouts in the final (a 2–0 win in Game 2 and the 4–0 capper in Game 7) and allowed but five goals in the four games he played against the Black Hawks that spring for a miniscule goals-against average of 1.25.

Jean Beliveau poses with the Stanley Cup and the Conn Smythe in 1965. It was the first time the NHL selected a playoff MVP.

Gump won three of the four games in which he faced Chicago, while back-up Charlie Hodge won the other.

Beliveau's 1965 victory may never have happened if it weren't for a talk with a close ally. "In 1962, when I felt that my personal fortunes were at their lowest ebb, I went to see Senator Hartland Molson, then the Canadiens' owner," Beliveau recounted in his autobiography, *Jean Beliveau: My Life in Hockey*. The Habs' captain was disgruntled with his play, and the stress of expectations placed on him had worn Jean down. "Senator, I'm starting to doubt that I'm ever going to play as well as I have in the past," he admitted to the man he regarded as a second father.

Molson buoyed Beliveau's confidence, stating, "Over the course of a career, there will be many ups and downs, especially for someone of your temperament. You take everything so seriously. When you're not performing to your standards, it's understandable that you would be disappointed. But any doubt that you are having now will pass with time. You have the talent and the strength of character to come back."

In his book, Jean told co-authors Chrys Goyens and Allan Turowetz, "I was cheered by his words and I took them to heart." He also took them to Hart, winning the league's most valuable player award in 1964 and, of course, the Conn Smythe Trophy in 1965.

Jean Beliveau went on to play on four more Stanley Cup championship teams with Montreal, totaling ten in all, before he retired at the conclusion of the 1970–71 season. Jean remained with the Canadiens as an executive and ambassador and was part of an additional seven Stanley Cup championships.

In 2009, Jean auctioned off the miniature version of the Conn Smythe Trophy with which he was presented in 1965. The award, in extraordinary condition, was purchased for $17,270., the proceeds of the sale of this and other hockey artifacts were being channeled to his grandchildren.

Dave Keon
1967

The Chicago Black Hawks ran away with the regular season in 1966–67, accumulating 94 points, 17 more than second-place Montreal, but when the dust settled, it was third-place Toronto who faced the Canadiens for the Stanley Cup.

It was a historically significant spring. First off, 1967 was the end of the Original Six era: Montreal, Toronto, Chicago, Detroit, New York and Boston had competed since 1942–43, but the National Hockey League would double in size for the 1967–68 season. It was also a milestone for another reason: 1967 was Canada's 100th birthday, and to have the two Canadian NHL franchises competing for the Stanley Cup was a dream come true for the country. The City of Montreal, hosting Expo 67, already had earmarked a spot for the Stanley Cup to be showcased after the Canadiens collected the hardware.

The teams battled fiercely, with Montreal taking Games 1 and 4, but the aged Maple Leafs, anchored by the tandem of Johnny Bower and Terry Sawchuk in goal, led the series three games to two going into Game 6 played at Maple Leaf Gardens on May 2, 1967. After a scoreless first period, Ron Ellis and Jim Pappin scored for Toronto, with former Leaf Dick Duff replying for Montreal in the third. Toronto captain George Armstrong secured the win with a late-game insurance marker, allowing the Maple Leafs to steal the Stanley Cup from beneath the collective noses of the Canadiens.

Although the NHL vowed to keep the winner of the Conn Smythe Trophy under wraps until 5:30 p.m. the next day, the worst-kept secret in hockey was that Dave Keon had been selected as recipient of the award. Each of the six league governors or their representatives had cast ballots for the Smythe Trophy before they left the arena. Although it wasn't official, the results of the voting circulated through Maple Leaf Gardens. In fact, NHL president Clarence Campbell took the sealed envelopes to Montreal, where they were counted. One ballot indicated Terry Sawchuk as the most valuable playoff performer, but five had selected Keon, the sprightly center of the Stanley Cup champions, the Toronto Maple Leafs, as recipient of the prestigious Conn Smythe Trophy.

During the celebration, *Hockey Night in Canada* announced that Keon had been named winner of the Conn Smythe Trophy. Broadcaster Foster Hewitt wasn't surprised. "I think he was

the top player in the playoffs this season," he stated. *Toronto Star* sportswriter Red Burnett concurred. "Leaf center Dave Keon was the outstanding player of the 1967 playoffs," he stated. "He dominated every center he faced, including Canadiens' great Jean Beliveau. No Leaf ever performed better than the Keon of that playoff."

Keon had not dominated offensively—the line of Jim Pappin (15 points), Peter Stemkowski (12) and Bob Pulford (11) had finished one, two and four in playoff production, but Keon's 3 goals and 5 assists told only part of the story. His exceptional two-way play had neutralized the Canadiens, and contributed significantly to the Stanley Cup victory for Toronto.

Following the tickertape civic parade on May 5, a very curious surprise unfolded at Maple Leaf Gardens that afternoon: another MVP trophy was awarded. Terry Sawchuk was awarded the J.P. Bickell Memorial Cup, a Maple Leaf-specific trophy for meritorious service to the franchise, as well as the Air Canada Trophy as the Maple Leafs' most valuable performer in that spring's playoffs. Why an MVP trophy was presented to Sawchuk while the Conn Smythe Trophy was awarded to Dave Keon is a mystery, but an even bigger mystery is, whatever became of this award? The Hockey Hall of Fame has no record of it. The Sawchuk family is aware that Terry won the award and believes that the Leaf players themselves voted on the recipient of the award. Alumni of the team during that era have no recollection of a team playoff MVP award. Maple Leaf Sports and Entertainment has never heard of it and Air Canada could find nothing in their files. On closer inspection, the Air Canada Trophy is actually engraved as the Trans-Canada Airlines Trophy, meaning that the trophy was created prior to January 1965 when Trans-Canada changed its name to Air Canada, and yet,

1971 Conn Smythe winner Ken Dryden watches the play as Serge Savard clears the front of the net.

through exhaustive research, there doesn't appear to be any winner before Sawchuk, and following his win in 1967, the trophy was apparently never awarded again.

Ken Dryden
1971

The Montreal Canadiens rode the exploits of a rookie goaltender to a Stanley Cup championship in both 1971 and in 1986. In 1971, it was Ken Dryden; in 1986, Patrick Roy. And in each case, the young netminder earned the Conn Smythe Trophy.

During the 1970–71 regular season, the Canadiens split goaltending duties between Rogie Vachon and Phil Myre, but coach Al MacNeil played a hunch and towards the end of the season, summoned Ken Dryden from the Montreal Voyageurs, the Habs' American Hockey League affiliate. With just six NHL games under his belt, Dryden led the Canadiens into the 1971 Stanley Cup playoffs.

The Boston Bruins were favored to win a second consecutive Stanley Cup championship that year, using the firepower of ten players who had scored twenty or more goals through the regular season, including Phil Esposito (76), Johnny Bucyk (51) and Ken Hodge (43) as well as Bobby Orr, who contributed 37.

The Bruins faced the Montreal Canadiens in the quarterfinals, and observers believed that Boston, after a 3–1 win in Game 1, was well on its way to rolling through the post-season. The Bruins were winning 5–1 midway through the second game but the Canadiens poured six unanswered goals past a stunned Gerry Cheevers and won the game 7–5.

The win reversed the momentum of the series. "It was a question of personal pride, team spirit and, of course, all the predictions that the Bruins would undoubtedly dominate the Canadiens with ease," Jean Beliveau stated in *La Patrie*.

The Bruins didn't go down without a fight. It took seven games, but the Canadiens persevered to eliminate Boston, and gained their own momentum in the process. They went on to defeat Minnesota, earning a spot in the Stanley Cup final against the Chicago Black Hawks.

The 1971 final extended to a full seven games, with the deciding contest played May 18 at Chicago Stadium. Tighter than the bark to a tree, Henri Richard's third period goal stood as the winner as the Canadiens won the Stanley Cup on enemy soil, edging the Hawks 3–2.

Who should win the Conn Smythe? Frank Mahovlich set a franchise record by recording 27 points in the post-season. Sentimentally, Jean Beliveau, appearing in the final for the last time, may have been a consideration. And then there were the opponents to consider. The Hawks' Bobby Hull had a terrific playoff. But it was the rookie netminder for Montreal who was awarded the prize. Dryden stood up to a barrage of shots through the playoffs, showed immense poise and led the Canadiens to the Stanley Cup. "I was a rookie that year and just being there was such a thrill," he said.

The following season, Dryden won the Calder Trophy as the NHL's best rookie, eligible because he had played just six games during the previous regular season. He remains the only NHL player to win the Conn Smythe *before* winning the rookie of the year honor.

Guy Lafleur
1977

The Montreal Canadiens' dynasty of the 1970s reached its zenith in 1976–77 when the Habs won 60, tied 12 and lost but 8 games, setting a record for fewest losses in an NHL season. They scored a staggering 387 goals through the season, while allowing just 171. At home, on the ice of the Montreal Forum, the Canadiens won 33 times, tied 6 and lost just once. Montreal finished with 132 points, 20 more than second-place Philadelphia. Canadiens goalie Ken Dryden, who shared the Vezina Trophy with Michel "Bunny" Larocque that season, commented, "There were an inordinate number of games we won without even a reasonable amount of difficulty."

The Canadiens had few obstacles through the post-season, sweeping the St. Louis Blues and then eliminating the New York Islanders in six games to reach the Stanley Cup final against the Boston Bruins.

The Bruins mounted their best effort, but offered little opposition to the powerful Canadiens. Montreal rolled over the Bruins, winning four consecutive games: 7–3, 3–0, 4–2 and then 1–0 on an overtime tally by Jacques Lemaire.

Guy Lafleur, who had dominated the regular season, did the same in the post-season. During the season, he won the scoring championship with 136 points on 56 goals and 80 assists. In the playoffs, he scored 9 goals and added 17 assists for 26 points, leading all other scorers, and was an easy choice for the Conn Smythe Trophy.

Lafleur joined Bobby Orr as the only player to have won both the Conn Smythe Trophy and the Hart Trophy during the same season. Wayne Gretzky joined them after his remarkable 1984–85 season and playoffs.

Mark Messier

1984

Why, in a season when Gretzky so dominated the NHL offensively, would the selection of Mark Messier as the 1984 Conn Smythe Trophy recipient hold such significance? Messier was the leader of the Edmonton Oilers both on and off the ice, and the intangibles he brought to the Oilers' victory—and the start of their dynasty—cannot be dismissed.

As Gretzky collected a staggering 205 points through the regular season, Messier's 101 points were greatly overshadowed. In fact, even with more than a hundred points, Messier still was just the fourth top scorer on the Oilers that season, falling in behind Gretzky, Paul Coffey (126 points) and Jari Kurri (113 points). The Oilers were a dominant first overall at the conclusion of the regular season.

The spirited team had learned a valuable lesson in the spring of 1983. Reaching the final, they were swept by the New York Islanders, who claimed a fourth consecutive Stanley Cup championship. In losing, the Oilers learned how to win.

Messier began his NHL career as a left winger, but was converted to a center during the 1984 playoffs. It was a shrewd move by Edmonton's coach, Glen Sather, and one that paid immense dividends for the franchise.

The Oilers made short work of the Winnipeg Jets, sweeping them in the best-of-five series. An on-going nemesis, the Calgary Flames, were next, and while it took Edmonton the full seven games to dismiss their provincial rival, they did,

and moved on to face the Minnesota North Stars. Messier and the Oilers snuffed out the North Stars in four straight games to earn a reunion final with the New York Islanders.

Ordinarily, the high-flying Oilers used their potent offense to extinguish opponents, but the tone was set in Game 1 when Grant Fuhr earned a 1–0 shutout against the Long Island squad. The determined Islanders bounced back with a 6–1 spanking of the Oilers in Game 2. And then up stepped Mark Messier.

In Game 3, Messier reversed the momentum with a massive hit on Islanders' star defenseman Denis Potvin. "At that time, when you hit Denis Potvin, you just went down," recalled Paul Coffey in Jeff Klein's book, *Messier*. We were all, 'Wow! Yeah, yeah!' It really brought our emotion up. We said, 'Hey, we can play with these guys,' because up to that point, the Islanders were so superior to our hockey club."

But it didn't end there. Trailing the Islanders by a goal in that same game, Messier made a sensational end-to-end rush that tied the score and sparked a remarkable comeback by the Oilers. "It really took the wind out of the Islanders' sails," stated Lee Fogolin. "You could tell. They sagged." Wayne Gretzky agreed. "It really took our team to a level of confidence where we never looked back."

Game 3 ended in a 7–2 Edmonton win, followed by another 7–2 win in Game 4 and a 5–2 win in Game 6 that clinched the Stanley Cup for the Oilers. In spite of Wayne Gretzky's playoff-best 35 points, including 7 in the final, it was Mark Messier who was the difference-maker, and as such, was named recipient of the Conn Smythe Trophy.

"In the trench warfare of the series against Calgary and especially the Islanders, it was Messier's physical play that carried the Oilers

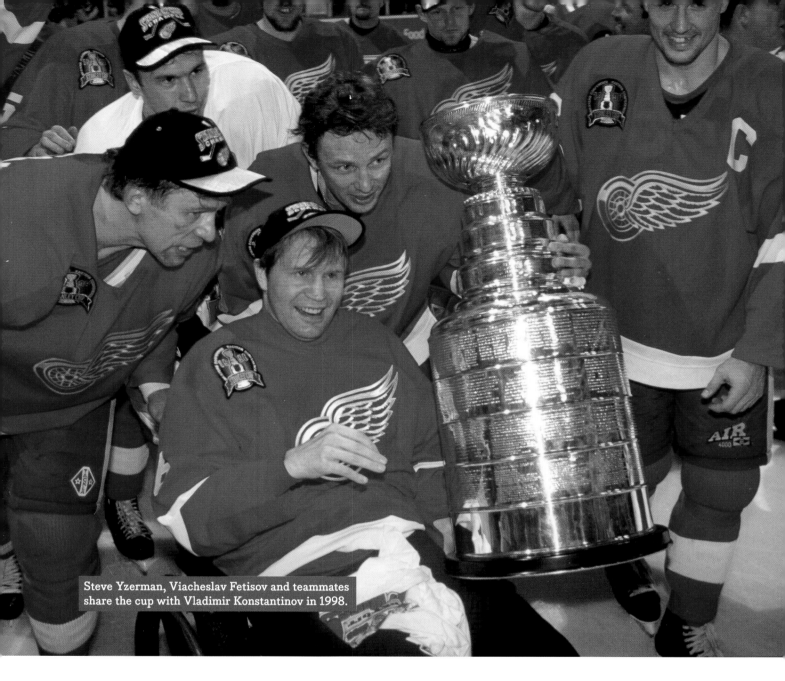

Steve Yzerman, Viacheslav Fetisov and teammates share the cup with Vladimir Konstantinov in 1998.

forward," wrote Douglas Hunter in *The Glory Barons: The Saga of the Edmonton Oilers*. "The weakness of Gretzky's style was revealed in the heavy traffic of an aggressive physical game. Unlike Messier, he could not fight his way through and still contribute to scoring. Messier's Conn Smythe win was not a repudiation of Gretzky's skills, but an indication that a championship team needs more than playmaking finesse. It was the first indication that the Oilers might be able to win without Gretzky, and that they could lose if Messier was not completely effective."

Steve Yzerman

1998

It was a challenging season for the Detroit Red Wings. The previous spring, the Stanley Cup celebration that Steve Yzerman had waited for fourteen seasons—and that had eluded the city of Detroit for 42 years—lasted but a week when a limousine carrying Viacheslav Fetisov, Vladimir Konstantinov and masseur Sergei Mnatsakanov crashed into a tree, rendering the latter two wheelchair-bound. The accident deeply impacted the Red Wings, but the team rallied and dedicated the 1997–98 season to their injured colleagues.

The Red Wings earned 103 points to finish third overall. Captain Steve Yzerman led Detroit in scoring in 1997–98, although his 69 points were well off the offensive totals he had once enjoyed. While age may have played a role, Yzerman's commitment to playing in both ends of the rink played the biggest role in the reduced point total, but also played an integral role in the Red Wings' success.

Detroit methodically eliminated Phoenix, St. Louis and Dallas, each in six games, to get a shot at the Stanley Cup for a second straight season. They faced the Washington Capitals, who had also enjoyed a fine season.

Yzerman led by example and was a powerhouse for the Red Wings. He earned an assist in Game 1, a 2–1 victory for Detroit. In Game 2, he scored twice, including a shorthanded tally, to help Detroit earn a 5–4 overtime win. From the opening faceoff of Game 3, Yzerman bulldozed through the Capitals' defense and got a great chance that Olaf Kolzig stopped, but Tomas Holmstrom banged in the rebound to give the Wings the very early lead, which held as Detroit won the third contest 2–1.

Game 4, played June 16, 1998, was a 4–1 victory for Detroit. With that win, the Red Wings won back-to-back championships. NHL commissioner Gary Bettman called Steve Yzerman to center ice and handed him the Conn Smythe Trophy. Stevie Y had led the playoffs with 24 points (6 goals and 18 assists).

Then, Bettman called the captain back to center ice and handed him the Stanley Cup. Yzerman accepted Lord Stanley's legacy, hoisted it over his head in victory, and then spun around, placing the giant trophy on the lap of Konstantinov, who had been wheeled out onto the ice to revel in the moment with his former teammates. Few will ever forget the poignant scene, one that serves as one of the most emotional moments in hockey's history.

Yzerman's competitive spirit had helped win a second Stanley Cup championship (he'd win three before his 2007 retirement)—a great achievement for him, for his teammates and for the franchise, and one dedicated to the fighting spirit of Vladimir Konstantinov and Sergei Mnatsakanov.

CHAPTER 14
Controversies and Surprises

Roger Crozier

As difficult as it may be to believe, Jean Beliveau was even better during the playoffs in 1965–66 than he was in his Conn Smythe-winning season the year before. But the trophy took a curious turn in its second year of existence.

The Canadiens finished the 1965–66 season in first place, a dominant eight points over Chicago. Toronto finished third and Detroit, in fourth place, claimed the final playoff spot, sixteen points behind the league leader.

Montreal steamrolled the Maple Leafs, eliminating the Toronto squad in four games. But the other semifinal series surprised even the most open-minded hockey fans. The Hawks had beaten the Red Wings eleven of the fourteen times they faced each other through the regular season, but by shadowing Hawks' star Bobby Hull with super-pest Bryan "Bugsy" Watson, and riding a hot netminder in Roger Crozier, Detroit upset Chicago in six games.

The final saw the Montreal Canadiens challenged by the upstart Detroit Red Wings. In Game 1, the acrobatic Crozier turned away terrific first-period chances by J.C. Tremblay and Bobby Rousseau to set the tone for the contest, which his Wings won 3–2. Game 2 ended with Detroit dumping Montreal 5–2, again spurred on by their diminutive netminder.

Bruised but undaunted, the Canadiens roared back in Games 3 and 4, both played in Detroit, in spite of Crozier turning away the Habs' attack time and time again. Game 3 resulted in a 4–2 Montreal win and Game 4, a 2–1 win for the Habs. But during the latter contest, Montreal forward Bobby Rousseau crashed into Crozier, who left the game with an injured ankle and was replaced by veteran Hank Bassen.

Crozier was a surprise starter in Game 5, returning to the crease after having work done on his twisted ankle. He appeared to be only slightly off his game, although Montreal poured on wave after wave of pressure, and the game ended with a 5–1 win for Montreal.

Game 6 concluded the 1965–66 season, but not without a momentous fight from the underdog Red Wings. Crozier again stood on his head, and at the end of sixty minutes, the teams were deadlocked in a 2–2 tie. Then, at 2:20 of overtime, Montreal's Henri Richard beat Crozier with a controversial goal that involved a collision with the netminder, and, what many Detroit fans thought was Richard's hand knocking the puck into the net.

While J.C. Tremblay and Jean Beliveau both had stand-out playoff performances, the NHL recognized valiant Roger Crozier of the Red Wings as the most valuable player in the playoffs of 1966. The Bracebridge, Ontario, native gave up just 18 goals to the powerful Canadiens in the six Stanley Cup final contests, and is credited with being the key reason the series was as close as it turned out to be.

To date, the Conn Smythe Trophy has been awarded five times to a player who was not a member of the Stanley Cup champions, and in May 1966, Roger Crozier, an NHL sophomore, became the first.

Ron Hextall

The Edmonton Oilers were in the midst of their dynasty in 1986–87, and it was going to take a Herculean effort to stop Gretzky and Company, no matter what team they faced in the Stanley Cup final. But they hadn't encountered the strength of Philadelphia's rookie goaltender, Ron Hextall.

The Oilers and the Flyers finished the regular season with the two best records in the NHL. The Oilers used their extraordinary offensive prowess to collect 106 points while the Flyers combined strong defensive play, grit and goaltending to finish with 100 points.

The Flyers' goaltending came from 22-year-old rookie Ron Hextall, a third-generation NHLer. Drafted by Philadelphia in 1982, he made his NHL debut in the 1986–87 season, playing in 66 games and posting a league-best 37 wins. He was later named to the NHL's First All-Star Team and was awarded the Vezina Trophy as the league's top netminder.

The Oilers and Flyers had met in the Stanley Cup final in 1985, with Edmonton collecting the silverware in five games. With a new netminder and a good offensive team, Philadelphia hoped to exact revenge on the Oilers, although they would have to do so without their leading scorer, the injured Tim Kerr. While Edmonton cruised into the final, the Flyers scrapped and scrambled to get past the Rangers, Islanders and Canadiens to earn their shot at Lord Stanley's Cup.

Edmonton won the opening two games at home, setting the stage for what they believed could be a relatively easy romp, but Hextall and the Flyers were having nothing to do with that. Philadelphia took Game 3 at home, but lost Game 4. The third period of that contest saw tensions boil over when Glenn Anderson of the Oilers tried to poke at a puck smothered by Hextall. The combative rookie had had enough and took a swing with his stick at the closest Oiler, who happened to be Kent Nilsson. Nilsson went down hard and the teams gathered around, pairing off, until cooler heads prevailed. Hextall was awarded a five-minute major and was later suspended for the first eight games of the following season.

With Edmonton up three games to one, the Flyers battled back, edging the Oilers in the following two games and setting up a classic seventh and deciding game.

The powerful Oilers peppered Hextall with shots, but the youngster turned back the waves of offense time and time again. While the Flyers only managed to test opposing goalie Grant Fuhr with 16 shots (and only two in the final period), Hextall stood up to 43 shots against. Although the final score was 3–1 for Edmonton, who won their third Stanley Cup championship in four years, it would be difficult to claim that any player during the playoffs in 1987 was more important to his team than Ron Hextall, and accordingly, the rookie netminder was presented with the Conn Smythe Trophy. Although fans at the Northlands Coliseum booed vociferously, Ron Hextall had earned the award over such candidates as Glenn Anderson, Grant Fuhr and Wayne Gretzky. Hextall led all goaltenders through the post-season in games played, shots faced, saves, save percentage and penalty minutes.

"Hextall is probably the best goaltender I've ever played against in the NHL," stated Wayne Gretzky during that year's playoffs. "Just when you think you'll bombard him, he comes up with the big saves."

Claude Lemieux

The dispute-shortened season, which had included just 48 regular season games, had seen the New Jersey Devils struggle to a record of 22 wins, 18 losses and 8 ties. Claude Lemieux, their feisty winger, had previously won the Stanley Cup with Montreal in 1986, and had endured a regular season in which he scored but six goals and 19 points. But Lemieux inexplicably went on a tear in the playoffs, astonishing even his own coach and teammates by scoring a playoff-best 13 goals, four more than second-place Vyacheslav Kozlov of the Red Wings.

With three assists, Lemieux finished with 16 points. But that was only the eighth best in the 1994–95 playoffs. Sergei Fedorov of Detroit was the scoring leader with 24 points. On the Devils team alone, Lemieux was eclipsed by Stephane Richer (21 points), Neal Broten (19 points, including a team-best of six in the final) and John MacLean (18 points).

Detractors would cite that while Lemieux was valuable, he wasn't the most valuable player of the playoffs. Goalie Martin Brodeur had been sensational in leading New Jersey to hockey's Promised Land. In the final, he had allowed just seven goals through the four game series. Scott Niedermayer had been strong from the blue line, and had contributed offensively. Both Broten and Richer enjoyed an excellent post-season, but when it comes to selecting a single recipient, it is hard to argue with Clause Lemieux's dominating goal-scoring run in the playoffs.

Joe Nieuwendyk

There are six great reasons why Joe Nieuwendyk was awarded the Conn Smythe Trophy in 1999—Joe scored a record-setting six of the Dallas Stars sixteen game-winning goals that spring, as his team went on to win the franchise's first Stanley Cup championship.

That, in itself, is a deciding factor when selecting a Conn Smythe Trophy winner. But well-argued cases can be made for Joe's Dallas teammate, Mike Modano, and for Buffalo's goaltender, Dominik Hasek.

Modano led the Cup-winning Stars with 23 points through the playoffs. He was used in offensive situations, but was also a key component of the penalty kill for Dallas. Nieuwendyk was also highly productive, collecting 21 points, 11 of which were goals. His faceoff prowess was sparkling.

Pundits argue that while Nieuwendyk was crucial to the Stars earlier in the post-season facing inferior opponents, it was Modano who was integral to the Cup win because of his efforts in the final against Buffalo. Nieuwendyk collected three points in the final—two goals and an assist. Both goals were scored in Game 3's 2–1 win over Buffalo. Conversely, Modano earned a team-best seven points (all assists) in the final, all garnered while playing with an injured wrist.

Mike Modano averaged 24:39 of ice-time through the playoffs, while Nieuwendyk was on the ice for an average of 18:15 per game. Much of the difference in playing time results from the extensive use of Modano in penalty killing situations.

But then, there is the suggestion that Dominik Hasek could have won the Smythe, too. The Buffalo goaltender was sensational in taking his team to the Stanley Cup final for just the second time in franchise history. On the back of their goalie, who won the Vezina Trophy that season and was named to the NHL's First All-Star Team, the Sabres defeated Ottawa (four games), Boston (six games) and Toronto (five games) with relative ease on the path to the Stanley Cup.

Each game of the final was exceptionally close. Buffalo edged Dallas 3–2 in overtime in Game 1. Dallas doubled Buffalo 4–2 in Game 2. Game 3 was a 2–1 Dallas win and Game 4, a 2–1 Buffalo win. Dallas shut out the Sabres 2–0 in Game 5 and it took Brett Hull's controversial goal at 54:51 of triple overtime for the Stars to win the contest 2–1 (and the Cup) in Game 6.

Dominik Hasek was Buffalo's most valuable player through the 1998–99 playoffs (include the regular season, too), but it was Joe Nieuwendyk who had his name engraved on the Conn Smythe Trophy that year. "I went ten years without even getting past the first round, which was just brutal," recalled Nieuwendyk. "To build that franchise up from nothing in the late nineties was just an incredible experience."

Jean-Sebastien Giguere

The Mighty Ducks of Anaheim finished the 2002–03 season with 95 points in the Pacific Division, eleventh best in the league. By contrast, the New Jersey Devils collected 108 points, finishing first in the Atlantic Division and fourth-best overall.

The Western Conference delivered surprise after surprise, but none were quite as astonishing as the Mighty Ducks elimination of the perennially strong Detroit Red Wings in the opening series. The Ducks got hot at just the right time and rode the sensational goaltending of Jean-Sebastien Giguere. In his first-ever NHL playoff game, J-S stole the victory from under the noses of the astonished Wings, stopping 63 of 64 shots in a thrilling 2–1 triple-overtime win. It was no fluke. The Ducks swept the Wings in four straight games, each won by a single goal.

While Anaheim went on to beat the Dallas Stars in six games (with Giguere earning one shutout), J-S was simply extraordinary against the upstart Minnesota Wild. He collected three consecutive shutouts and stopped 122 of 123 shots he faced to earn a robust save percentage of .992, and led his Ducks to the Stanley Cup final.

Meanwhile, New Jersey rolled over the Boston Bruins, Tampa Bay Lightning and the Ottawa Senators, setting the stage for an unlikely, but very exciting series.

New Jersey dominated, winning the first two games by identical 3–0 scores at Continental Airlines Arena in New Jersey. But Anaheim had no intention of giving up, and battled hard back at home to take Game 3 with a 3–2 overtime win. In Game 4, Anaheim's Giguere and New Jersey's Martin Brodeur both shut out the opposition through overtime, but a Steve Thomas tally just 39 seconds into the extra frame gave the Ducks a 1–0 victory.

The teams (and scores) opened up in Games 5 and 6. The Devils took the former by a 6–3 margin, while the Mighty Ducks took the latter by a 5–2 count.

No one could have predicted that the upstart Ducks would be participating in a Game 7 in the Stanley Cup final, but there they were, ready to face the Devils in a winner-take-all scenario. The game ended with New Jersey topping Anaheim, 3–0, and Commissioner Gary Bettman presented the Stanley Cup to Devils captain Scott Stevens. But just prior to that was the announcement of the winner of the Conn Smythe Trophy. The New Jersey crowd gasped when it was announced that Jean-Sebastien Giguere had been selected as the playoff's most valuable player.

How could the voters have selected Giguere when his New Jersey counterpart, Martin Brodeur, had won the requisite sixteen games, a record seven by shutout and three in the final alone? Or, there was a case for Scott Niedermayer, who tied teammate Jamie Langenbrunner as the playoff scoring leader with 18 points. Scott Stevens was also a rock on defense for New Jersey. But while the Devils got the trophy they wanted, Giguere was a more than appropriate winner, carrying his team through the post-season to their first appearance in a Stanley Cup final. The New Jersey fans booed the selection, but hockey experts concur that the Devils votes may simply have been distributed among several contenders who excelled through the playoffs. Nevertheless, Jean-Sebastien Giguere became just the fifth recipient of the Conn Smythe Trophy to be selected from a team other than the Stanley Cup champions.

Cam Ward hoists the Cup as a rookie in 2006.

Cam Ward

Great surprises always seem to emerge from first round match-ups. After finishing the 2005–06 season one point behind the first-place Ottawa Senators in the Eastern Division, the Carolina Hurricanes found themselves facing the Montreal Canadiens in the opening series. But they had no idea that they would have to proceed through the post-season with a rookie netminder. Veteran Martin Gerber started, but was battling a stomach ailment. Carolina lost Game 1 at home by a decisive 6–1 score.

Montreal tallied three quick goals in Game 2, and Canes coach Peter Laviolette was forced to make a pivotal decision: he pulled Gerber and inserted Cam Ward, the 22-year-old rookie who had a total of 28 games of NHL experience. It was a gamble that paid huge dividends for the Hurricanes. Carolina rebounded in that second game and at the end of sixty minutes, they found themselves tied 5–5. It took a goal in the second overtime for Montreal to earn the win.

Laviolette stuck with Ward as the series shifted to Montreal for Game 3. Carolina eked out a 2–1 overtime win, and then edged their hosts 3–2 in Game 4. Ward continued to come up big as Carolina returned home and beat Montreal 2–1. Then, they won their fourth straight game, a 2–1 overtime squeaker, to eliminate Montreal.

Cam Ward astonished the hockey world. Playing with poise and confidence, he displayed his ability to battle, helping Carolina take a 3–0 series lead over the New Jersey Devils in the Eastern Conference semifinal, earning a shutout in Game 1 of the series. He faltered in Game 4, allowing four unanswered goals, but showed good bounce-back abilities, helping the Hurricanes to a 4–1 victory in Game 5 to claim the series.

The Eastern Conference final was a showdown between the Hurricanes and the Buffalo Sabres. The teams traded wins in Games 1 and 2, and in Game 3 Ward was again pulled and replaced by Martin Gerber. Although Gerber didn't allow a goal, the Canes lost 4–3.

The Hurricanes started Gerber in goal for Game 4, and the veteran backstopper responded with a 4–0 shutout. He played poorly in Game 5, and after surrendering a third goal early in the second period, Ward was again summoned to the net for the Hurricanes. He held the fort and helped carry the game to overtime. A goal by Cory Stillman won Game 5 for the Hurricanes.

The series went seven games, with Carolina earning their second trip to the Stanley Cup final in four seasons.

It was a battle royal between the Carolina Hurricanes and the Edmonton Oilers for the Stanley Cup that needed seven games to decide a winner. The seesaw battle concluded with Cam Ward and the "Cardiac 'Canes" dominating the final contest, 3–1.

There was no clear-cut recipient for the Conn Smythe Trophy. Eric Staal had enjoyed a superb playoff, leading all playoff scorers with 28 points in 25 games (9 goals and 19 assists) including a fifteen-game point streak. Rod Brind'Amour, Carolina's captain, had been a forceful leader, collecting a team-best 12 goals to go along with his rugged play and faceoff wizadry. Cory Stillman also played well, scoring 9 goals and 17 assists to finish second to teammate Staal in the playoff scoring race.

But Cam Ward stood above them all. His numbers were solid—a 2.14 goals-against average and a .920 save percentage with two shutouts—but it was his coolness as a rookie in the highly stressful situation of an NHL playoff series that swayed the voters, in spite of having been pulled in favor of Martin Gerber on two occasions.

"I truly feel that you could have given it to anybody on this hockey team," suggested Ward, who was just the fourth rookie to collect the Smythe, following Ken Dryden, Patrick Roy and Ron Hextall, all goaltenders. "But to tell you the truth, the Cup is the trophy that matters the most."

CHAPTER 15
Conn Smythe Trophy Winners

1964—65
Jean Beliveau
MONTREAL CANADIENS

The Montreal Canadiens, led by their captain, Jean Beliveau, finished the regular season in second place in 1964–65. They defeated the Maple Leafs in six games in the semifinal and moved on to face the Chicago Black Hawks for the Stanley Cup. The two teams faced off in a battle that went the distance, with Beliveau scoring the Stanley Cup-winning goal at the fourteen-second mark of the first period in Game 7 on the way to a 4–0 win for the Canadiens. Jean Beliveau, the inaugural winner of the award, had scored 8 goals, 8 assists and 16 points through thirteen playoff games. In the Chicago series alone, Jean scored 5 goals and 10 points.

1965—66
Roger Crozier
DETROIT RED WINGS

The Montreal Canadiens finished first in the regular season and had eliminated Toronto with a four-game sweep in the first round of the playoffs. The Detroit Red Wings, meanwhile, defeated the powerful Chicago Black Hawks in six games, setting up a confrontation that no one gave Detroit much of a chance of winning. However, they underestimated sophomore goaltender Roger Crozier, who had led the NHL with seven shutouts during the regular season. Detroit took Games 1 and 2, but the Canadiens roared back and won Games 3, 4 and 5. Game 6 went into overtime, and just past the two-minute mark, Henri Richard scored on a breakaway, giving the Canadiens the Stanley Cup. However, the Conn Smythe was awarded to Crozier for his stellar play, making him the first recipient not to be on the winning side.

1964–65 **JEAN BELIVEAU**

1965–66 **ROGER CROZIER**

1966–67
David Keon
TORONTO MAPLE LEAFS

Dave Keon's modest scoring contributions during the 1967 playoffs (3 goals and 5 assists) were overshadowed by the all-around play that made him the recipient of the Conn Smythe Trophy that spring. Keon, diligent in both ends of the rink and a force to be reckoned with no matter which role he was playing, led the third-place Maple Leafs past the first-place Chicago Black Hawks in a stunning opening round upset. Then, in a fitting tribute to Canada's 100-year birthday, Toronto faced Montreal for the Stanley Cup. Again, Keon skated miles in suppressing the Canadiens attack, and in six games, his Leafs were handed the Stanley Cup.

1967–68
Glenn Hall
ST. LOUIS BLUES

A six-team league since 1942, the NHL doubled in size in the 1967–68 season. The new expansion teams formed a Western Conference, while the original six NHL teams remained together in the Eastern Conference. Montreal finished first in the east, beat Boston and Chicago and earned a spot in the Stanley Cup final. In the west, the St. Louis Blues first defeated the Philadelphia Flyers and then the Minnesota North Stars to earn the right to face the Canadiens for the Stanley Cup. While the series was a mismatch, veteran goaltender Glenn Hall, who had spent most of his career with the Chicago Black Hawks, made the final exciting. The Montreal Canadiens swept the Blues, but each of the four games ended with a one goal differential, two of which ended in over-time. For his heroics, Glenn Hall was awarded the Conn Smythe Trophy, although in a losing cause.

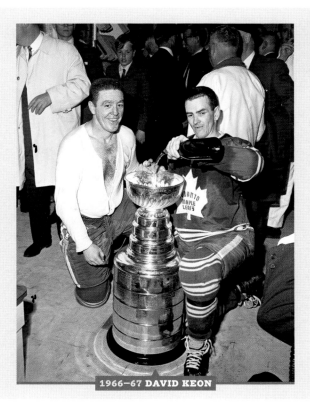

1966–67 **DAVID KEON**

1968–69
Serge Savard
MONTREAL CANADIENS

In the 1969 playoffs, the St. Louis Blues in the west first defeated the Philadelphia Flyers and then the Los Angeles Kings. Meanwhile, in the east, the Montreal Canadiens were eliminating the New York Rangers and dumping the Boston Bruins, to set up a Stanley Cup rematch between the previous spring's participants. For the second year in a row, however, the Canadiens swept the Blues to win the Cup. In only his second NHL season, Serge Savard had become a dominant team player, and in the playoffs, he was outstanding, blocking shots and clearing the zone, while collecting points. His four goals in the playoffs were one shy of an NHL record by a defenseman in a single season and helped earn Savard the Conn Smythe Trophy.

Pre-Trophy Winners

While the Conn Smythe Trophy was introduced in 1965, the Society for International Hockey Research (SIHR) delved into earlier playoffs and provided their collective opinion on who might have won the trophy had it been introduced at the inception of the National Hockey League. The list was created in 2001 by a five-person committee of hockey historians, who researched newspaper accounts for every playoff season going back to the NHL's inception in 1917. The committee studied every aspect of the playoffs—not only scoring points and goaltending statistics, but the comments of coaches and writers covering the games—to ascertain the relative importance of players during the post-season.

1918
Alf Skinner
TORONTO ARENAS
Alf Skinner led the playoffs with eight goals and ten points for Toronto, the NHL champions, in the best-of-five series against the PCHL's Vancouver Millionaires. He scored a hat trick in Game 2, a 6–4 loss.

1919
The NHL playoffs were cancelled due to the influenza pandemic.

1920
Jack Darragh
OTTAWA SENATORS
Jack Darragh scored the game-winning goals in all three of Ottawa's wins over the Seattle Metropolitans of the PCHL. On April 1, 1920, Darragh tallied three times in the 6–1 game that earned the Stanley Cup for Ottawa.

1921
Jack Darragh
OTTAWA SENATORS
The Senators faced the Vancouver Millionaires for the Stanley Cup in 1921. In order to get permission for Jack Darragh to play in the series, Ottawa mayor Frank Plant had to seek approval from the Ottawa Dairy Company to get the required time off for the Senators veteran star. Once granted, Darragh starred throughout the best-of-five series, scoring in each of the three Ottawa victories. Jack finished the series with five goals, including the tying and winning goals in the deciding contest.

1922
Cecil Dye
TORONTO ST. PATS
Cecil "Babe" Dye set a record by scoring nine goals

1967–68 GLENN HALL

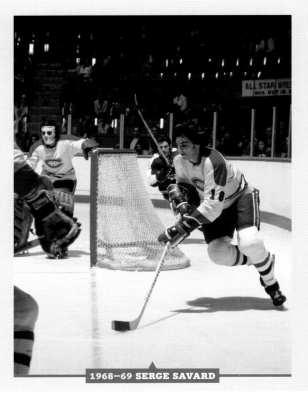

1968–69 SERGE SAVARD

1969–70
Bobby Orr
BOSTON BRUINS

In the spring of 1970, after a decade of futility, the Boston Bruins reached the Stanley Cup final for the first time since 1958. They did so by defeating the New York Rangers and then the Chicago Black Hawks. Their competition, the St. Louis Blues, pushed aside the Minnesota North Stars and Pittsburgh Penguins to earn a third consecutive shot at winning the Stanley Cup. For a third straight season, the Blues were denied in four straight games, with the Bruins outscoring St. Louis 20–7 in the final. Bobby Orr scored 9 goals and 11 assists throughout the playoffs, including a goal and 4 assists in the final. That goal, the Stanley Cup winner, is forever remembered as one of the greatest goals in NHL history.

1970–71
Ken Dryden
MONTREAL CANADIENS

The Montreal Canadiens had used Rogatien Vachon throughout most of the season, but playing a hunch toward the end of the season, coach Al MacNeil summoned young Ken Dryden from the American Hockey League. Then, unexpectedly, MacNeil called on Dryden, who had played just six NHL games, to start the playoffs against the Boston Bruins. Montreal astonished everyone, including the high-flying Bruins (who had earned 121 points during the regular season) by eliminating them in seven games. The Canadiens then beat the Minnesota North Stars to earn a berth in the final against the Chicago Black Hawks, which Montreal won, four games to three. Dryden backstopped Montreal to that Stanley Cup championship and was awarded the Conn Smythe Trophy for his jaw-dropping exploits.

1969–70 · 1971–72 BOBBY ORR

1971–72
Bobby Orr
BOSTON BRUINS

Boston was again the NHL's elite squad during the regular season, finishing first overall with 119 points. Orr led the post-season in scoring with 5 goals and 19 assists as the Boston Bruins eliminated the Toronto Maple Leafs and then demolished the St. Louis Blues, outscoring them 28–8. The final pitted Orr's Bruins against long-time rivals, the New York Rangers. It took six games, but Boston emerged victorious, with Orr scoring the Stanley Cup-winning goal. Bobby Orr accepted the Conn Smythe Trophy for the second time, the first player to enjoy multiple wins of the playoff MVP award.

in the best-of-five championship series between Toronto and the Vancouver Millionaires. In Game 2, he was awarded a penalty shot—the first-ever—but was unsuccessful, although he did score that game's winner in overtime. Dye was anything but unsuccessful as the series progressed. In Game 5, he single-handedly won Toronto the Stanley Cup, scoring four goals, including the winner, in a 5–1 victory.

1923
Punch Broadbent
OTTAWA SENATORS

The NHL champions, the Ottawa Senators, first defeated the Vancouver Maroons of the PCHL to earn the right to face the WCHL champions, the Edmonton Eskimos, for the Stanley Cup. Punch Broadbent led all playoff scorers with six goals, including the Stanley Cup winner, to earn MVP honors.

1924
Howie Morenz
MONTREAL CANADIENS

The Montreal Canadiens, NHL victors, first defeated the PCHL's Vancouver Maroons before facing the Calgary Tigers, champions of the WCHL. It took just four games for Montreal to win both best-of-three series, with Howie Morenz scoring four times. Morenz

was at his exciting best, dominating with end-to-end rushes, and scoring the Stanley Cup-winning goal against Calgary.

1925
Jack Walker
VICTORIA COUGARS

Jack Walker had goals in six consecutive playoff games, and was the Victoria Cougars scoring leader in the final. In the best-of-five series against the defending Stanley Cup champions, the Montreal Canadiens, he tallied four times, including the game-winning goal in Game 1 and two goals in Game 2. In addition to scoring, Walker contributed defensively, utilizing an effective sweep check to minimize Montreal's scoring chances.

1926
Nels Stewart
MONTREAL MAROONS

While there could have been a substantial argument for choosing Maroons netminder Clint Benedict as the series MVP—he earned shutouts in each of the three victories in Montreal's best-of-five win over the Victoria Cougars in the Stanley Cup final—Nels Stewart was the choice to earn the honor. Scoring six of Montreal's ten goals, he led the Montreal Maroons to the Stanley Cup in the last series to feature a non-NHL team.

1970–71 KEN DRYDEN

1972–73 YVAN COURNOYER

1972–73
Yvan Cournoyer
MONTREAL CANADIENS

The Montreal Canadiens dominated the NHL's regular season, finishing with 120 points, thirteen more than second-place Boston. In the playoffs, the Canadiens first bumped Buffalo and Philadelphia out of their way, before meeting the Chicago Black Hawks in the final. The two teams battled in an exciting series that saw the Canadiens win the Stanley Cup in six games. Yvan "The Roadrunner" Cournoyer, after a superb regular season (40 goals and 39 assists), went into hyper-drive in the playoffs. He was the post-season's leading scorer, registering 25 points, including a record 15 goals, one of which was the Stanley Cup winner.

1973–74
Bernie Parent
PHILADELPHIA FLYERS

The Philadelphia Flyers topped the West Division with 112 regular season points. The Boston Bruins finished first in the east with 113 points. When the teams faced each other for Stanley Cup supremacy, there was no doubt that it was going to make for a sensational series. The Flyers had ridden Bernie Parent's exceptional goaltending throughout the playoffs and in the final, Parent continued his superb play. He kept Boston to a total of three goals in Games 3 and 4, and then in Game 6, the single goal by the Flyers and Bernie Parent's shutout gave Philadelphia the Stanley Cup. Parent won the MVP award, and Philly was the first expansion squad to be NHL champions.

1973–74 · 1974–75 **BERNIE PARENT**

1974–75
Bernie Parent
PHILADELPHIA FLYERS

The "Broad Street Bullies," having tasted Stanley Cup champagne in 1974, were determined to repeat their success in 1975. Bernie Parent earned the Vezina Trophy for the best goals-against average, and in the playoffs, Parent stepped up his game even further. The Philadelphia Flyers defeated the Toronto Maple Leafs and the New York Islanders to reach the Stanley Cup final against the Buffalo Sabres. The Flyers were triumphant in six games, and Parent finished the post-season with a remarkable goals-against average of 1.89 including four shutouts. For a second consecutive spring, Bernie Parent was awarded the Conn Smythe Trophy, the first recipient to win it in consecutive seasons.

PRE-TROPHY WINNERS

1927
Alex Connell
OTTAWA SENATORS

The 1927 Stanley Cup final between the Ottawa Senators and the Boston Bruins was intended to be a best-of-three series. However, as the series played out, it took four games for the Senators to beat the Bruins—by winning two games and tying the other two—and claim the Cup. Ottawa goalie Alex Connell earned a shutout in Game 1 and surrendered just three goals in the four games.

1928
Frank Boucher
NEW YORK RANGERS

Frank Boucher led the playoffs in scoring with ten points, including a playoff-best four goals in the final. Boucher scored the winning goals for the Rangers in Games 2, 4 and 5 of the best-of-five series against the Montreal Maroons to lead the Rangers to their first Stanley Cup championship.

1929
Tiny Thompson
BOSTON BRUINS

The Stanley Cup final in 1929 was a best-of-three affair, and featured two American teams (the Boston Bruins and New York Rangers) for the first time in NHL history. Tiny Thompson replaced the retired Hal Winkler in the Boston goal, and allowed just three goals in the playoffs, including just one in the Stanley Cup final.

1930
George Hainsworth
MONTREAL CANADIENS

For the second straight year, a netminder was chosen as the most valuable player of the playoffs. George Hainsworth of the Canadiens allowed just six goals in six games and collected three shutouts to lead Montreal to the Stanley Cup over Boston.

1931
Johnny Gagnon
MONTREAL CANADIENS

The Montreal Canadiens won the Stanley Cup for the second straight year, and much of the credit must be attributed to Johnny "Black Cat" Gagnon. Playing on a line with Aurel Joliat and Howie Morenz, the rookie scored six playoff goals, including the Cup winner, to lead all NHL scorers.

1932
Charlie Conacher
TORONTO MAPLE LEAFS

Playing in the newly-built Maple Leaf Gardens, the Toronto Maple Leafs collected their first Stanley Cup championship in 1932, sweeping the New York Rangers in the best-of-five

1975–76 REGGIE LEACH

1976–77 GUY LAFLEUR

1975–76
Reggie Leach
PHILADELPHIA FLYERS

The Montreal Canadiens dominated the regular season with a record-setting 127-point campaign, but a determined Philadelphia Flyers squad finished second overall with 118 points. Montreal defeated Chicago and the New York Islanders to reach the Stanley Cup final, while the Flyers beat Toronto and Boston for the opportunity to go for a third straight Stanley Cup. Although the Canadiens swept Philadelphia in the series, the talk of the post-season was Reggie Leach of the Flyers. Clearly the most valuable player that spring, Leach led the playoffs with 24 points and scored an NHL-best 19 goals in 16 games (five of those markers came in Game 5 of the semifinal against the Bruins).

1976–77
Guy Lafleur
MONTREAL CANADIENS

The Canadiens enjoyed an extraordinary 1976–77 season, winning 60 games, tying 12 and losing only 8, establishing the record for fewest losses in a season. The momentum carried into the post-season, too. Montreal swept St. Louis and defeated the Islanders in six games, to reach the Stanley Cup final for the second straight spring. Facing the Bostons Bruins, the Canadiens easily defeated their opponents in four games to lay claim to their second consecutive Stanley Cup championship. Guy Lafleur, who had a league-leading 136 points in the regular season, also led in the playoffs with 26 points (9 goals and 17 assists). He was the fifth Hab to win the Conn Smythe Trophy.

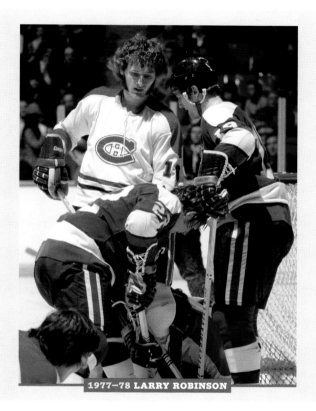

1977–78 LARRY ROBINSON

1977–78
Larry Robinson
MONTREAL CANADIENS

The Montreal Canadiens powered through the 1977–78 season, completing the season with 129 points, 16 more than second-place Boston. The two teams met in the Stanley Cup final, Montreal having dusted Detroit and triumphed over Toronto in the process, to earn a shot at a third straight Stanley Cup championship. Guy Lafleur had led the regular season in scoring, but defenseman Larry Robinson was the surprising scoring star of the post-season. He scored 2 goals and 4 assists in the final against Boston, helping the Canadiens to Stanley Cup victory in six. Robinson tied teammate Guy Lafleur with 21 playoff points, including a playoff-best 17 assists, and for his gargantuan efforts both offensively and defensively, was named the Conn Smythe winner.

series. "The Big Bomber," Charlie Conacher, earned the nod as the best player in the playoffs. Conacher tied Bun Cook of the Rangers with six playoff goals and finished second (one behind New York's Frank Boucher) for most post-season points.

1933
Cecil Dillon
NEW YORK RANGERS

The Rangers and Maple Leafs met in the Stanley Cup final for a second straight year in 1933, but this time the Rangers emerged as the victors. Taking the best-of-five in four games, Cecil Dillon led all playoff scorers with eight goals and ten points, including three goals and an assist in the final.

1934
Lionel Conacher
CHICAGO BLACK HAWKS

Lionel "The Big Train" Conacher was chosen as the most valuable player in the 1934 playoffs. In his first season with the Black Hawks, Conacher was a First All-Star Team selection and was runner-up for the Hart Trophy. During the playoffs, the big defenseman helped guide Chicago past both the Montreal Canadiens and Montreal Maroons, and then Detroit, dumping them three games to one in the best-of-five final. He blocked shots, led

rushes and scored a pair of goals to earn the MVP distinction.

1935
Lawrence Northcott
MONTREAL MAROONS

The Montreal Maroons met the Toronto Maple Leafs in the Stanley Cup final of 1935, and swept the series to emerge victorious. Lawrence "Baldy" Northcott led all playoff performers by scoring four goals, two of which were tallied in the final. Three of his four goals were game winners, including the Stanley Cup-winning goal.

1936
Normie Smith
DETROIT RED WINGS

To reach the final, Detroit had to eliminate the Montreal Maroons, and did so, including a monstrous opening game that took 116:30 of overtime to decide a winner—the Wings—in a record-breaking 1–0 conclusion. Netminder Normie Smith recorded a shutout in his next game, too, and was a solid backstop as Detroit defeated Toronto three games to one in the best-of-five series.

1978–79 **BOB GAINEY**

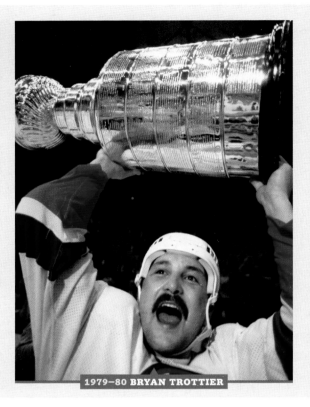

1979–80 **BRYAN TROTTIER**

1978–79
Bob Gainey
MONTREAL CANADIENS

The powerful Montreal Canadiens won the Norris Division for the fifth time, collecting 115 points in the process. The Habs swept Toronto in the first round, but Boston proved to be a more challenging opponent. The Canadiens finally edged the Bruins in seven games to claim a spot in the final against the New York Rangers. The Rangers won Game 1, but Montreal then took four straight to win the Stanley Cup for the fourth consecutive season. Bob Gainey was superb throughout the post-season, both offensively and defensively. He finished the playoffs with 16 points in sixteen games, including 3 goals and 2 assists in the five-game final, and was rewarded with the Conn Smythe Trophy for his efforts.

1979–80
Bryan Trottier
NEW YORK ISLANDERS

The Philadelphia Flyers, who had finished first in the Patrick Division, beat Edmonton, the New York Rangers and Minnesota to stake claim to a spot in the Stanley Cup final. After finishing second to Philadelphia in the Patrick during the regular season, the New York Islanders dumped Los Angeles, Boston and Buffalo to earn their chance at Stanley Cup glory. It took six games, but when Bob Nystrom's overtime shot entered the net at 7:11, it gave the New York Islanders their first franchise Stanley Cup championship. Bryan Trottier was awarded the Conn Smythe Trophy after leading the playoffs in scoring with 29 points, including 12 goals and 17 assists.

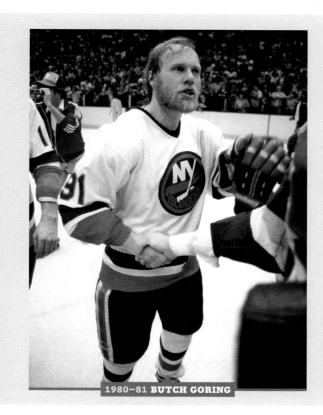

1980–81 **BUTCH GORING**

1980–81
Butch Goring
NEW YORK ISLANDERS

The powerful New York Islanders were ready to defend their 1980 Stanley Cup championship, proving it by finishing first overall in the regular season. The Long Island squad eliminated the Toronto Maple Leafs, Edmonton Oilers and the New York Rangers to face the Minnesota North Stars in the final. The Islanders scored 26 goals, taking the Cup in five games. Butch Goring, who had been acquired by the Islanders in 1980, and had helped his new team to its first Stanley Cup championship, was named the Conn Smythe Trophy winner. Goring had played an inspired two-way game, finishing the post-season with 10 goals and 20 points, with two of his tallies standing up as game winners.

PRE-TROPHY WINNERS

1937
Marty Barry
DETROIT RED WINGS

For a second consecutive spring, the Red Wings skated away with the Stanley Cup, this time edging the New York Rangers three games to two in the best-of-five series. While Detroit's principal goalie, rookie Earl Robertson, collected back-to-back shutouts in Games 4 and 5 of the final, it was Marty Barry who earned selection as the playoff MVP, leading all post-season scorers with 11 points. He scored three goals in the final, including the game winners in Game 4 and Game 5.

1938
Gordie Drillon
TORONTO MAPLE LEAFS

The 1938 Chicago Black Hawks can boast the worst regular season record for a Stanley Cup-winning squad. After winning 14, losing 25 and tying 9, the Hawks beat the Canadiens and the New York Americans to earn a berth in the final against Toronto. Gordie Drillon scored the winning goals in Games 2 and 3 of the semifinal versus the Bruins. Drillon led the playoffs in scoring (eight points in eight games) and scored half of the Leafs' 14 playoff goals. While the underdog Hawks won the Stanley Cup, honors

for most valuable playoff performer go to Gordie Drillon of Toronto.

1939
Bill Cowley
BOSTON BRUINS

For the first time, the NHL adopted a best-of-seven format for post-season play. Mel "Sudden Death" Hill earned his nickname, scoring the overtime winner for Boston in three games to get past the New York Rangers in the semifinal. The Bruins then went on to defeat Toronto in five games to capture the Stanley Cup. Bill Cowley's consistency earned him the most valuable player designation. He collected seven points in the semifinal and another seven in the final.

1940
Phil Watson
NEW YORK RANGERS

The New York Rangers knocked the defending Stanley Cup champions, the Boston Bruins, out of contention in the semifinal, in large part because the line of Phil Watson, Dutch Hiller and Bryan Hextall was able to hold the Bruins' explosive Kraut Line to a single goal. The line then faced Toronto's first line of Syl Apps, Bob Davidson and Gordie Drillon in the Stanley Cup final and kept them off the score sheet. Watson

1981–82 MIKE BOSSY

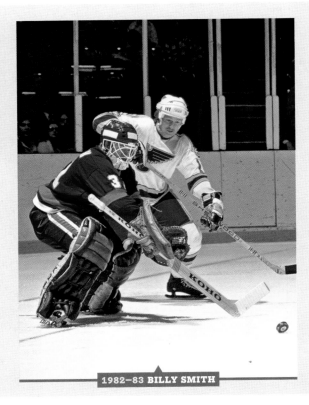

1982–83 BILLY SMITH

1981–82
Mike Bossy
NEW YORK ISLANDERS

The New York Islanders finished the regular season in first place yet again, and fans wondered if there was any way to stop the high-flying squad. The Pittsburgh Penguins couldn't in the first round of the playoffs and the New York Rangers couldn't, in spite of a tough six-game series. The Quebec Nordiques were then swept in four, leading to a showdown between the Islanders and Vancouver Canucks in the final. New York's Mike Bossy dominated, helping the Islanders win a third consecutive Stanley Cup championship. Bossy scored 7 goals in the final, a record for a four-game series. Throughout the playoffs, he fired 17 goals and 10 assists for 27 points, earning the MVP award as the most valuable performer in the playoffs.

1982–83
Billy Smith
NEW YORK ISLANDERS

After finishing first overall in 1980–81 and 1981–82, the New York Islanders slipped to sixth overall in 1982–83. Nevertheless, the Long Island crew knew what it took to win and had the tools to do it. They beat the Washington Capitals, the New York Rangers and the Boston Bruins for a chance to once again capture the Stanley Cup. Although the Islanders did collect the Cup after defeating the Edmonton Oilers in four straight games, it was a heated and bitter series. Conn Smythe Trophy winner Billy Smith, aggressively protecting his crease, kept Edmonton scoreless in seven of the twelve periods of the final, including a shutout in Game 1. The Islanders held the Oilers to just six goals, giving Billy Smith a sensational 1.50 goals-against average.

1983–84 **MARK MESSIER**

1983–84
Mark Messier
EDMONTON OILERS

After being soundly defeated by the New York Islanders the previous year in the Stanley Cup final, the Edmonton Oilers refused to be denied in 1984. The Oilers finished the season in first place, and were ready for the playoffs with their high octane offense. Their path took them past Winnipeg, Calgary and Minnesota, setting up a showdown again with the Islanders. The teams traded wins in the first two games and the Islanders were leading 2–1 in Game 3 when Mark Messier grabbed the puck and made an end-to-end dash to score and tie the game, igniting the team to a 7–2 win. Messier snarled, growled, battled, won faceoffs and scored to lead his Oilers to their first Stanley Cup, one they achieved in five games. While Wayne Gretzky led the playoffs in scoring, it was Mark Messier who earned the Conn Smythe Trophy.

tied for the playoff scoring title. He had a goal and four assists in the final, with three of those assists coming in a 6–2 win in Game 2.

1941
Milt Schmidt
BOSTON BRUINS

The Bruins were dealt a serious blow when NHL scoring leader Bill Cowley injured a knee in the first playoff game and was out for the duration of the post-season. But others stepped into the breach to assist the Bruins cause. Milt Schmidt was one, leading all playoff scorers with 11 points, including three goals and four assists in the four-game sweep of the Detroit Red Wings in the final.

1942
Syl Apps
TORONTO MAPLE LEAFS

The Toronto Maple Leafs eliminated the New York Rangers to earn the opportunity to face the Detroit Red Wings in the Stanley Cup final. The entire Toronto team, including its captain, was quiet in the first three games, all won by Detroit, but then Toronto erupted. In Game 4, Syl Apps scored a goal and an assist on the way to a pivotal 4–3 win. Then, in Game 5, Apps scored twice and added three assists to lead his Leafs to a 9–3

victory. The Maple Leafs rebounded from the brink of elimination to win four straight games, and in doing so, won the Stanley Cup in a most suspenseful fashion. Apps tied for the playoff point lead with 14, including an NHL-record 9 assists.

1943
Jack Stewart
DETROIT RED WINGS

The Detroit Red Wings returned to the Stanley Cup final in 1943, beating the Maple Leafs in order to face Boston for the championship. The selection of playoff MVP went to "Black Jack" Stewart, a stalwart on defense, who played more than forty minutes per game and held the Bruins to just five goals in four games. The veteran defenseman added a goal and an assist, his only points in the final, in Game 1 against Boston.

1944
Toe Blake
MONTREAL CANADIENS

Toe Blake was on fire in 1943–44. He won the scoring race during the regular season and followed that by finishing as the playoff scoring leader, collecting an NHL-record 18 points. Montreal first brushed aside the Toronto Maple Leafs in five games, with Blake picking up five assists (Maurice Richard scored all five

1984–85 · 1987–88 **WAYNE GRETZKY**

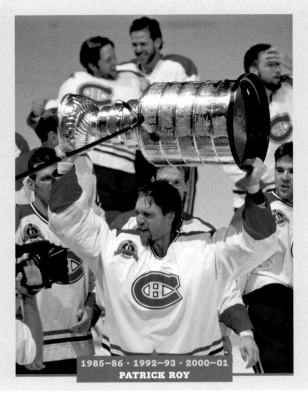

1985–86 · 1992–93 · 2000–01
PATRICK ROY

1984–85
Wayne Gretzky
EDMONTON OILERS

The Oilers, led by superstar Wayne Gretzky, were at their powerful best in the early 1980s. In 1984–85, Gretzky led the NHL in scoring for an astonishing sixth time. Meanwhile, Edmonton enjoyed a fourth straight first-place finish in the Smythe Division. The Oilers dusted L.A. in three straight games (best of five) and then polished off Winnipeg in four and Chicago in six. That victory set up the series final between Edmonton and the Philadelphia Flyers, who had finished first overall during the regular season. The Flyers won Game 1, but Edmonton took the next four to claim the Stanley Cup for a second consecutive season. Gretzky scored an eye-popping 47 points in eighteen games to establish an NHL playoff record. Seven of his 17 goals were scored in the final against the Flyers.

1985–86
Patrick Roy
MONTREAL CANADIENS

All eyes were on the Edmonton Oilers after they finished first overall in the regular season, but a shocking loss to the Calgary Flames extinguished Edmonton's dreams of a third Stanley Cup win. The Montreal Canadiens, meanwhile, went into the playoffs with Patrick Roy in goal and—shades of Ken Dryden in 1971—the rookie was outstanding, as the Canadiens were victorious over the Boston Bruins, Hartford Whalers and the New York Rangers. The Canadiens then met the Calgary Flames for the 1986 Stanley Cup, the first all-Canadian final since Montreal and Toronto had met in 1967. The Flames won the opening contest, but the Canadiens took the next four to claim hockey's greatest prize. Patrick Roy, the rookie goaltender, made all the difference in the post-season, posting a playoff goals-against average of 1.92.

1986–87 **RON HEXTALL**

1986–87
Ron Hextall
PHILADELPHIA FLYERS

The 1987 Stanley Cup final pitted the two teams that finished atop the NHL during the regular season against each other: the Edmonton Oilers and the Philadelphia Flyers. On the march to the final, Edmonton, with its run-and-gun offense, lost just twice as they pushed aside L.A., Winnipeg and Detroit, while Philly used grit and the great goaltending of netminder Ron Hextall (that season's Vezina Trophy recipient) to take the Rangers, Islanders and Canadiens. The final series went to a seventh game, with Hextall stopping 40 shots, before the Oilers finally won 3–1 to claim the Stanley Cup for the third time in four years. Rewarded for his extraordinary goaltending, Ron Hextall of Philadelphia was presented with the Conn Smythe Trophy, just the fourth time the award went to a player on the losing team.

goals) in Game 2's 5–1 win. Then, the Canadiens swept the Chicago Black Hawks, with Blake recording five assists and scoring three goals, including the Stanley Cup winner in overtime in Game 4.

1945
Ted Kennedy
TORONTO MAPLE LEAFS

In the semifinal against Montreal, Ted Kennedy opened the scoring with the game winner with just 22 seconds remaining in Game 1, and the Leafs proceeded to upset the Canadiens in six games. The final pitted Toronto against the Detroit Red Wings. Kennedy scored the game winner in Game 2 and then scored a hat trick in Game 4's 5–3 loss. Kennedy led the low-scoring playoffs with seven goals and two assists to guide the Maple Leafs to an unlikely Stanley Cup victory.

1946
Elmer Lach
MONTREAL CANADIENS

The Canadiens breezed through the 1946 playoffs like they coasted through the regular season. After finishing first for the third straight season, the Habs swept Chicago, with Elmer Lach picking up ten points, including eight assists. In the final, it took Montreal five games against the

Boston Bruins to win the Stanley Cup. Lach continued his point spree, finishing the post-season with a record 12 assists, and had 17 points in nine games to earn status as that spring's most valuable performer.

1947
Ted Kennedy
TORONTO MAPLE LEAFS

With World War II concluded, the National Hockey League returned to some sense of normalcy. The second-place Maple Leafs first eliminated Detroit in order to compete in the Stanley Cup final against the Montreal Canadiens. Ted Kennedy finished second in playoff scoring while leading the Leafs with nine points. He scored two game-winning goals, including the Stanley Cup winner, to lead the Leafs to victory.

1948
Ted Kennedy
TORONTO MAPLE LEAFS

The Maple Leafs were in the midst of their first dynasty, and this was arguably the strongest season from that successful run. Toronto finished first overall, and then powered past the Bruins, eliminating them in five games. The final was staged with first-place Toronto meeting second-place Detroit, but it was no contest—the Leafs

1988–89 AL MACINNIS

1989–90 BILL RANFORD

1987–88
Wayne Gretzky
EDMONTON OILERS

The high-flying Oilers went into the playoffs expecting to win a fourth Stanley Cup championship in five years. With a potent offense led by Wayne Gretzky, who had finished the season second in scoring, the Oilers pushed aside the Winnipeg Jets, the Calgary Flames and the Detroit Red Wings, to face the Boston Bruins for the Cup. The Bruins proved little competition to Edmonton who won the final in four games. Gretzky was awesome in that post-season, collecting 43 points, including an NHL record 31 assists. He recorded 3 points alone in the last game, including the Stanley Cup-winning goal. Since Gretzky would no longer be an Oiler after that summer, this Conn Smythe Trophy win was particularly poignant.

1988–89
Al MacInnis
CALGARY FLAMES

The potent Calgary Flames offense took them to a first-place regular season finish and was an omen of things to come. In the first round, the Flames fought the Vancouver Canucks to a seventh-game victory, then rolled over the Los Angeles Kings and Chicago Blackhawks to earn their spot in the final against the Montreal Canadiens. It took six games, but the Flames emerged victorious to capture the franchise's first Stanley Cup championship. Calgary's Al MacInnis was the post-season's top scorer with 31 points, making him the first defenseman to lead the playoffs in scoring. He was particularly lethal in the final for the Cup, scoring 5 goals and 4 assists.

1990–91 · 1991–92 **MARIO LEMIEUX**

1989–90
Bill Ranford
EDMONTON OILERS

In the 1990 playoffs, the Oilers first defeated the Winnipeg Jets, next pushed aside Gretzky and the L.A. Kings and then dumped the Chicago Blackhawks in the third round. The final saw the Boston Bruins challenge Edmonton, but it took just five games for the Oilers to win their fifth Stanley Cup in seven years. Goalie Bill Ranford, who had seen little action when the Oilers won the Cup in 1988, became Edmonton's number one netminder in 1989–90. During the playoffs, he went 16–6 with a 2.53 goals-against average, and was especially strong in the final, carving his average down to 1.35. It may have been the least expected of the franchise's five Stanley Cup victories, and much of the credit for that went to goalie Bill Ranford.

swept Detroit, winning four straight and outscoring the Wings 18 to 7. Ted Kennedy was dominant for the Leafs, showing an intensity that saw him win battles in the corners and in front of the net, but he contributed to the team scoring, too, leading the playoffs in goals (8) and points (14).

1949
Turk Broda
TORONTO MAPLE LEAFS

After a sub-par regular season, the Maple Leafs rebounded in the 1949 playoffs to win an unprecedented third straight Stanley Cup championship. It took the Leafs just nine games to win that spring, first overpowering Boston in five games and then four straight to claim the Cup against a powerful Detroit Red Wings squad. Much of this can be attributed to goalie Turk Broda. He allowed but fifteen goals in nine playoff games, and just five in the final to carry his team to its third consecutive Stanley Cup.

1950
Charlie Rayner
NEW YORK RANGERS

Charlie Rayner and the New York Rangers finished fourth during the regular season, but much to the astonishment of everyone, eliminated the second-place Montreal Canadiens in five games, and moved on to the final to face the Red Wings. The Rangers did not play a single game at home during the seven-game series, as the circus was making Madison Square Garden its home. The Rangers played Games 2 and 3 in Toronto as a neutral site, and the other five games were played in Detroit's Olympia. It took a goal by Pete Babando in the second overtime of Game 7 to finally win the Stanley Cup for Detroit. Although a member of the losing team, Rayner was the top performer in the playoffs of 1950, giving a group of journeymen a legitimate shot at a Stanley Cup championship.

1951
Maurice Richard
MONTREAL CANADIENS

Maurice Richard was at the zenith of his productivity, and although his Canadiens lost to Toronto, Richard was the most valuable player. He scored two overtime winners in Montreal's semifinal against Detroit, and another OT winner in Game 2 of the final. The Rocket finished the playoffs tied with Max Bentley for the playoff scoring championship, but his thirteen points included an incredible nine goals.

1990—91
Mario Lemieux
PITTSBURGH PENGUINS

The Pittsburgh Penguins, although missing their captain Mario Lemieux for the first 50 games of the 1990–91 season due to back problems, still managed to take their division title. (Lemieux, playing in just 26 games, still contributed 45 points to his team's surge.) In the playoffs, Lemieux went on a tear, driving his team past New Jersey, Washington and Boston. The Stanley Cup final pitted the Penguins against the Minnesota North Stars, which the Pens won in six games. The Pittsburgh captain played a total of 23 games in the playoffs, scoring 16 goals and 28 assists, while leading the Penguins to Stanley Cup victory. There was little debate—Mario Lemieux was the MVP of the playoffs.

1991—92
Mario Lemieux
PITTSBURGH PENGUINS

The Pittsburgh Penguins, rocked by the death of their coach Bob Johnson in November 1991, went on a mission to repeat as Stanley Cup champions. The Penguins met the Chicago Blackhawks in the final after eliminating the Washington Capitals, the New York Rangers and the Boston Bruins. Pittsburgh swept the Chicago Blackhawks with Mario Lemieux collecting 5 goals and 8 points in the four-game series. He led all playoff performers in scoring with 34 points, even though he missed six games due to injury, and was awarded the Conn Smythe Trophy for a second consecutive season, the first since Bernie Parent (in 1974 and 1975) to accomplish such a feat.

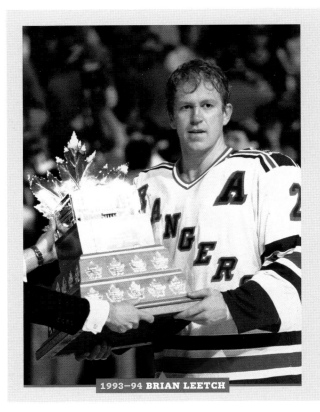

1993–94 **BRIAN LEETCH**

1992—93
Patrick Roy
MONTREAL CANADIENS

Patrick Roy was the Conn Smythe Trophy recipient in 1993 after backstopping his Montreal Canadiens to the Stanley Cup in the trophy's 100th anniversary. Roy was spectacular as the Canadiens defeated the Quebec Nordiques (two OT wins), the Buffalo Sabres (three OT victories), the New York Islanders (two OT wins) and then, to earn the Stanley Cup, the Los Angeles Kings (three OT wins). The ten overtime victories established an astonishing NHL record. Patrick Roy, with a goals-against average of 2:13, was awarded the MVP trophy and joined Bernie Parent as the only netminders to win the award twice (he would go on to win a third in 2001).

1994–95 **CLAUDE LEMIEUX**

1993–94
Brian Leetch
NEW YORK RANGERS

After finishing last in the Patrick Division in 1992–93, the New York Rangers bounded back the following season, not only to be first in their division, but first overall. The Rangers beat the Islanders, Capitals and Devils to stake their spot in the Stanley Cup final against the Vancouver Canucks. It took the full seven games, but New York eventually won the Stanley Cup championship, their first since 1940. No one was more important to the team that spring than Brian Leetch. Throughout the season, the defenseman had provided both offense and defense, but in the playoffs his worth skyrocketed as he led all scorers with 34 points, with 11 of those coming in the seven-game final. Leetch was the first American-born player to be awarded the Conn Smythe Trophy.

PRE-TROPHY WINNERS

1952
Terry Sawchuk
DETROIT RED WINGS

During the 1952 playoffs, goalie Terry Sawchuk was unbelievable, shutting out the Maple Leafs twice and surrendering but three goals in the semifinal. The superb netminding carried into the final as Detroit faced the Montreal Canadiens. Sawchuk blanked the Habs in Game 3 and again in Game 4 to lead his Wings to victory. The Canadiens scored just two goals against Detroit during their series. Sawchuk's goals-against average in the final was a microscopic 0.50, and for the entire post-season was 0.63. His playoff save percentage was an extraordinary .977. "He is their team," shrugged Maurice Richard after the Stanley Cup presentation to Detroit.

1953
Ed Sandford
BOSTON BRUINS

Although the Montreal Canadiens collected the Stanley Cup in 1953, the committee selected Boston's Ed Sandford as the best performer in the 1953 playoffs. Sandford scored 8 goals and 11 points to lead all playoff scores. Montreal won Game 1 of the final, but when the Bruins struck for a 4–1 win in Game 2, with Sandford scoring the winner,

Canadiens goaltender Jacques Plante was replaced in net by Gerry McNeil. McNeil earned shutouts in Games 3 and 5 to confirm the Canadiens Cup win. Had Gerry McNeil played more than three games, he would have been a candidate for MVP status.

1954
Terry Sawchuk
DETROIT RED WINGS

While he didn't win the Vezina Trophy as the NHL's best goaltender, Terry Sawchuk still had been spectacular all season, recording twelve shutouts. The Wings met the Maple Leafs in the semifinal, eliminating them in five games with Sawchuk limiting Toronto to just eight goals. Detroit and second-place Montreal faced off in the final. Sawchuk was a star, battling the powerful Canadiens onslaught and leading Detroit to a Stanley Cup victory. He allowed just twelve goals in the final.

1955
Gordie Howe
DETROIT RED WINGS

In the Stanley Cup final, the Wings were challenged by the Montreal Canadiens. Montreal had finished just two points behind Detroit during the regular season. Gordie Howe set a record with 20 points in the play-offs, twelve of them in the

1995-96 JOE SAKIC

1996-97 MIKE VERNON

1994-95
Claude Lemieux
NEW JERSEY DEVILS

In 1994–95, the NHL endured a lock-out that reduced the regular season to just 48 games. During the shortened season, Claude Lemieux collected just 19 points for the New Jersey Devils, but he established himself as a top performer during the playoffs. The Devils first beat Boston before upsetting Pittsburgh and then Philadelphia to reach the Stanley Cup final for the first time in franchise history. The Devils then went on to sweep the Detroit Red Wings to win their first Stanley Cup championship. The team hero was Claude Lemieux, who, in addition to his grit and forechecking, exploded for 13 goals to lead all playoff performers, adding 3 assists for 16 points in 20 games.

1995-96
Joe Sakic
COLORADO AVALANCHE

The Colorado Avalanche (formerly the Quebec Nordiques) finished atop the Pacific Division in 1995–96. The playoffs saw the Avalanche defeat Vancouver, Chicago and Detroit in consecutive six-game series to establish their spot in the Stanley Cup final, facing the upstart Florida Panthers. The pain was over quickly for the Panthers, as the Avalanche swept them in four straight games (although the final game wasn't decided until Uwe Krupp scored in the third overtime period) to win the first Stanley Cup for the franchise. Team captain Joe Sakic, who had finished third in scoring with 120 points during the regular season, including 51 goals, led all playoff performers with 18 goals and 34 points.

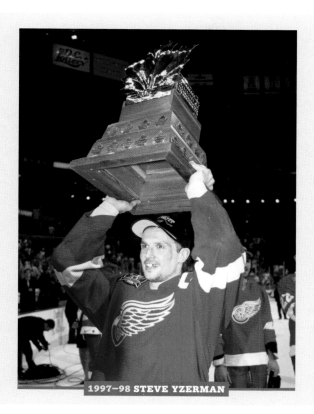

1997–98 STEVE YZERMAN

1996–97
Mike Vernon
DETROIT RED WINGS

Mike Vernon was not the Red Wings number-one goalie in 1996–97. Chris Osgood had played the majority of games for Detroit; however, in the playoffs, the veteran Vernon was handed the starting job. Detroit eliminated St. Louis, Anaheim and Colorado, and earned the right to face the Philadelphia Flyers in the Stanley Cup final. It developed into a sweep, with Detroit rolling over Philadelphia in four straight, giving the Red Wings their first Stanley Cup championship since 1955. For his excellent performance, Vernon was selected as the winner of the Conn Smythe Trophy, going 16–4 in the post-season, compiling a 1.76 goals-against average and save percentage of .927.

PRE-TROPHY WINNERS

final. Howe also led all post-season participants with nine goals, five of which were against the Canadiens. He had three game-winning playoff goals, giving the Red Wings a second-straight Stanley Cup championship.

1956
Jean Beliveau
MONTREAL CANADIENS

Montreal star Dickie Moore called the 1955–56 edition of the Canadiens "the best team I ever played on." Montreal was virtually unstoppable, finishing the regular season with 100 points, 24 more than second-place Detroit. Jean Beliveau led all NHL players in goals (47) and points (88), and continued his furious pace into the playoffs. In the semifinal, Montreal put away the New York Rangers in five games and defeated the Red Wings in the final four games to one. Beliveau was on fire, scoring seven goals against Detroit to finish with a playoff-best twelve tallies. He also picked up ten points in that final for a total of nineteen.

1957
Bernie Geoffrion
MONTREAL CANADIENS

A bad elbow hampered Bernie "Boom Boom" Geoffrion throughout much of the 1956–57 regular season, but he was at his

dominant best during the playoffs. First, the Canadiens dumped the New York Rangers in five games. Geoffrion and his teammates rolled to a second straight Stanley Cup championship by winning the final series against Boston in five games. Boom Boom led all playoff scorers in both goals (11) and points (18). Geoffrion had three game-winning goals through the playoffs and set up three others.

1958
Maurice Richard
MONTREAL CANADIENS

In the semifinal against Detroit, Maurice Richard scored seven goals, including a hat trick in Game 4, to eliminate the Wings. Then, in the final versus Boston, he added four more goals, including the overtime winner in Game 5, to help his Canadiens win their third consecutive Stanley Cup, defeating the Bruins in six games. Richard was the leading goal scorer of these playoffs with eleven.

1959
Marcel Bonin
MONTREAL CANADIENS

Marcel Bonin, who had scored thirteen goals during the regular season, scored seven goals in the semifinal as the Canadiens ousted Chicago. Then, Montreal faced the upstart Toronto

1997–98
Steve Yzerman
DETROIT RED WINGS

The defending Stanley Cup winners, the Detroit Red Wings, reached the final for a second straight spring in 1998 by pushing aside the Phoenix Coyotes, the St. Louis Blues and the Dallas Stars. The championship series saw Detroit facing the Washington Capitals for hockey glory. Captain Steve Yzerman led his charges in a series dedicated to their fallen comrades, Vladimir Konstantinov and Sergei Mnatsakanov who had both been severely injured in a limo accident after the previous Stanley Cup win. Detroit won the first three games by a single goal each time, but in Game 4 they won 4–1 to sweep Washington and earn a second consecutive Stanley Cup. Yzerman scored 6 post-season goals and led all playoff scorers with 18 assists and 24 points.

1998–99
Joe Nieuwendyk
DALLAS STARS

The Dallas Stars reached the Stanley Cup final after defeating the Edmonton Oilers, St. Louis Blues and Colorado Avalanche. It was the third time the franchise had competed in the final, but the first as the Dallas Stars (the previous two visits had been while the team was located in Minnesota). The Stars won the Stanley Cup on a controversial goal by Brett Hull in triple-overtime of Game 6 that gave them hockey's big prize. Joe Nieuwendyk had a superb playoff, scoring 6 of Dallas' 16 game-winning goals that spring and finishing with a playoff-best 11 goals, and with an additional 10 assists, for a total of 21 points.

1998–99 JOE NIEUWENDYK

1999–2000
Scott Stevens
NEW JERSEY DEVILS

The New Jersey Devils concluded the 1999–2000 regular season as the Eastern Conference champions. In the playoffs, they swept the Florida Panthers, took the Toronto Maple Leafs in six games and the Philadelphia Flyers in seven to earn a spot in the Stanley Cup final against the Dallas Stars. Scott Stevens, an intimidating presence on the blue line, led the Devils to the Stanley Cup championship, one of just nine players remaining from New Jersey's 1995 Stanley Cup win. Stevens scored 11 points in the 2000 playoffs, but it was his leadership, his work in his own end and his thundering body checks that earned Stevens the Conn Smythe Trophy.

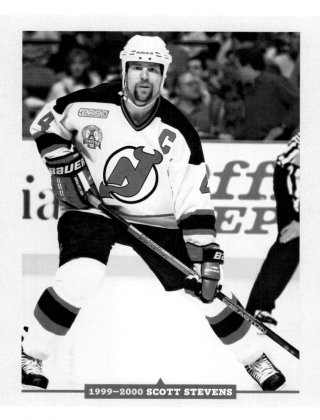

1999–2000 **SCOTT STEVENS**

2000–01
Patrick Roy
COLORADO AVALANCHE

The Colorado Avalanche were first at the conclusion of the regular season and heavily favored to win the Stanley Cup, but success didn't come easily. The Avalanche had to defeat the Canucks, the Los Angeles Kings (two shutouts by Roy) and the St. Louis Blues (three overtime contests) before facing the New Jersey Devils for the Cup. Patrick Roy kicked off the series with a shutout in Game 1 and a second shutout in Game 6, but the final had to go the full seven games before the Avalanche emerged victorious. Roy won an unprecedented third Conn Smythe Trophy, having previously won with the Montreal Canadiens in 1986 and 1993.

Maple Leafs. The Leafs put up a modest fight to conclude their Cinderella season, but Bonin and the Habs were too strong. Bonin scored another three goals as Montreal won the Stanley Cup for a fourth time by winning four of five games in the final. Marcel Bonin, who scored the Stanley Cup-winning goal, finished with fifteen points in the eleven games.

1960
Jacques Plante
MONTREAL CANADIENS

The Montreal Canadiens had won the Stanley Cup in each of the previous four springs, and, with Jacques Plante in goal, were expected to win once again. Montreal defeated the Chicago Black Hawks in the semifinal, facing the Toronto Maple Leafs for a second straight spring. Plante and the Canadiens allowed but five goals in a four-game sweep to earn an unprecedented fifth straight Stanley Cup championship. Jacques Plante shut out the Hawks twice and the Leafs once to emerge as the leading candidate for recognition as the most valuable player of the 1960 playoffs.

1961
Pierre Pilote
CHICAGO BLACK HAWKS

Even with forwards like the explosive Bobby Hull and dynamic Stan Mikita, in 1961 it was defenseman Pierre Pilote who led the team's production, setting an NHL record for playoff points by a defenseman with 15 (3 goals, 12 assists), tying him with Gordie Howe of the Red Wings for the playoff scoring championship. Pilote assisted on six of Chicago's eight winning goals and had at least one point in eleven of their twelve playoff games. Chicago defeated the Red Wings in six games in the final to win their first Stanley Cup championship since 1938.

1962
Stan Mikita
CHICAGO BLACK HAWKS

The Hawks eliminated the first-place Montreal Canadiens in six games to once again return to the Stanley Cup final, this time against the Maple Leafs. Toronto set the stage, winning the first two games at home before the Black Hawks took the next two in Chicago. The Leafs then doubled Chicago 8–4 in Game 5, finishing the season with a 2–1 win against the Hawks in Game 6 in Chicago. However, it was Stan Mikita who was the

2001–02 **NICKLAS LIDSTROM**

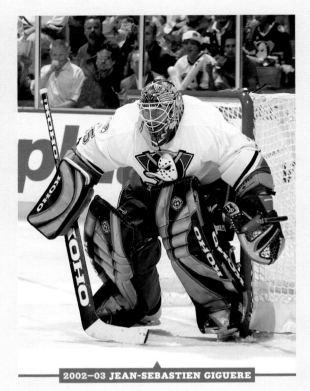

2002–03 **JEAN-SEBASTIEN GIGUERE**

2001—02
Nicklas Lidstrom
DETROIT RED WINGS

The Detroit Red Wings won the President's Trophy as the team finishing the regular season with the most points The Wings proceeded to defeat Vancouver, St. Louis and Colorado, before facing the Carolina Hurricanes, who were making their first trip to the Stanley Cup final. Detroit lost the first game, but took the next four, winning the Cup for the third time in six seasons. Nicklas Lidstrom quietly dominated for Detroit, scoring 5 goals (including two game-winners and a short-handed tally) and adding 16 assists to earn the playoff MVP award. Lidstrom was the first European to win the Conn Smythe Trophy.

2002—03
Jean-Sebastien Giguere
MIGHTY DUCKS OF ANAHEIM

The Mighty Ducks would not have had the opportunity to reach the final in the spring of 2003 had it not been for their sensational goalie Jean-Sebastien Giguere. He stoned Detroit in four games, helped defeat the Dallas Stars in six and then, incredibly, allowed just one goal in the series as Anaheim swept the Minnesota Wild. The Mighty Ducks then took the New Jersey Devils to a seventh game in the final before losing. Giguere won 15 playoff games for the Ducks, including five shutouts, and led all netminders with a goals-against average of 1.62 and a staggering save percentage of .945. J-S Giguere was highly lauded for his extraordinary performance, even in a losing cause.

2003–04 **BRAD RICHARDS**

2003–04
Brad Richards
TAMPA BAY LIGHTNING

Brad Richards enjoyed one of the greatest playoffs ever in 2004. He led all playoff performers with 26 points (12 goals and 14 assists) and scored an NHL-record seven game-winning goals. The Tampa Bay Lightning didn't lose a playoff game in which he scored. The Southeast Division champions cruised past the New York Islanders and the Montreal Canadiens before battling the Philadelphia Flyers to earn a spot in the Stanley Cup final against the Calgary Flames. The series went seven games and in the deciding contest, Richards assisted on both of Ruslan Fedotenko's goals in a 2–1 win that brought the franchise its first Stanley Cup championship.

standout playoff performer, setting a new playoff scoring record with 21 points in a losing cause. He had points in eleven consecutive playoff games and scored two game-winning goals while setting up two others.

1963
Johnny Bower
TORONTO MAPLE LEAFS

The Leafs netminders were outstanding from the opening faceoff of the season through to the awarding of the Stanley Cup on April 18, 1963. Johnny Bower, assisted by Don Simmons, led his team to a first-place finish, and then moved through the post-season with relative ease. Toronto erased the Canadiens in five games, including two shutouts by Bower, and then faced the Detroit Red Wings for the Stanley Cup. The Leafs outscored the Wings 17 to 10, and took the best-of-seven series in five games. Johnny Bower was determined to be the most valuable performer in the 1963 playoffs.

1964
Bob Pulford
TORONTO MAPLE LEAFS

Although this Stanley Cup is remembered as the series in which Toronto's Bob Baun scored an overtime winner on a broken leg, it was teammate Bob Pulford who earned selection as the post-season's most valuable player. In the semifinal against Montreal, Pulford was outstanding, checking, killing penalties and, in a 3–2 loss, scoring both Leaf goals. In the final against the Red Wings, Pulford scored the winning goal in Game 1 and had two goals and an assist in a 4–3 Game 6 victory. Pulford had five points in the final series, but it was his overall effort that contributed significantly to Toronto's Cup win.

2005–06 **CAM WARD**

2006–07 **SCOTT NIEDERMAYER**

2005–06
Cam Ward
CAROLINA HURRICANES

Unexpectedly inserted into the starting role due to Martin Gerber's stomach ailment, 22-year-old rookie netminder Cam Ward played with the poise of a veteran. He backstopped the Carolina Hurricanes to victories over Montreal, New Jersey and Buffalo before facing the Edmonton Oilers in the final. In 23 games on the path to the Stanley Cup, Ward won 15 games (two shutouts), with a goals-against average of 2.14 and a sensational save percentage of .920. He was the first rookie goaltender since Patrick Roy in 1986 to lead his team to a Stanley Cup championship, and was the first rookie since Ron Hextall in 1987 to claim the Conn Smythe Trophy.

2006–07
Scott Niedermayer
ANAHEIM DUCKS

In the 2007 playoffs, the Anaheim Ducks (the former Mighty Ducks) first defeated Minnesota and then got past Vancouver after captain Scott Niedermayer scored the winning goal in double overtime of the fifth game to end the series. Anaheim next met Detroit. Scott scored the winning goal in Game 2 and in Game 5 he scored with 47 seconds left to tie the game. Anaheim subsequently won that game in overtime and went on to put Detroit out in six. The Ducks then faced the Ottawa Senators for the Stanley Cup championship, defeating them in five games. Niedermayer's calm leadership and his three critical goals in the playoffs resulted in the MVP award.

2007–08 HENRIK ZETTERBERG

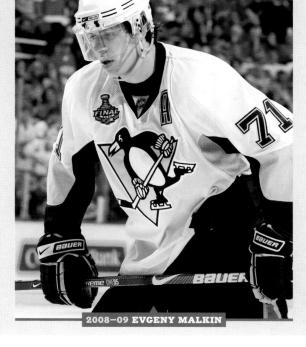

2008–09 EVGENY MALKIN

2007–08
Henrik Zetterberg
DETROIT RED WINGS

After a career-high 92 points in the regular season, Henrik Zetterberg excelled at both ends of the rink in the playoffs. The Detroit Red Wings systematically eliminated the Nashville Predators, Colorado Avalanche and Dallas Stars before going on to face the Pittsburgh Penguins for the Stanley Cup championship. The Wings won the final with Zetterberg scoring the series-winning goal in the sixth and deciding game. It was one of 13 he scored in the post-season, and combined with 14 assists, his total of 27 points tied him with Pittsburgh's Sidney Crosby as the playoff scoring leader. Zetterberg was just the second European to receive the Conn Smythe Trophy.

2008–09
Evgeny Malkin
PITTSBURGH PENGUINS

In the 2008–09 post-season, the Pittsburgh Penguins defeated the Philadelphia Flyers in six games, the Washington Capitals in seven, and the Carolina Hurricanes in four before meeting the Detroit Red Wings in the final to claim hockey's biggest prize. Evgeny Malkin was not only the NHL's regular-season scoring leader with 113 points, but also led the post-season in scoring, too. His 36 points (14 goals and 22 assists) were the highest total in the playoffs since Wayne Gretzky got 40 in 1993. For his accomplishments he was rewarded with the Conn Smythe Trophy.

2009–10 JONATHAN TOEWS

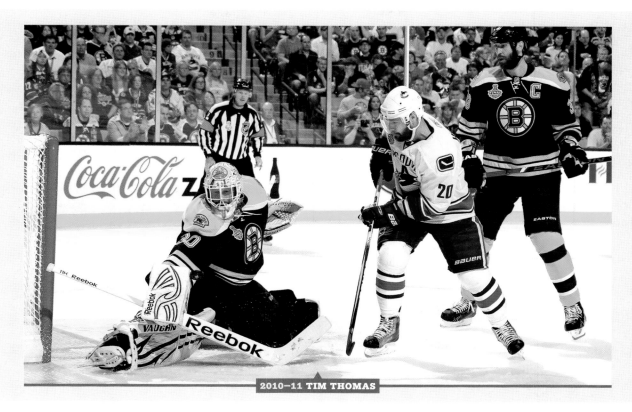

2010–11 TIM THOMAS

2009—10
Jonathan Toews
CHICAGO BLACKHAWKS

The Chicago Blackhawks needed only six games to triumph over Nashville and Vancouver in the quarterfinals and semifinals. They then went on to sweep San Jose to win the Western Conference championship before facing the Philadelphia Flyers in the final. It then took the Blackhawks six games to win the Stanley Cup, their first since 1961. Twenty-two-year-old Jonathan Toews, the youngest NHL captain, demonstrated remarkable poise throughout the playoffs, finishing second in scoring with 29 points (7 goals and 22 assists), one point behind Daniel Briere of the Philadelphia Flyers. He was the second youngest player and the youngest captain to win the Conn Smythe Trophy.

2010-11
Tim Thomas
BOSTON BRUINS

Pundits had already decided that Tim Thomas was going to win the Conn Smythe Trophy whether Boston won the Stanley Cup or not—he was that dominant. The 37-year-old netminder, drafted by the Quebec Nordiques in 1994, didn't make his NHL debut until 2002–03 with the Bruins, and even then, he didn't become a regular until 2005–06. He even lost his starting job during the 2009–10 season, the season after he won his first Vezina Trophy. Needless to say, Thomas' return to form in the 2010–11 season and his playoff run provided hockey fans everywhere a feel good story. Thomas posted a 1.98 goals-against average and a .940 save percentage, while setting an NHL record for most saves in a single post-season. He earned shutouts in Games 4 and 7 and allowed the Vancouver Canucks only eight goals in the seven-game Stanley Cup final.

Acknowledgments

I'D LIKE TO offer thanks to Phil Pritchard, Craig Campbell, Kelly Masse and all the staff at the Hockey Hall of Fame for their assistance with this project, as well as to all of the NHL players, past and present, who willingly shared their thoughts and opinions on the subject. Thanks to authors Andrew Cohen and Martin Harris for sharing their knowledge of Lester B. Pearson, and to the members of the Society for International Hockey Research for their help uncovering the history of the Hart family. It was a pleasure to work on the project with such a fine professional as Kevin Shea. Much appreciation also goes to the tireless and often under appreciated work of editor Steve Cameron. Most of all, I'd like to thank my wife, Shira, and daughter, Cecilia, for their support during the research and writing of this book, as well as their patience and understanding when deadlines hovered over me.

—Bob Duff

I WOULD LIKE to thank all of the Conn Smythe Trophy recipients who took the time to discuss this honor with me. Special thanks to the Society for International Hockey Research (SIHR) for allowing me to use their subjective list of playoff MVPs prior to the introduction of the Conn Smythe Trophy in 1965. For more information on SIHR, I encourage you to look them up online at www.sihrhockey.org. I'd also like to thank the Hockey Hall of Fame and the Hockey Hall of Fame Resource Centre—for research into hockey's glorious history, there is no better place. To my friend Paul Patskou, an extraordinary researcher who has partnered with me on many books, thanks again for your splendid work. Personal thanks to Steve Cameron and the team at Firefly Books, Bob Duff, my partner on this project, and my wonderful wife, Nancy Niklas, who tolerates my obsession with the game of hockey.

—Kevin Shea

Photo Credits

Index